The Irrational Season

Also by Madeleine L'Engle

The Summer of the Great-grandmother
A Circle of Quiet
Ladder of Angels
The Sphinx at Dawn

THE CROSSWICKS JOURNAL · BOOK 3

The Irrational Season

MADELEINE L'ENGLE

THE SEABURY PRESS • NEW YORK

Ninth Printing

1983
The Seabury Press
815 Second Avenue
New York, N.Y. 10017

Printed in the United States of America

Library of Congress Cataloging in Publication Data

L'Engle, Madeleine   The irrational season.

1. Church year—Meditations. 1. Title.
BV30.L46   242'.3   76-46944
ISBN 0-8164-0324-4   ISBN 0-8164-2261-3 pbk

For Carmen Gomezplata

Acknowledgements

NONE OF THIS would have been written had not Reid Isaac, then with The Seabury Press, come to me and asked, "Don't you want to write a book for us?" My immediate and vocal response was, "No." But then this book tapped me on the shoulder and said, "Here I am. Write me," and when this happens I have little choice.

Several names have been changed and a few incidents "translated" in order to protect privacy. Nevertheless this book is as "true" as I can make it.

The last third was completed while I was a Visiting Fellow at the Episcopal Seminary of the Southwest in Austin, Texas. My debt to my friends there is incalculable. Not only was I given time to write, and an opportunity to share in the life and worship of the seminary, but I was also fed, chauffered, and consistently ministered to.

Contents

1... The Night Is Far Spent

NEW YORK.

Two o'clock in the morning. A thin, chill November rain is falling. I stand at the dining-room window, holding a comforting mug of hot bouillon, and look out at the never-wholly-asleep city. A taxi moves slowly along West End Avenue. A young woman walks down the middle of 105th Street with a very large Great Dane. My Irish setter is asleep in the bedroom; he knows that it is much too early to get up.

I enjoy these occasional spells of nocturnal wakefulness, and I am never awake alone. Across West End Avenue there is an apartment building where the eleventh-floor windows are always lit, no matter what time it is. This night, in another building, someone is studying by a single light bulb suspended from the ceiling. The Hudson River is visible through television aerials and between two tall apartment buildings on Riverside Drive. Ours is a restricted view, but it is a view, nevertheless, and I love it. There is a small ship, a freighter, I think, moving slowly along the dark water, its lights both warmly greeting and mysterious. What looks like a star grows brighter and reveals itself to be a plane coming in to land at La Guardia; but there is a star left behind in the wake of the plane, a pale city star.

I sip hot bouillon and feel relaxed and at peace at this beginning of a new year—a new year for me. I have had another birthday, and this is always like opening a brand-new journal to the first page, or putting a clean sheet of paper into the typewriter as I start a new book; it is all ahead of me, clear and bright, the first smudges and mistakes not yet made. I know that they will come, and soon—I don't think

I've ever typed a full page without making at least one error; however, beginnings are always exciting and full of hope.

The beginning of my personal new year comes as the Christian Church's new year, Advent, begins, the four weeks before Christmas. The Jewish New Year is over; it is not yet time for the secular New Year or the Buddhist New Year; the academic year is already well started. Has there ever been a culture or a religion where there has not been a special day to mark the beginning of a new year? I still function more in terms of the academic year than any other, and probably will continue to do so even when we no longer have children in school or college.

A new year can begin only because the old year ends. In northern climates this is especially apparent. As rain turns to snow, puddles to ice, the sun rises later and sets earlier; and each day it climbs less high in the sky. One time when I went with my children to the planetarium I was fascinated to hear the lecturer say that the primitive people used to watch the sun drop lower on the horizon in great terror, because they were afraid that one day it was going to go so low that it would never rise again; they would be left in unremitting night. There would be weeping and wailing and gnashing of teeth, and a terror of great darkness would fall upon them. And then, just as it seemed that there would never be another dawn, the sun would start to come back; each day it would rise higher, set later.

Somewhere in the depths of our unconsciousness we share that primordial fear, and when there is the first indication that the days are going to lengthen, our hearts, too, lift with relief. The end has not come: joy! and so a new year makes its birth known.

In the Christian Church these weeks leading up to Christmas, this dark beginning of our new year, is also traditionally the time of thinking of the last things, of the 'eschaton,' the end.

The night is far spent. The day is at hand.

That day when all nights will be spent, when time will end: we all know it's coming. Scientists know it, and tell us the various ways that it could happen, but as of now they aren't predicting when. Various religious groups have predicted the end of the world off and on for hundreds of years. Whenever one of these groups tells us that Dooms-day is going to come at midnight on a certain day, I always feel a little queasy. Maybe this time they're right. It has to happen sometime.

It was a long time before I could begin to think of this ending of all known things, all matter, the stars in their courses, music, laughter, sunrise, daisies and dynasties, starfish and stars, suns and chrysanthemums, as being in any way something to look forward to with joy and hope. It was a long time before I could turn my thoughts to the eschaton without terror. Long before I'd heard about the atom bomb or the hydrogen bomb, or fission or fusion, I feared the end of the world in much the same way that I fear a nuclear holocaust. And the description of the last day in the New Testament sounds very much like atomic devastation: "The present sky and earth are reserved for fire. . . . The Day of the Lord will come like a thief, and then with a roar the sky will vanish, the elements will catch fire and fall apart, and the earth and all that it contains will be burned up."

A nuclear holocaust would probably mean the end of human life on planet earth, but not the rest of the solar system, or the galaxy, or any of the hundreds of billions of other galaxies in the universe. And nuclear warfare would be man's pride and folly rather than God's anger.

The end of the world in the eschatological sense has nothing to do with pride or anger and it is not just the end of this one planet, but of all planets, all solar systems, all galaxies.

And what then? Is that it? Annihilation?

No. Annihilation might follow an intergalactic nuclear battle, but annihilation is the opposite of what the eschaton is about. It is not nearly so much a going as a coming, an ending as a beginning. It is the redemption, not the destruction, of Creation. We've heard the phrases so often and from so many denominations that they've become distorted until the meaning is nearly bled from them:

The Second Coming. The Coming of the Kingdom.

What does that mean?

My son-in-law Alan was asked once by a pious woman if our feet would be wafted from the earth, at the time of the Second Coming, before Jesus's feet touched ground. Ouch. That kind of literalism is not what it's about.

For the simple fact is that we are not capable of knowing what it's about. The Coming of the Kingdom is creation coming to be what it was meant to be, the joy and glory of all creation working together with the Creator. In literal language none of it makes much sense, and

I can only go once again to my adolescent analogy of the planet on which all sentient life was sightless. If nobody could see, other senses would take over, and everybody would get along perfectly well. But if you tried to explain the joy of sight to anybody on that planet you couldn't do it. Nobody could understand something so glorious and so totally out of an eyeless frame of reference. Multiply that gap between a blind planet and a seeing one a billion times and we'll still be far from understanding the difference between creation, now, and creation in the fullness of the kingdom. But I am slowly learning that it is something to be awaited with joy and not terror.

When I try to grasp the nature of the universe with my conscious mind, my humanly limited intellectual powers, I grope blindly. I come closer to understanding with the language of the heart, sipping hot bouillon and relaxing, standing by the dining-room window where I can no longer sit on the window sill because of our accumulation of plants—coleus and Swedish Ivy and ferns and alligator pears and philodendron and anything else we can coax to grow in the polluted air of the city—than when I think with mind alone.

The night is far spent. The day is at hand.

Yes. It's nearly three o'clock in the morning. But I'm not ready to go back to bed yet. I'll be sorry when the alarm goes off in the morning. Meanwhile, I want to stay here a little longer.

Before I can contemplate the end I have to think about the beginning, and no one is very certain about the beginning, that moment when God created the universe out of sheer *joie de vivre.* There are three conflicting theories of the creation of the universe. First, there's the big-bang theory. Once upon a time all matter was One, an incredibly compact mass of unmeasurable compression. And suddenly—and the cosmologists don't know why—it burst asunder and particles of it flew out wildly and eventually became galaxies, and within the galaxies suns, and planets, and planetary satellites like our moon. And all these fragments of the original Oneness are still flying out, out, out into—what? farther and farther away from each other (how lonely outer space must be), so that the distances between galaxies are becoming greater and greater . . .

Then there's the theory of continuous creation. In the vast hydrogen clouds all over the universe, stars are constantly being born, as stars are constantly dying. It's an attractive theory, but where did those hydrogen clouds come from in the first place?

And then there's the flux theory: once upon a time all matter was One. And suddenly there was an explosion and particles of this original Oneness went flying out in every direction, stars and galaxies growing farther and farther apart—and then the direction reverses and there is an implosion and everything moves inward, together, eventually becoming the original One, and then there's another big bang and the Unity explodes and particles go flying out in all directions, and this explosion/implosion continues to repeat itself . . .

Forever?

And none of these theories answers the question of why there's anything at all. Why isn't there just nothing?

My children asked me these things and I was hard put to answer their questions, which are still my own questions.

Why is there anything?

Well, God made something out of nothing.

Why? Didn't he like nothing?

Well, God is love, and it is the nature of love to create.

Could he have created anything he wanted to?

Of course. He's God.

Do you like what he created?

Yes. Yes, I do.

Battlefields and slums and insane asylums?

Well, he didn't create those.

Who did?

We did.

Who's we? I didn't create them.

Mankind did. And you're part of mankind and so am I.

But God created mankind?

Yes.

Why did he create mankind if mankind was going to create battlefields and slums and insane asylums?

I don't suppose that's what he created man *for.*

What did he create him for, then?

Well, it's the nature of love to create . . .

So.

What does that do to all Love? It is the nature of love to create, and what do the children of this Love do? We make battlefields and slums and insane asylums.

Out of all this original nothingness wouldn't you think he could have done better?

Maybe he did. I don't know why we have the conceit to think we're the flower of his Creation. Maybe not all life went wrong—and even with all our wrongness there's the Bach *St. Matthew Passion* and Shakespeare's plays and Rembrandt's paintings and . . .

The morning star is low on the horizon. There are three more stars pulsing faintly in the city sky. But even if I can't see a skyful of stars they are there above me nevertheless; the Milky Way, our own galaxy, swings somewhere in the vast dark above the city lights.

All those stars. Suns. More suns than can be imagined. Great flaming brilliant atomic furnaces, the bursting of their atoms providing life instead of death. Providing life for their planets. Perhaps most of the inhabited planets are different from ours, with no battlefields or slums or insane asylums. Perhaps there are planets where that which was created by love returns love, and there is joy and worship and praise and man sings with the angels—not pink and blue and cute, not angels with weak faces and weaker wings—but

> *O sing unto God*
> *and sing praises unto his Name*
> *magnify him that rideth upon the heavens*
> *praise him in his name*
> *JAH!*
> *shout it*
> *cry it aloud upon the wind*
> *take the tail of his steed*
> *and fling across the sky*
> *in his wild wake*
> *JAH!*
> *he cannot be caught*
> *he cannot be fled*
> *nor his knowledge escaped*
> *the light of his Name*
> *blinds the brilliance of stars*
> *JAH!*
> *catch the falling dragon*
> *ride between his flailing wings*

leap between the jaws of the lion
grasp the horn of the unicorn
calling with mighty voice
JAH!
caught in star flame
whipped by comet lash
rejoice before him
cry above the voices of the cherubim
shout alongside the seraphim
JAH!
bellowing joy behind kings
scattered by the quaking of his hills
fleeing before his fire
rush like snow through his thunderous flame
crying with gladness
adoration of his Name
He is Lord
JAH!*

I'm going to be thinking about man, and his part in the world, fairly frequently in these pages, and I want to make it quite clear, right away, that I, Madeleine, sex: f, wife and mother, am just as much *man* as is Hugh, sex: m, husband and father, and that I'm not about to abdicate my full share in mankind. One of the most pusillanimous things we of the female sex have done throughout the centuries is to have allowed the male sex to assume that mankind is masculine.

It is not. It takes both male and female to make the image of God. The proper understanding of mankind is that it is only a poor, broken thing if either male or female is excluded. The result of such exclusion is that in terms of human sexuality the English language is presently inadequate. The word *man* has been so taken over by the male sex that I'm not sure it's redeemable. In the old days the familiar word for male was *wer*—as in werwolf; and the familiar word for female was *wif*—and not just as in housewif; the Amazons were wifs, too.

But if I try to use *wer* and *wif,* or if I make up new words which would be useful, these unusual words would stick out and the meaning of the sentence might easily be lost. So I'll stick with our present mutilated generic vocabulary.

I realize how fortunate I was to have grown up in a household

*From L'Engle, *Lines Scribbled on an Envelope,* copyright © 1969. Reprinted with permission of Farrar, Straus & Giroux.

where I never encountered sexism, where it never occurred to me that female was in any way less than male; different, yes; but equal. In my work, both in the theatre and in writing, I have been in worlds which are not sexist. The reason the mothers in my children's books are usually professional women, respected in their chosen fields, is that this is the kind of woman I've always known best. In my marriage, sexism has never been a barrier. So I realize that it's easy for me to be casual about the words for gender. If I had grown up in an atmosphere where the female was put down, where my sex was relegated to an inferior place, I would not be able to be so casual.

I will have to struggle along with the old, tattered words, trying never to forget that *man* is as much a feminine as a masculine word, and if I abandon my share in it, *that* would be to kowtow to the 'm.c.p.,' who would like to hog the whole human gender for himself, and is aided and abetted by the more thoughtless members of the female sex who do not realize that they are not more free by insisting on falling down personholes, but are blindly relinquishing their true identity. And so the male is given his usual opportunity to say, "It was the woman's fault. She made me eat of the fruit of the tree"— a sniveling and cowardly alibi which immediately broke the proper joyful and creative relationship between male and female.

The Church with blithe disregard of the folly of sexism calls itself the Body of Christ (masculine), and affirms itself also to be the Bride of Christ (feminine), and just as it takes male and female to make the image of God, so it takes male and female to make the Church.

Because I am a female and my sexuality is fulfilled by the male of the species, it is easy for me to respond joyfully to the maleness of the Godhead, but that does not make me see it as exclusively masculine; that would be just as much of a dead end as not acknowledging the essential male genes in myself, or the female genes in my husband, Hugh, which are an important part of our full sexuality.

If, when we were married, Hugh and I became a new entity, he as much as I, then, when Mary conceived by the power of the Holy Spirit, that mighty action affirmed forever the sexual wholeness of Creation. I do not mean that a young and very human girl became one of the persons of the Trinity, but surely the most holy Birth-giver should make us understand that the Trinity embraces all sexuality in a complete and unfragmented manner.

We make complicated what is simple, and the powers of darkness rejoice. But because I, too, am woman and mother, it is my joy and privilege to identify with this young girl who contained within her womb the Power of the universe.

> *O thou who bears the pain of the whole earth,*
> *I bore thee.*
> *O thou whose tears give human tears their worth,*
> *I laughed with thee.*
> *Thou who, when thy hem is touched, give power,*
> *I nourished thee.*
> *Who turns the day to night in this dark hour,*
> *Dayspring for me.*
> *O thou who held the world in thy embrace,*
> *I dandled thee,*
> *Whose arms encircle all men with thy grace,*
> *I once held thee.*
> *O thou who laughed and ate and walked the shore,*
> *I played with thee.*
> *And I, who with all others, thou died for,*
> *I now hold thee.*
>
> *May I be faithful to this final test:*
> *For the last time I hold my child, my son,*
> *Thy body close enfolded to my breast,*
> *The holder held, the bearer borne.*
> *Mourning to joy: darkness to morn.*
> *Open, my arms; the work is done.*

The original relationship between male and female was meant to be one of mutual fulfillment and joy, but that relationship was broken, to our grief, and turned into one of suspicion and warfare, misunderstanding and exclusion, and will not be fully restored until the end of time. Nevertheless, we are given enough glimpses of the original relationship so that we should be able to rejoice in our participation in mankind.

Rejoice I do, and I'm not willing to relinquish one iota of my share!

Mankind: male and female created he them,

and in his image.

Whose image? God's. And *God* is a word as abused and battered as the gender words.

Martin Buber defends the word *God* passionately; soiled though it is, it is the word we have by which to call the One who is so glorious that no one knows his real name. Year by year the word becomes more abused, and still it is the one I cry out in despair or anguish or joy. So it pains me when people try to narrow down the One to whom I cry as no more than a sexist symbol. Certainly domineering males have tried to take God over and make him in their own image, but I do not understand why we accept that image. Juliana of Norwich, with casual casting aside of the sexism of her day (far worse than ours), calls Christ her mother—mother, father, brother, sister, it doesn't matter. The Power behind the universe is all in all. Jesus called the Father *Abba,* a name so personal it might almost be translated daddy—except for what we've done to the word daddy.

The thought of the Original Oneness which preceded the big bang keeps returning to me, the Original Oneness which preceded galaxies and stars and planets and Adam and Eve and you and me. Was that the primordial fall? Are the stars in their courses singing the Lord's song in a strange land?

There was war in heaven: Michael and his angels fought against the dragon; and the dragon fought, and his angels, and prevailed not; neither was their place found any more in heaven. And the great dragon was cast out, that old serpent called the Devil, and Satan, who deceives the whole world; he was cast out into the earth, and his angels with him . . .

So goes the old song, and what does it mean?

The dragon and his angels did not want to be One; they wanted independence and individuation and autonomy, and they broke wholeness into fragments . . .

When will we once again be one?

Perhaps galaxy by galaxy, solar system by solar system, planet by planet, all creation must be redeemed.

Where were we when the morning stars sang together, and all the sons of God shouted for joy?

During my journey through life I have moved in and out of agnosticism and even atheism, as I become bewildered by what mankind has done to God; and so, too often, I see God in man's image, rather than the other way around. But I cannot live for long in this dead-end world, but return to the more open places of my child's intuitive love of God, where I know that all creatures are the concern of the God who created the galaxies, and who nevertheless notes the fall of each sparrow. And from the darkness I cry out: God!

And it is enough.

Come, Lord Jesus! Do I dare
Cry: Lord Jesus, quickly come!
Flash the lightning in the air,
Crash the thunder on my home!
Should I speak this aweful prayer?
Come, Lord Jesus, help me dare.

Come, Lord Jesus! You I call
To come, come soon, are not the child
Who lay once in the manger stall,
Are not the infant meek and mild.
You come in judgment on our fall.
Help me to know on whom I call.

Come, Lord Jesus! Come this night
With your judgment and your power,
For the earth is dark with blight
And in sin we run and cower
Before the splendid raging sight
Of the breaking of the night.

Come, my Lord! Our darkness end!
Break the bonds of time and space.
All the powers of evil rend
By the radiance of your face.
The laughing stars with joy attend.
Come, Lord Jesus, be my end!

When I think of the incredible, incomprehensible sweep of creation above me, I have the strange reaction of feeling fully alive. Rather than feeling lost and unimportant and meaningless, set against galaxies which go beyond the reach of the furthest telescopes, I feel that my life has meaning. Perhaps I should feel insignificant, but instead I feel a soaring in my heart that the God who could create all this— and out of nothing—can still count the hairs of my head.

Our tininess has nothing to do with it. The peculiar idea that bigger is better has been around for at least as long as I have, and it's always bothered me. There is within it the implication that is more difficult for God to care about a gnat than about a galaxy. Creation is just as visible in a grain of sand as in a skyful of stars.

The church is not immune from the bigger-is-better heresy. One woman told of going to a meeting where only a handful of people turned out, and these faithful few were scolded by the visiting preacher for the sparseness of the congregation. And she said indignantly, "Our Lord said *feed* my sheep, not count them!" I often feel that I'm being counted, rather than fed, and so I am hungry.

The glory of the incarnate world is briefly visible for me as I look through the sleeping plants to the planets, to the quiet of streets which will soon be waking; this glory is too often obscured in the city because of what we human beings have done to it. Hugh and I live in a melting pot of a neighborhood which was once solid, respectable, moneyed; Jewish on West End and Riverside Avenues, Irish on Amsterdam; and which is now white, black, yellow, tan; where one hears English in a multitude of accents, as well as Spanish, German, Creole, Taiwanese, Chinese, Japanese, Korean, Hindustani, Yiddish, Hebrew, French—and probably other languages I don't recognize. It is a far more realistic world than the world of New England farmland where we lived for a near decade when our children were little, and now know only in the summer.

The old ethnic stamp of the Bloomingdale section of Manhattan Island, the Upper West Side between the old academic elegance of Morningside Heights and the new cultural elegance of Lincoln Center, is still reflected in the observance of holidays. Markets are open on Sundays, even Easter Sunday, but are closed for the Jewish Holy Days. One Puerto Rican *bodega* placed a sign in the window which read: CLOSED FOR YOM KIPPER. What a delicious red herring!

Sometimes I think in wonder of our years in a New England village, a village still small enough so that everybody was known by name. It was not easy to get lost in our village; it wasn't exactly like living in a goldfish bowl, but there wasn't much that people didn't know about their neighbors. This has its disadvantages, but it's more human than the anonymity of the city where an old man or woman, living alone, can fall and break a hip and not be discovered for weeks. If anybody in our village had an accident, everybody knew about it; a lot of people prayed about it; almost everybody cared, wanted to help. But if I pass an accident in the city while I'm riding a bus or walking along the street, I, like everybody else around me, will stare in horrified curiosity as we pass by; it may be a *momento mori,* but we'll never know who was in that buckled car, who lay on the street after having been hit by that bus; it happens so often that we won't even read about it in the paper. We are forced to be as passive as though we were viewing it on television, and this frightens me. Our cities get more crowded daily; we build bigger and better housing developments where neighbors are strangers and anonymity is a disease and not a privilege. It was predicted that we would feel the radical changes of overpopulation by the end of the century, but overpopulation in the cities has already plunged us into a new dark age. There are rats in the streets, fat and sleek and sinister as sharks.

I think of my children asking me why God created mankind if mankind was going to make battlefields and slums and insane asylums. The city around our pleasant apartment building is not an easy place in which to see the hand of God. Mankind has imposed its imprint of ugly buildings and dirty streets and desperate people. But if I cannot see God's love here on the Upper West Side of New York where we seem to have done everything possible to destroy the beauty of creation, it is going to do me little good to rejoice in beauty in the uncluttered world of the country.

My breath steams the window but I see a young man walking along the street, his head bowed against the wind. It is cold, but for the moment the city is quiet. No sirens shrieking, no grinding of brakes. A light goes on in a window across the street.

It is the nature of love to create, and no matter what we do to creation, that love is still there, creating; in the young man who is holding his jacket closed across his chest; in you; in me.

The last of the bouillon is lukewarm in the bottom of the mug. It's time for bed.

Time: why are we so timebound?

Why should I go to bed?

You'll be tired in the morning if you don't.

Yes. But maybe it's worth it. I don't want to get imprisoned by the clock, that arbitrary, man-made definer of the hours.

Let us view with joy and mirth
All the clocks upon the earth
Holding time with busy tocking
Ticking booming clanging clocking
Anxiously unraveling
Time's traveling
Through the stars and winds and tides.
Who can tell where time abides?

Foolish clocks, all time was broken
When that first great Word was spoken.
Cease we now this silly fleeing
From earth's time, for time's a being
And adoring
Bows before him
Who upon the throne is seated.
Time, defeated, wins, is greeted.

Clocks know not time's loving wonder
Day above as night swings under,
Turning always to the son,
Time's begun, is done, does run
Singing warning
Of the morning
Time, mass, space, a mystery
Of eternal trinity.

Time needs make no poor apology
For bursting forth from man's chronology
Laughs in glee as human hours
Dance before the heavenly powers.
Time's undone
Because the Son
Swiftly calls the coming light
That will end the far-spent night.

Advent.

Waiting for the end. The eschaton.

The night is far spent.

And now I'm sleepy and ready for bed.

In the dark bedroom Timothy, our Irish setter, sighs deeply in his sleep. I can hear my husband's peaceful breathing. I crawl into bed beside him, reaching out as always to touch, very lightly, the reassuring warmth of his flesh, flesh I have known intimately for over three decades.

Who is he, this man I have slept beside for lo these many years?

> *You are still new, my love. I do not know you,*
> *Stranger beside me in the dark of bed,*
> *Dreaming dreams I cannot ever enter,*
> *Eyes closed in that unknown, familiar head.*
> *Who are you? who have thrust and entered*
> *My very being, penetrated so that now*
> *I can never again be wholly separate,*
> *Bound by shared living to this unknown thou.*
> *I do not know you, nor do you know me,*
> *And yet we know each other in the way*
> *Of our primordial forebears in the garden.*
> *Adam knew Eve. As we do, so did they.*
> *They; we; forever strangers: austere, but true.*
> *And yet I would not change it. You are still new.*

Good night.

2... Sometimes I Forget to Tell You How Much I Love You

THE NATIVITY IS a time to take courage. How brave am I? Can I bear, without breaking apart, this extraordinary birth?

The end is the beginning. We have come to the shortest day, the longest night of the year. Christmas is coming, the goose is getting fat. I can turn from contemplation of the eschaton and Christ's return to *anamnesis,* the living memory, the memory in untimebound *kairos* of what has already been.

I've never been to seminary nor taken any religion courses; in college I was through with the religious establishment; so my interpretation of theological words is not always correct. Anamnesis is important to me, but my understanding of it is largely literary.

Anamnesis: against amnesia. This kind of memory is one of the most important of the storyteller's tools. If I am to write about young people in my novels, as well as those my own age, it is essential that I remember exactly what it was like to be young. I have sometimes been asked if my young protagonists are based on my children; no, of course they are not; I would not presume to write out of my children. My protagonists, male and female, are me. And so I must be able to recall exactly what it was like to be five years old, and twelve, and sixteen, and twenty-two, and.... For, after all, I am not an isolated fifty-seven years old; I am every other age I have been, one, two, three, four, five, six, seven ... all the way up to and occasionally beyond my present chronology.

When I am writing in a novel about a fourteen-year-old girl, I must remember what I was like at fourteen, but this anamnesis is not a looking back, from my present chronological age, at Madeleine, aged fourteen. If there is all this distance of years between us, my memory is only from the outside. When I am writing about a fourteen-year-old girl I will not succeed unless I am, during the time of writing, Madeleine: fourteen. The strange wonder of it is that I am also Madeleine: fifty-seven, with all the experience I have gained in the intervening years. But I am not, in the ordinary sense, remembering what it was like to be fourteen; it is not something in the past; it is present; I am fourteen.

I was talking to a psychiatrist friend about the importance of memory, and he said that many of his patients are afraid to remember, because they are afraid to learn who they really are.

I don't know what has kept me from being afraid, because the minute he spoke I understood the fear. Perhaps there's no getting around the fact that if I am to be a storyteller I must have a trained memory. No memory, no story. And so the joy of memory has remained mine.

As I understand anamnesis in my writing, so I understand it in the Holy Mysteries. When we are truly remembering, when we know anamnesis, suddenly the mighty acts of God are present.

And then we are in *kairos*. Kairos. God's time, which isn't really time at all in the sense that we know man's time, *chronos*. It is impossible, while we are living in time, to define *kairos;* it is to be understood by intuition, rather than intellect, and recognized only afterwards, by anamnesis when we are back in time again, for in *kairos* we are completely unselfconscious. Whenever I have loved most truly and most spontaneously, time has vanished and I have been in *kairos*.

The second Christmas of our marriage, and the first with our six-month-old baby, the beautiful flesh of our child made the whole miracle of incarnation new for me, and that newness touched on *kairos*.

Now, all these years later, I plunge into the delightful business of painting Christmas ornaments with my grandchildren; I hear the hammer as Bion puts together a dolls' house which looks remarkably like Crosswicks, our house in the country; the New York kitchen smells fragrant with Christmas cookies: this, for me, is incarnation.

The enfleshing of the Word which spoke the galaxies made the death of that Word inevitable. All flesh is mortal, and the flesh assumed by the Word was no exception in mortal terms. So the birth of the Creator in human flesh and human time was an event as shattering and terrible as the eschaton. If I accept this birth I must accept God's love, and this is pain as well as joy because God's love, as I am coming to understand it, is not like man's love.

What one of us can understand a love so great that we would willingly limit our unlimitedness, put the flesh of mortality over our immortality, accept all the pain and grief of humanity, submit to betrayal by that humanity, be killed by it, and die a total failure (in human terms) on a common cross between two thieves?

What kind of flawed, failed love is this? Why should we rejoice on Christmas Day? This is where the problem lies, not in secular bacchanalias, not in Santa Clauses with cotton beards, loudspeakers blatting out Christmas carols the day after Thanksgiving, not in shops full of people pushing and shouting and swearing at each other as they struggle to buy overpriced Christmas presents.

No, it's not the secular world which presents me with problems about Christmas, it's God.

Cribb'd, cabined, and confined within the contours of a human infant. The infinite defined by the finite? The Creator of all life thirsty and abandoned? Why would he do such a thing? Aren't there easier and better ways for God to redeem his fallen creatures?

And what good did it all do? The heart of man is still evil. Wars grow more terrible with each generation. The earth daily becomes more depleted by human greed. God came to save us and we thank him by producing bigger and better battlefields and slums and insane asylums.

And yet Christmas is still for me a time of hope, of hope for the courage to love and accept love, a time when I can forget that my Christology is extremely shaky and can rejoice in God's love through love of family and friends.

Christology: I'm all right through the first verses of John's Gospel, verses which are in the language of poetry which breaks through reason and strengthens my courage. My heart lifts at that first great cry which brought creation into being; Christ, the second person of the Trinity making all those galaxies burning with incredible brightness, those brilliant flaming suns which themselves are not the light which made them: I rejoice. It's the Word, the Light coming to us as Jesus of Nazareth, which confounds my imagination.

Most of the time the fact that this fact is impossible doesn't bother me. I live by the impossible. Like the White Queen, I find it a good discipline to practice believing as many as seven impossible things every morning before breakfast. How dull the world would be if we limited ourselves to the possible.

The only God who seems to me to be worth believing in is impossible for mortal man to understand, and therefore he teaches us through this impossible.

But we rebel against the impossible. I sense a wish in some professional religion-mongers to make God possible, to make him comprehensible to the naked intellect, domesticate him so that he's easy to believe in. Every century the Church makes a fresh attempt to make Christianity acceptable. But an acceptable Christianity is not Christian; a comprehensible God is no more than an idol.

I don't want that kind of God.

What kind of God, then?

One time, when I was little more than a baby, I was taken to visit my grandmother, who was living in a cottage on a nearly uninhabited stretch of beach in northern Florida. All I remember of this visit is being picked up from my crib in what seemed the middle of the night and carried from my bedroom and out of doors, where I had my first look at the stars.

It must have been an unusually clear and beautiful night for someone to have said, "Let's wake the baby and show her the stars." The night sky, the constant rolling of breakers against the shore, the stupendous light of the stars, all made an indelible impression on me. I was intuitively aware not only of a beauty I had never seen before but also that the world was far greater than the protected limits of the small child's world which was all that I had known thus far. I had a total, if not very conscious, moment of revelation; I saw creation bursting the bounds of daily restriction, and stretching out from dimension to dimension, beyond any human comprehension.

I had been taught to say my prayers at night: Our Father, and a long string of God-blesses, and it was that first showing of the galaxies which gave me an awareness that the God I spoke to at bedtime was extraordinary and not just a bigger and better combination of the grownup powers of my mother and father.

This early experience was freeing, rather than daunting, and since it was the first, it has been the foundation for all other such glimpses of glory. And it is probably why the sound of the ocean and the sight of the stars give me more healing, more whole-ing, than anything else.

We are meant to be whole creatures, we human beings, but mostly we are no more than fragments of what we ought to be. One of the great evils of twentieth-century civilization is the rift which has come between our conscious and our intuitive minds, a rift which has been slowly widening for thousands of years, so that now it seems as unbridgeable as the chasm which separated Dives, suffering the torments of hell, from Lazarus, resting on Abraham's bosom.

And this gap, separating intellect from intuition, mind from heart, is so frightening to some people that they won't admit that it exists. I heard an otherwise intelligent man announce belligerently that there was no gap whatsoever between his conscious and below-conscious mind; his conscious mind was in complete control of his unconscious mind, thank you very much.

We haven't learned much since Paul of Tarsus admitted quite openly that his conscious mind was not successful in dictating to his below-the-surface self. If anything, the gap between consciousness and super- sub- or un-consciousness is even wider now than it was then. How can we possibly bridge the chasm?' How can we become free?

I turn again to the night sky, this time to a planet, one of the planets in our own solar system, the planet Mercury. Mercury revolves around our mutual parent sun in such a way that one face is always turned toward the sun and is brilliantly lit and burningly hot; and the other side is always turned toward the cold dark of interstellar space. But Mercury oscillates slightly on its axis, and thereby sunside and nightside are integrated by a temperate zone which knows both heat and cold, light and dark. So the two disparate sides of Mercury are not separated by a chasm; the temperate zone mediates.

Where, in ourselves, can we find this temperate zone which will integrate and free us? The words *freedom* and *liberation* have been used frequently during the last decade, and this would certainly seem to imply that we are less free, less liberated, than we want to admit.

People who are already free don't need to talk about liberation. It is a great mistake to equate freedom with anarchy, liberation with chaos. It has been my experience that freedom comes as the temperate zone integrates sunside and nightside, thereby making wholeness instead of brokenness.

Art is for me the great integrater, and I understand Christianity as I understand art. I understand Christmas as I understand Bach's *Sleepers Awake* or *Jesu, Joy of Man's Desiring;* as I understand Braque's clowns, Blake's poetry. And I understand it when I am able to pray with the mind in the heart, as Theophan the Recluse advised. When we pray with the mind in the heart, sunside and nightside are integrated, we begin to heal, and we come close to the kind of understanding which can accept an unacceptable Christianity. When I am able to pray with the mind in the heart, I am joyfully able to affirm the irrationality of Christmas.

As I grow older
I get surer
Man's heart is colder,
His life no purer.
As I grow steadily
More austere
I come less readily
To Christmas each year.
I can't keep taking
Without a thought
Forced merrymaking
And presents bought
In crowds and jostling.
Alas, there's naught
In empty wassailing
Where oblivion's sought.
Oh, I'd be waiting
With quiet fasting
Anticipating
A joy more lasting.
And so I rhyme
With no apology
During this time
Of eschatology:
Judgment and warning
Come like thunder.

But now is the hour
When I remember
An infant's power
On a cold December.
Midnight is dawning
And the birth of wonder.

But what is that wonder? The marvel of Christianity is its particularity, and if I am to say anything about Christmas it must be through the particular, so let me tell the story of one particular Christmas.

The Thanksgiving before, we were expecting our usual mob for dinner. I dressed the turkey and put it in the oven, and lay down for a brief nap. But I couldn't rest and after a while I wandered back out to the kitchen to baste the turkey. I opened the oven door and was met with a fading glow of dying heat. The oven had gone off with the turkey not half cooked. We took the oven apart, but the gas pilot light would not relight. We called the 'super,' apologetically, explaining that it really was an emergency, and he left his own Thanksgiving dinner and came up. But it was quickly apparent that the problem with the oven was not a minor one, and we were not going to be able to finish cooking our turkey in the oven that day.

"But we have twenty people coming for dinner!" I cried in horror.

There was nothing the 'super' could do except go downstairs to his own dinner, explaining that his oven wasn't large enough for our turkey.

So we began calling friends in our apartment building. Some were away—we got no answer; others still had their own turkeys in the oven. Finally we got friends who had just started to carve their turkey and immediately offered to let us finish cooking ours in their oven.

On one of our various trips up and down the back stairs between apartments, I remarked to our son, Bion, home from college for vacation, "Oh, well, it's just another typical Thanksgiving at the Franklins'."

So if I say that the Christmas I am about to describe was 'typical,' it was not that the events themselves were typical, but that this Christmas evoked in me that response which makes me continue to struggle to understand, with the mind in the heart, the love of God for his creation, a love which expressed itself in the Incarnation. That tiny, helpless baby whose birth we honor contained the Power behind the universe, helpless, at the mercy of its own creation.

We had our usual full house of family and friends. Bion was again home from college. Our second daughter and son-in-law, Maria and Peter, were home from England, where Peter has a research job in theoretical chemistry at the University of Warwick. Our elder daughter and son-in-law, Josephine and Alan, had recently moved into a large and comfortable apartment at the General Theological Seminary, where Alan is associate professor of ascetical theology, and there was a good deal of going back and forth between the two households.

Maria and Peter had not expected to come home for Christmas; it seemed an unwarranted expense. But when Peter's mother, Dorothy, had a heart attack they came immediately. We all visited Dorothy in the hospital, Peter and his sisters daily, and she expected to be home shortly after Christmas, though she told all of us firmly that when she did die she wanted to be buried alongside her parents in an Orthodox Jewish Cemetery. But the present anxiety seemed to be over, so the weekend before Christmas Peter went to Poughkeepsie to visit cousins.

Saturday night the rest of our household went to bed rather late, after a lovely long evening of conversation. We were deep in sleep when the phone rang; it was one of Peter's sisters. One of the hospital nurses had gone to check on Dorothy and found her dead in her sleep.

Maria and Bion stayed up to wait for Peter while he drove from Poughkeepsie. Hugh and I felt that we would be more useful the next day if we got some sleep, so we turned out the light with heavy hearts.

In the morning I was awake before Hugh, so I slipped out quietly. Maria's and Peter's door was open and their lights on, so I knocked and went in. Peter was lying in bed, looking drawn and dry-eyed, although Bion and Maria told me later that he had done a lot of crying the night before, which relieved me, and I knew that he would need to do more crying later.

I sat beside him and took his hand.

"Madeleine, are you going to church this morning?"

"No, Peter, I want to stay here with you."

Peter, as head of the family, was in charge of his mother's funeral. Immediately he said that he wanted Alan to do as much as possible, but since Dorothy would be buried in a Jewish cemetery, the service would have to be led by a rabbi, so Peter asked me to call one of the rabbis from the temple where I recently had been the lay Christian on a panel about Christians and Jews. I did so, and everything was arranged for the following morning, Christmas Eve.

Peter was very torn within himself about his mother's funeral, and Christmas the next day. The loss of a mother is always a grief, but Dorothy had lived her life, and had died as she would have wished to die, with none of the pain and terror she had dreaded. So I put my arms about Peter and said, "On Christmas Day I think it's all right for you to relax and enjoy being with so many people you love, and to help us all make it a happy day for Léna and Charlotte." Peter is very fond of his two little Anglican nieces, and his misconceptions of Christianity had by and large disappeared. He agreed willingly.

Was that advice to a bereaved son all right? Is it proper to grieve and rejoice simultaneously?

If the love I define in my own heart as Christian love means anything at all; yes. If the birth of Christ as Jesus of Nazareth means anything at all; yes.

I don't think any of us will ever forget that Christmas Eve. We sat around the apartment in the morning drinking coffee and waiting for time to go to the funeral parlor.

I have an inordinate dread of funeral parlors. A horror of great darkness falls on me, and I feel further from home than did Abraham; I no longer even know where home is. In a funeral-parlor service I feel dragged into an ultimate pit of darkness. This is an irrational reaction, but I am convinced that the undertakers' lobby is personally led by Satan, who has as chief helpers a group of priests, rabbis, and ministers.

I didn't mention my dread. Instead, I dressed in my most elegant black, and wore high-heeled black pumps in order to please Peter and Maria. Then it was time to go to the funeral parlor with Alan and Josephine. Alan had got out of a sickbed and looked pale and half ill; he had a bad sore throat and he was to preach the midnight Christmas Eve service at St. Paul's Chapel.

Peter's family, sisters, aunts, uncles, cousins, started arriving. The rabbi spent half an hour with Peter and his sisters before the service, while the rest of us chatted in the desultory and fragmentary way of such places.

I felt cold and isolated from reality during the service, which the rabbi conducted with as much dignity as possible, given the setting. Then we got into funeral cars to drive to the cemetery in New Jersey. The rabbi couldn't come, but the cantor did, and Alan was to say the prayers for the dead at the graveside.

The traffic was heavy and we crawled slowly through a chill grey day. When we finally reached the cemetery I was appalled to see a carpet of fake green grass carefully covering the good earth which had been dug to make Dorothy's grave. This isn't a Jewish custom; the phony green is seen in Christian cemeteries, too, trying to conceal the reality of dust to dust. It is a travesty of truth and only makes death more brutal. What it is covering is earth, clean earth, real earth, which is going to cover the coffin. Grass will grow out of it again, and it will be real grass, not plastic.

If the Word coming to dwell in human flesh means anything, it means that Dorothy's flesh is real flesh, that it will now decay; it must be buried, as the seed is buried, before the flower, the plant, the tree, the true flesh, can be born.

We stood in a small circle around the grave while the cantor and Alan recited the service. When it came to the Kaddish—the beautiful Hebrew prayer for the dead—Alan was able to read and recite it in Hebrew. These rich, extraordinarily beautiful syllables moved me to the heart and were, for me, the reality of this other mother's funeral.

When we got back to the city it was time for me to dash down to the seminary, pick up my little grandaughters, and bring them all the way back uptown for the blessing of the crib at the convent of the Sisters of the Community of the Holy Spirit, who run the school where they were in kindergarten, and from which their mother was graduated.

The chapel is small, and in this smallness, holding Charlotte in my arms, with Léna leaning against me, I began to move into Christmas. The Sisters sang Solemn Vespers for Christmas Eve, and their high, clear voices, moving antiphonally back and forth across the chapel, contained for me the same reality I felt in the strong words of the

Kaddish. Then we all gathered round the crèche, the children on tiptoe to see the shepherds, the animals, Mary and Joseph and the infant in the crib, the helpless thing containing the brilliance of the galaxies and the shadow of the cross.

It was impossible, but for the moment I was the White Queen, and the loving and beautiful bodies of my grandaughters made it possible for me to believe: they have not been created to be discarded like dross; the baby lying between the ox and ass affirms the ultimate value of all life.

After the blessing of the crib there was a party: hot cider and cookies and homemade lemon bread. I had to hurry the little girls into their snowsuits and away from this warmth of love and laughter, and then we almost ran home so that I could cook dinner quickly, and once again it was all the way back downtown to the seminary, where Hugh baby-sat so that the rest of us could go to St. Paul's. Peter spent the evening with his sisters, but Maria came with us to church.

And there, in the peace and quiet, Christmas came into even clearer focus for me. We were very early because of Alan, and it was a strangely solemn joy for me to sit there in silence in the beautiful gold and white church where George Washington came to pray after his Inauguration.

The service began with a concert of chamber music, played on ancient instruments. I closed my eyes as the music wove gently about me. My thoughts wove along with the loveliness of sound. I was sitting between my two daughters in an extraordinary clarity of love, having buried so short a time ago the mortal remains of another mother who had beheld with joy her first-born babe. And the memory was vivid that two thousand years ago a young girl bore a child as helpless as any child, a child who would show us that the greatest power is in weakness, the greatest majesty in meekness, a child whose growing up was then, and always will be, out of tune with the tenor of the times.

The birth of my own babies (every woman's Christmas) shows me that the power which staggers with its splendor is a power of love, particular love. Surely it takes no more creative concentration to make a galaxy than a baby. And surely the greatest strength of all is this loving willingness to be weak, to share, to give utterly.

Oh, yes, according to Scripture the Lord throws a few thunderbolts when he is angry, but by now we must have angered him so much that it's a wonder he hasn't wiped us out entirely, at least on this recalcitrant planet. We are surely one of his failures. He loved us enough to come to us, and we didn't want him, and this incredible visit ended in total failure, and this failure gives me cause to question all failure, and all success.

And even after failure he continues to be concerned for us. We can, if we will, recognize him as he is manifested in love, total, giving love. And I believe that in one way or another we are all meant to receive him as Mary did.

The church is quiet. There is no room for sentimentality here after Dorothy's funeral in the sterile atmosphere of the mortuary. It would be easy now for me to close off, to say no, no, to the pain. But the name of the pain is love, love so great that it was willing to share and redeem our living and dying. It was a very small gift that God gave us for Christmas two thousand years ago: only a baby: only himself.

In the funeral parlor that morning I had been alienated from myself in cold and darkness; now I was thrown into myself in a loveliness of light.

When Alan got up into the white and gold pulpit to preach, his voice was hoarse—it was the beginning of an abcess on his tonsils—but his words were clear and part of the light; and the meaning of the Word made flesh was itself the light.

As we got back to the seminary we sat down to relax and have a drink together, and Hugh said that when he had been putting the children to bed Léna had turned to him and said, "You know, Gum, sometimes I forget to tell you how much I love you, but I do."

And that, too, was Christmas.

> *This is the irrational season*
> *When love blooms bright and wild.*
> *Had Mary been filled with reason*
> *There'd have been no room for the child.*

3... Rachel Weeping

THE DAYS BETWEEN Christmas and Epiphany slide by too quickly. We eat turkey sandwiches and cold stuffing—almost the best part of the turkey. The living room is full of the fragrance of the tree.

Every day is a festival. The twenty-sixth is St. Stephen's Day (I find it impossible to think of Stephen as someone who wasn't quite bright enough to go on beyond the diaconate and make it to the priesthood). The twenty-seventh is the feast of St. John, John who speaks most closely to my understanding, who helps put the mind in the heart to bring wholeness.

And on the twenty-eighth of December, Holy Innocents' Day. Holy Innocents' Day is a stumbling block for me. This is a festival? this remembering the slaughter of all those babies under two years of age whose only wrong was to have been born at a time when three Wise Men came out of the East to worship a great King; and Herod, in panic lest his earthly power be taken away from him by this unknown infant potentate, ordered the execution of all the children who might grow up to dethrone him.

Jesus grew up to heal and preach at the expense of all those little ones, and I have sometimes wondered if his loving gentleness with small children may not have had something to do with this incredible price. And it causes me to ask painful questions about the love of God.

St. Catherine of Siena said, "Nails were not enough to hold God-and-man nailed and fastened on the cross, had not love kept him there."

What kind of love was that? More like folly. All the disciples except John had abandoned him. His mother was there and a few women as usual, and a gaping mob, also as usual, and some jeering soldiers. That's all. The cross represented the failure of his earthly mission. God came to the world and the world didn't want him and threw him out by crucifying him like a common criminal. God—God the Father —loved the world he had created so much that he sent his only son —that spoken Word who called forth something from nothing, galaxies from chaos—he sent him to dwell in human flesh, to accept all earthly limitations, to confine himself in mortal time; and when this beloved son begged in agony that he might be spared the cross, what did the Father do? No thunderbolts, no lightning flash. Silence was the answer to the prayer. NO was the answer. And Jesus of Nazareth died in agony on the cross; the love of God echoing back into the silence of God.

That is love? How can we understand it? Do we even want it?

I sometimes get very angry at God, and I do not feel guilty about it, because the anger is an affirmation of faith. You cannot get angry at someone who is not there. So the raging is for me a necessary step toward accepting that God's way of loving is more real than man's, that this irrational, seemingly unsuccessful love is what it's all about, is what created the galaxies, is what keeps the stars in their courses, is what gives all life value and meaning.

But what kind of meaning? It's not a meaning that makes any sense in a world geared to success and self-fulfillment.

Remember the children in the school bus hit by a train? Remember the Vietnamese orphans dying in a flaming plane? What about all the holy innocents throughout time? It was this extraordinary God of love who personally killed all the first-born of the Egyptians in order to belabor a point which surely should have been obvious long before.

First God changed the waters of the Egyptians' river into blood; then he sent a plague of frogs which weakened Pharaoh's nerve considerably so that he almost let Moses and the Israelites go; then God sent mosquitoes against the Egyptians, and then gadflies, and then he killed all the Egyptians' livestock, but spared the beasts of the children of Israel. Then God sent boils to torment the Egyptians, and Pharaoh said, "Go ahead, leave in safety," and God, mind you, God, hardened Pharaoh's heart so that he changed his mind and would not let the people go.

The boils were followed by hail, and Pharaoh begged Moses to stop the thunder and hail and he would let them go, and God stopped the storm and then he hardened Pharaoh's heart again. And this kept right on. Next God sent locusts, and next he blotted out the light of the sun and sent darkness over the Egyptians, and whenever Pharaoh was ready to let the children of Israel go, God hardened his heart again, so that God could send one more horrible plague, and the worst of these was the death of the first-born children of the Egyptians, and these children were no more sinful or guilty than the children in the school bus or in the huge plane or the children under two years of age slaughtered by Herod.

Only a story? But there is no better way to search for the truth of history than to look in poetry and story.

This story really bothers me. I struggle with it.

Sometimes in this groping dark of knowing my not-knowing
I am exhausted with the struggle to believe in you, O God.
Your ways are not our ways. You sent evil angels to the Egyptians
and killed countless babies in order that Pharaoh—
whose heart was hardened by you (that worries me, Lord)
might be slow to let the Hebrew children go.
You turned back the waters of the Red Sea
and your Chosen People went through on dry land
and the Egyptians were drowned, men with wives and children,
young men with mothers and fathers (your ways are not our ways),
and there was much rejoicing, and the angels laughed and sang
and you stopped them, saying, "How can you laugh
when my children are drowning?"

When your people reached Mount Sinai you warned Moses
not to let any of them near you lest you break forth and kill them.
You are love—if you are God—and you command us to love,
and yet you yourself turn men to evil, and you wipe out nations
with one sweep of the hand—the Amorites and the Hittites and the
Perizzites—
gone, gone, all gone. Sometimes it seems that any means will do.
And yet—all these things are but stories told about you by fallen man,
and they are part of the story—for your ways are not our ways—
but they are not the whole story. You are our author,
and we try to listen and set down what you say, but we all suffer
from faulty hearing and we get the words wrong.

One small enormous thing: you came to us as one of us
and lived with us and died for us and descended into hell for us

and burst out into life for us—:
and now do you hold Pharaoh in your arms?

The love of God reveals itself in extraordinary ways. What kind of love kept him nailed to the cross? What kind of a Father did Jesus of Nazareth have?

Are we too intellectual and too reasonable to understand? Jesus said, "I bless you, Father, Lord of Heaven and earth, for hiding these things from the learned and the clever and revealing them to mere children."

We're a learned and clever generation, we of the late twentieth century. Those of us with the heritage of the Anglican Communion are a learned and clever group of people. Did those first-born of the Egyptians, those Holy Innocents in Bethlehem, those Vietnamese orphans in the flaming plane know something that God is deliberately hiding from us? Why would a God of love do such things, permit such things? What does all this teach us about how we are to love one another?

For some time my husband played the father in *The Diary of Anne Frank,* the father who was the only one of the group of people hiding from the Nazis in an attic in Amsterdam who survived concentration camp. One evening while they were still in hiding, they heard a terrible crash downstairs, and they thought the Nazis had found them, and they held their breaths in terror. Nothing. Silence.

So the father goes downstairs to investigate, and they all know that he may never come back. While they are in an agony of waiting, the mother drops to her knees and says the 121st Psalm: *I will lift up mine eyes unto the hills. . . .* She says it all, all those comforting words: *The Lord shall preserve thy going out, and thy coming in, from this time forth and even forevermore.* But the Lord didn't preserve them. He let the Nazis find them and send them to concentration camp and they all died there except the father, a whole group of innocent people guilty of nothing except being chosen of God. The mother who had cried for help died. Anne, the innocent child, died. God, the God they trusted, let it happen. In human terms it would seem evident that the love and faith of the mother who cried out for help was far greater than the love of God.

Do I want this kind of God? Until I saw my husband in *The Diary of Anne Frank*—and I saw it several times—the 121st Psalm used to be strong and comforting to me. Now I say it daily with a kind of terror. Hugh's performance in that play brought about a crisis in my understanding of the love of God, and the saying of the Psalm is a cry in the dark that I still affirm that God's love is more real than mine.

For men make the cozy and comfy promises; not God.

Yes, but how can a God of love stand by and let Anne Frank die, and all the holy innocents in the children's leukemia wards and in rat-infested tenements? Why doesn't he stop the slaughter? If he's God, he can do anything. What kind of love is this?

Okay, Madeleine, but if God interferes every time we do wrong, where's our free will?

But Anne Frank didn't do wrong.

But the Nazis did. When they built concentration camps that was a very big wrong and a lot of innocent people suffered. But it was man who did the wrong, not God.

But he could have stopped it.

And if he did? Do I want to adore a God who allows me no free will, and therefore no potential for either evil or good? Do I want a cosmic dictator, ruling a closed, finished cosmos?

Sometimes when I think of our battlefields and slums and insane asylums, I'm not sure, and I ask: why does God treat in such a peculiar way the creatures he loves so much that he sent his own Son to them?

And what about that son whose love kept him on the cross?

Deep in our hearts most of us really wish that Jesus hadn't resisted the temptations; if he had only been a reasonable son of man and turned those stones into bread, then all the poor of the earth could be fed and we wouldn't have inner cities or ghettos in this country, or children with bloated bellies dying of starvation in India or Cambodia or Venezuela. If he had only come down from the cross in a blaze of power, then we wouldn't have any trouble understanding the Resurrection—why did he have to be so *quiet* about it?—and we wouldn't be afraid of death. If he had only worshipped the prince of this world, he could have ruled and ordered the earth, and legislated our lives so that we needn't make decisions, and he could have taken away all pain (there is no coming to life without pain) and organized our old age so that we could be senior citizens in some happy home, going on happy buses for happy excursions. . . . Our churches and government agencies think that this kind of manipulation is a good thing, and so they're trying to do it themselves, since Jesus failed to take the opportunity offered him.

Why, why did he turn it down?

All those innocent little children . . .

All the hungry . . .

All the old men and women struggling to live alone and being mugged as they bring in their inadequate groceries (we see it on television every night), little girls raped and murdered, little boys mutilated . . .

cancer and blindness and senility . . .

battlefields and slums and insane asylums . . .

He could have stopped it all if only he'd listened to Satan in the wilderness. What kind of love is he teaching us? And who are we in the Church listening to? The tempter, or the one who put the temptations behind him? Oh, he healed a few blind people and lepers, but certainly not all, and he drove out a few unclean spirits, but not all, and he announced that the poor will be always with us.

No wonder the Church often thinks that he was wrong and turns, with ardent social activism, to the promises of Satan. But why hasn't the social activism worked? It ought to have worked. But the social activism of the sixties has, after all, produced the seventies, which are galloping to their anguished end. Have we, then, failed—because we've fed only a few starving children, rescued only a few war orphans, taken care, like Mother Thersa of Calcutta, of only a few indigent dying people?

And who is this Church I keep referring to? It is not limited to my own denomination, or even the Anglican Communion. When I talk of the Church I mean all of us—Episcopalians, Presbyterians, Lutherans, Baptists, Methodists, all, all of the denominations and all of the sects, all who in any organized way call themselves Christians.

St. Paul said, "I was given a thorn in the flesh, an angel of Satan to beat me and stop me from getting too proud. About this thing, I have pleaded with the Lord three times for it to leave me, but he has said, 'My grace is enough for you: my power is at its best in weakness.' "

And there, for me, is a clue, another tiny piece in the incomprehensible puzzle. Man's pride and God's weakness. And if this is to make any sense to me at all, it must be in terms of my own experience, not what I read about, see on television, but what touches me personally.

Of course, that's what this book is about. It may be a small and inadequate response of experience, but it's my own. My profession is writing—stories, novels, fantasy, poetry, thoughts. Writing is not just my job, but a vocation, a total commitment. I started to write when I was five, and as I look back on fifty years of this work, I am forced to accept that my best work has been born from pain; I am forced to see that my own continuing development involves pain. It is pain and weakness and constant failures which keep me from pride and help me to grow. The power of God *is* to be found in weakness, but it is God's power.

He has a strange way of loving; it is not man's way, but I find evidence in my own experience that it is better than man's way, and that it leads to fuller life, and to extraordinary joy.

Nails were not enough to hold God-and-man nailed to the cross had not love kept him there.

Because I am a writer I live by symbol, and because I was born in the Western World my symbolism is largely Judaeo-Christian, and I find it valid, and the symbol which gives me most strength is that of bread and wine. Through the darkness of my uncomprehending, through my pain and weakness, only thus may I try to become open to God's love as I move to the altar to receive the body and blood, and accept with friend and neighbor, foe and stranger, the tangible assurance that this love is real.

It is real, but it is not like our love.

I keep thinking about those Holy Innocents, all those little ones who died that Jesus might live.

And one night I woke up thinking about the nobleman from Capernaum whose son Jesus saved from death, and I wondered if perhaps this man's first-born son might not have been one of the slaughtered little ones, and the memory of that death would stay with him as long as he lived, even if he became a very old man. . . .

... AND THE OLD MAN BECAME AS A LITTLE CHILD ...

He could not sleep.
The tomb was dark, and the stone heavy that sealed it.
He could not sleep for all the innocent blood he had seen shed.
He was an old man. Too old for tears.
Not yet young enough for sleep. He waited and watched.

Thrice he had spoken to him whose body had been sealed
within the tomb, thrice had the old man spoken,
he who was a disciple, but not one of the twelve,
older, gentler in all ways,
and tired, worn with time and experience and the shedding of blood.
He came from Capernaum
and after that his son
who touched the edge of death
was drawn back from the pit
and made whole,
the old man returned to Jesus and said,
"O thou, who hast today been the consolation of my household,
wast also its desolation.
Because of you my first-born died
in that great shedding of innocent blood.
Nevertheless, I believe
though I know not what
or how or why
for it has not been revealed to me.
I only know that one manchild was slain
and one made to live."

And a second time he spoke
when the Lord kept the children beside him
and suffered them not to be taken away:
"These are the ones that are left us,
but where, Lord, is the Kingdom of Heaven?
Where, Lord, are the others?
What of them? What of them?"
And he wept.

And a third time he spoke
when the Lord turned to Jerusalem
and laughter turned to steel
and he moved gravely
towards the hour that was prepared
and the bitterness of the cup:
then the old man said,
"All your years you have lived

under the burden of their blood.
Their life was the price of yours.
Have you borne the knowledge and the cost?
During those times
when you have gone silent in the midst of laughter
have you remembered all the innocence
slaughtered that you might be with us now?
When you have gone up into the mountain apart to pray,
have you remembered that their lives were cut down
for your life, and so ours?
Rachel's screams still shatter the silence
and I cannot sleep at night for remembering.
Do you ever forget your children that sleep?
When will you bring them out of the sides of the earth
and show mercy unto them?
Who will embrace them until you come?
I cannot sleep.
But because I have already tasted of the cup
I cannot turn from you now.
I, who live, praise you.
Can those who have gone before you into the pit
celebrate you or hope for your truth?
Tell me, tell me, for I am an old man
and lost in the dark cloud of my ignorance.
Nevertheless, blessed is he
whom thou hast chosen and taken, O Lord."

He did not speak again.

But he was there when the rocks were rent
the veil of the temple torn in twain
the sun blackened by clouds
the earth quaked with darkness

the sky was white and utterly empty.
The city gaped with loss.

Then, out of the silence,
the Lord went
bearing the marks of nails and spear
moving swiftly through the darkness
into the yawning night of the pit.
There he sought first
not as one might have supposed
for Moses or Elias
but for the children
who had been waiting for him.

So, seeking, he was met
by the three Holy Children
the Young Men
burning bright
transforming the fire into dew as they cried:
"Blessed art thou, O Lord God, forevermore."

And all the children came running
and offering to him their blood
and singing: "With sevenfold heat
did the Chaldean tyrant in his rage
cause the furnace to be heated
for the Godly Ones
who wiped our blood like tears
when we were thrust here
lost and unknowing.
The Holy Three
waited here to receive us
and to teach us to sing your coming
forasmuch as thou art pitiful
and lovest mankind."
So they held his hand
and gave him their kisses and their blood
and, laughing, led him by the dragon
who could not bear their innocence
and thrashed with his tail
so that the pit trembled with his rage.
But even his roaring could not drown their song:
"For unto Thee are due all glory, honor, and worship,
with the Father and the Holy Spirit, now, and ever,
and unto ages of ages, Amen."

And the holy children were round about him,
the Holy Innocents and the Holy Three.
They walked through the darkness of the fiery furnace
and the dragon could see their brightness,
yea, he saw four walkers loose
walking in the midst of the fire and having no hurt
and the form of the fourth was like the Son of God.

And he saw the Son of God move through hell
and he heard the Holy Children sing:
"Meet is it that we should magnify thee,
the life-giver
who has stretched out thy hands upon the cross
and hast shattered the dominion of the enemy.
Blessed art thou, O Lord God, forevermore.

> *O Jesus, God and Saviour,*
> *who didst take upon thee Adam's sin*
> *and didst taste of death*
> *(the cup was bitter),*
> *thou hast come again to Adam*
> *O compassionate One*
> *for thou only art good*
> *and lovest mankind,*
> *Blessed art thou, O Lord God, forevermore."*

> *So hell was shriven*
> *while the holy children, singing,*
> *transformed the flames to dew,*
> *and the gates of Heaven opened.*

> *Then, by the empty tomb,*
> *the old man slept.*

If the dark prophets who infuriated the people of the Establishment in their own day have anything to say to me today, it is through their constant emphasizing that God is so free of his own creation that he can transform us in our pain into a community of people who are able to be free of the very establishments which are formed in his name. For these establishments inevitably begin to institutionalize God's love and then he teaches us (put my tears in your bottle) what love really is—not our love, not what we want God's love to be, but God's love.

4... To a Long-Loved Love

WHEN I WAS a little girl in France I put out my shoes on the Eve of Epiphany. They were only ordinary shoes, not proper sabots, so I wasn't sure that they would be noticed by the three Wise Men; but in the morning one shoe held a new drawing pad, and the other a box of colored pencils. I like the idea of presents and feasting on Twelfth Night, so that Christmas can follow quietly on Advent. Christmas doesn't start until Christmas Eve, and then it can go on and on and the tree shines as brightly on Epiphany as on Christmas Day.

And there's more time to make things, which is one of the joys of Christmas. Our favorite presents are the homemade ones. Several years ago we decided that we were not going to be bullied by the post office or the Greeting Card Establishment into mailing our cards well before Christmas. We make our own cards, and I may not get an idea for one well before Christmas, for one thing. And there are a goodly number of people we write to only once a year, tucking the letter in with the card. So for the past several years we've taken our time, and as long as the last Christmas letter gets mailed before Lent, that's all I worry about, and Epiphany is a season of joy instead of exhaustion.

EPIPHANY

Unclench your fists
Hold our your hands.
Take mine.
Let us hold each other.
Thus is his Glory
Manifest.

Epiphany is a special time to me in another and extra-special way, because Hugh and I were married during the Epiphany season, thirty years ago, and my wedding anniversary is part of my personal calendar of the Church year. My attitude toward the promises Hugh and I made is a fundamental part of my theology of failure, and the freedom and laughter and joy which this brings.

During Advent, when I contemplate the four last things, I think not only of the end of all time and matter, but of my own end, Hugh's end. A friend of mine said that when two people truly love each other, each one has to be willing to let the other die first. I try to be willing, but it's not easy.

And it's not part of the American atmosphere where the amoeba, rather than the human being, would be the logical symbol of success. Amoebas never betray each other by dying. Nor is there any sexism in the amoeba's culture—though this may be because there isn't any sex. The amoeba produces by dividing and subdividing, which doesn't sound like much fun.

However, fun or no fun, the amoeba is a success—and when I consider the world's definition of success, I doubt if there's ever much fun involved. But the amoeba is way ahead of the human being, because it is immortal. It has no normal life span. Unless killed by some unforeseen accident, the amoeba lives forever.

Radio and television commercials seem directed more to the amoeba than to the human being, especially those for life insurance, where the announcer says, ". . . but in case something should happen to you . . ."

It strikes me forcefully as I listen to those unctuous words that something is indeed going to happen to me, and to that announcer, and to everybody who buys or does not buy insurance. We are going to die. We have a life span, and sooner or later, by accident or disease or attrition, we are going to come to the end of our mortal lives.

Why do we have a life span instead of being like the amoeba? Because of sex. It wasn't until it took two members of a species to produce offspring that a life span came into the evolutionary system. Sex and death came into the world simultaneously. All creatures with a complicated cellular system have a life span: it may be a few days, a few years, or threescore years and ten.

Obviously we are all failures, we human beings. We may have fun, but we're flops. But maybe I'm happy because I *am* a failure, a human failure who enjoys sex, has a limited life span, and who made marriage vows which have added both to the fun and the failure. I wish the American marriage service had not deleted the words of the English service, where the man says to the woman, "With my body I thee worship," because I think the basic difference between Christian and secular marriage is that Christian marriage affirms the pleasures of the body, of creation. Too many people would like to forget that Jesus's first miracle was turning water into wine at a marriage feast, in a glorious affirmation of human love, human joy, human pain. Wine is a word which has meaning upon meaning for the Christian: water into wine; the baptism of water and blood; and it is only when I think of the wedding at Cana that I come close to understanding the words of the ancient prayer: *Blood of Christ inebriate me.* At the Eucharist I pray that our souls may be washed in this precious blood, and that it will preserve our souls and bodies into everlasting life. These are terrible prayers, and it is small wonder that so many of us are afraid to say them, and that many of the new translations try to water them down.

I was taken aback to have a well-known liberal theologian say that he wished that people would not think of sex in terms of morals, and I replied that I had never thought of sex and morals in conjunction, and he said, "You're very lucky. Most people still think that sex is not very nice." What a strange, revealing remark, and what a totally un-Christian point of view. And yet I think that it is often a factor in the breakup of a marriage.

A year ago on our anniversary I had occasion to take a taxi, and the driver and I got to talking, and we talked about marriage, and I said that it was pretty much of a record for a writer and an actor to have been married for twenty-nine years. He turned completely around, disregarding the traffic and the snowy streets, and said, "Lady, that's not a record. That's a miracle."

He's probably right. It's an extraordinary thing to me that Hugh and I have been married for this long. It is also, I believe, a good marriage, although much of it would not seem to be so in terms of the kind of success commercials would hold out to us. However, our own expectations of marriage were false to start out with. Neither of us knew the person we had promised to live with for the rest of our lives. The first bitter lessons of marriage consisted in learning to love the person we had actually married, instead of the image we wanted to have married.

I was twenty-seven. I had been living in Greenwich Village and working in the theatre. I had made a lot of mistakes and failures in love already, and had learned that structure and discipline were essential in my life if I wanted the freedom to write. Shortly before I met Hugh, I had painfully but totally cut loose from an undisciplined group of friends, and I assumed that the kind of pattern needed in my single writing life would also be essential to my married writing life. I was too involved in the ecstasy of love to think much about the inevitable conflicts ahead, and I don't think it would have made any difference if I had been aware of them. I don't ever remember living without conflict of one kind or another, and I'm not at all convinced that life without conflict is desirable. There's not much conflict in the grave, but while we're alive the only creative choice is choice of conflict.

I realize how fortunate I was in the terms with which I started my marriage; I had had one novel published; the second was already in galleys; I had made a good start as a professional writer. When Hugh asked me to marry him, and talked about children, I said that I, too, wanted children, but that he had to understand that I could not stop writing, that he was marrying me as a writer, marrying all of me, not just the part of me which would bear his children. And I rather naïvely told him that writing takes a lot of time, and that I would be glad to do the cooking but he'd have to do the dishes.

The division hasn't been that straight down the line, but we've always shared household chores, and we have also shared the nurture of our babies. Hugh showed a generosity and understanding as rare then as it is now when he accepted me on these terms, and never expected me to be only an appendage, an *et ux.* I have never had to struggle against my husband to be me. This doesn't mean that we haven't had struggles and conflicts in our marriage—we have—but they have been in different areas.

It is the nature of love to create, and Hugh and I did want to make babies together. In my conception of love, something always has to be created during the act of intercourse, but this something may be simply a strengthening of love, a love which is participation, not possession. Daniel Day Williams, in *The Spirit and the Forms of Love,* was the one to bring to my attention the idea of love which is participatory, and not long after I had read this book I was able to talk with him about it, and was taught even more. Just as our friendship was a'birthing he died, and I look forward to learning more from him in heaven.

Too often, love is seen in terms of possession, and this destroys marriage. Until Hugh and I started our first baby, our love-making was a discovery of each other, was creating this strange new creature, a marriage.

I'm glad that I'm a human mother, and not a sea horse; the sea horse might well be a symbol for the more extreme branches of women's lib, because the female sea horse lays her eggs in the male's pouch, and then he has to carry the eggs to term, go through labor pains, and bear the babies.

I don't understand why some women consider childbearing a humiliation; it's an extraordinary act of creativity, and men suffer a great deprivation in being barred by their very nature from this most creative of all experiences. But there's a price on it, as with all good things, especially for a woman who feels called to do something as well as being wife and mother.

I actively enjoyed the whole magnificent process of having children, the amazing months of pregnancy when suddenly one becomes aware that one is carrying life, that a new human being is being created. While I was carrying Josephine, our first-born, I felt quickening while I was in an eye-and-ear hospital with a recurring eye problem; a young nurse happened to come into my room as I felt the first small flutterings, and I cried, "I think I feel the baby!" She ran to the bed and put her hand on my belly, and her joy in feeling the new life was almost as great as my own. From then on, there was a lovely procession of nurses and doctors coming to feel the baby; the quickening of new life is something which doesn't often happen in an eye-and-ear hospital.

I find the birthing of babies even more fantastic. And here I feel profoundly that the husband should be given the privilege of being with his wife during the birth, that he should not be excluded. This didn't happen with Hugh and me until our son, Bion, was born in a small New England village, and delivered by an old-fashioned general practitioner. Hugh was with me to rub my back during pains, to hold my hand, suddenly to see the crowning of his son. Our first baby was born in a big New York hospital, delivered by an eminent obstetrician, and I spent hours left alone and in pain and afraid. It's enough to make the whole process seem degrading.

And nursing: I loved nursing my babies, but when Josephine was born, nursing was not yet popular again in New York City; it's more trouble for the nurses, and I had to fight for the right to nurse my baby: "But nobody nurses babies nowadays." "I do."

My husband's theatre hours are definitely not nine to five. I had seen other young wives up at six with the baby, and unable to manage to be awake and ready to listen and talk when their husbands got home from the theatre, and I was determined that this was not going to happen with us. Our baby was a strong, healthy specimen, so, while I was still in the hospital, the head nurse told me that they had decided that the baby didn't need the 2 A.M. feeding and they were going to cut it out. "But my husband's an actor and we're up at 2 A.M. Let's cut the 6 A.M. feeding." This wasn't hospital procedure at all, and I had my first hospital fight to be a human being and not a cog in routine. I was told in no uncertain terms that it was the 2 A.M. feeding which would be cut. I replied in equally certain terms that if my baby was brought to me at 6 A.M. I would turn my breasts to the wall. I won.

I had made a choice, a free yet structured choice. Why should a man come home at all if his wife isn't awake and available? I had seen other actors go to the local bar instead of coming home to a dark apartment. This choosing the structure of our day was not being an unliberated woman. I chose it for my own pleasure, too; I enjoyed this time with my husband; it was no sacrifice. And I profoundly disbelieve in the child-centered household. What happens to the parents when it is time for the children to leave the nest if all of life has been focused on the fledglings?

We had such fun with Josephine that we wanted more children, and this was when Hugh decided to leave the theatre—it didn't seem fair to our children to have two parents in precarious professions. But I don't think that either of us realized what this complete uprooting was going to involve. I know that I had a glamorous and completely unrealistic vision of life in the country, based on romantic English poetry, and my illusions were shattered in short order.

In refusing to nurse my baby at 6 A.M. I was already moving toward what is now called 'choosing an alternative life style.' And when Hugh and I left New York and the theatre to continue raising our growing family, and went to live in a small village in New England, and ran a general store, we did what was later to be called 'downgrading'—though we certainly didn't think of it as such. Nor was it.

When the children were little I was often on edge with sheer frustration. I was trying to run a big two-hundred-year-old house with no help; for three hours a day I helped my husband in the store—my shift was from noon to three in the afternoon, so that he could go home for lunch and a nap. Two of our best-sellers were teat dilators and bag balm—these are for cows; over half our customers were farmers, many of whom are still our good friends.

Writing was not easy during those years. I struggled to write under the worst possible conditions, after the children were in bed, often falling asleep at my desk. During the early school years Hugh got up with the children in the morning, so that I could sleep a little later in order to be able to write at night, and without that understanding help I don't think I could have managed. Even so, it was not easy, particularly when I ventured into new ways of writing. So I was prickly and defensive, because during the near-decade we lived year-round in the country, almost nothing I wrote sold, and rejection slips for work you believe in are bitter indeed.

I know that I'm a better writer now because of the conflict and frustration of those years, and some of that conflict was in our marriage, and I don't minimize any of the pain.

During the years of Hugh's leaving the theatre forever—thank God forever lasted only nine years—our time together, alone, was the hour before dinner, when we sat in front of the fire and had a quiet drink and talked. At dinnertime we were the whole family, gathered around the table, but the hour before dinner was our quiet hour, our grownup hour, and I do not think that the children felt rejected because of it. But it was a choice, a deliberate choice, and it was part of the structure of the day.

Even if we had had money for servants, I don't think I would have wanted anybody else to have brought up our children; I was an only child and for many reasons I did not see a great deal of my parents when I was very young, and this may explain my feelings. But children and store meant that if I were to hope to write, something had to go—lots of things, in fact. I eliminated all kinds of housewifely virtues. Our house was tidy—I cannot write in a filthy nest—but I will never win an award as Housekeeper of the Year. I did not scrub the kitchen floor daily; commercials for various floor waxes, furniture polishes, and window-cleaning sprays go right over my head; they are not within my frame of reference or the seasons of my heart. It is more important that I have at least an hour a day to read and study; that I walk at least a couple of miles a day with the dog—this is thinking and praying time; that I have an hour a day at the piano. Practicing the piano, rather than just playing at it, got eliminated with the advent of our third child; I'm only now properly getting back to it, and playing the piano is one of the best consciousness and memory expanders there is.

I'm asked with increasing frequency, "But why marry?" a question to be taken seriously, especially when it comes from young people who have seen their parents' marriages end in divorce, or in constant bickering and hostility, which is almost worse. The desire to make sure that there is integrity in love, that neither partner wants to use or manipulate the other, is a healthy one. But ultimately there comes a moment when a decision must be made. Ultimately two people who love each other must ask themselves how much they hope for as their love grows and deepens, and how much risk they are willing to take.

I'm glad that I was twenty-seven when Hugh and I married. As I look back on the men I might have married, I shudder. I needed the time not only to wait to meet the man who was to become my husband, but to do enough growing up so that I was a mature enough human being to enter into the depths of a lifelong partnership. I matured slowly, and I know that I was not adult enough before I met Hugh—and hardly, then.

After all these years I am just beginning to understand the freedom that making a solemn vow before God, making a lifelong commitment to one person, gives each of us. Thirty years ago on a cold morning in January—very cold, it was 18° below zero—when Hugh and I made those vows, we were deliberately, if not very consciously, leaving youth and taking the risk of adulthood and a permanent partnership. It is indeed a fearful gamble. When I looked into the future I knew that there would be more than glorious nights, longed-for babies, someone to come home to. I knew that an actor and a writer are a poor risk. But we had committed ourselves, before a God neither of us was at all sure about, that we wouldn't quit when the going got rough. If I was not fulfilled by my relationship with this particular man, I couldn't look around for another. And vice versa. No matter how rough the going got, neither of us was going to opt out.

Because it is the nature of love to create, a marriage itself is something which has to be created, so that, together, we become a new creature. There are many glorious ways of intercourse besides the sex act, but the emphasis of this country's culture today is focused on the physical, genital act of sex, rather than love, whole love, and so we've lost a lot of these other ways of completion. The intercourse of that quiet hour in front of the fire with my husband; or walking, as we love to do, on the beach, hand touching hand, can be as electrifying as the more obvious forms of love.

To marry is the biggest risk in human relations that a person can take. All the rather pompous sociological jargon about the advisability of trial marriages or short-term relationships as part of the new freedom is in actuality a result of our rejection of freedom and our fear of risk—I had learned this through experience in the Greenwich Village years before I was twenty-seven.

There isn't much risk in a one-night stand except venereal disease, and penicillin will cope with that. The pill has almost eliminated the risk of unexpected babies, and liberal abortion laws will take care of the few surprises. In trial or short-term commitment we don't have to risk all of ourselves; we can hold back.

If we commit ourselves to one person for life this is not, as many people think, a rejection of freedom; rather, it demands the courage to move into all the risks of freedom, and the risk of love which is permanent; into that love which is not possession but participation.

And there is the risk of failure. It doesn't always work. There are marriages which for one reason or another simply do not become marriages. There are times when two people who have taken the risk have to accept the brutal fact of failure, and separation, and divorce. But, far too often, people quit simply because the going is rough, and this is almost more sad than the marriage manqué.

It takes a lifetime to learn another person. After all these years I still do not understand Hugh; and he certainly does not understand me. We're still in the risky process of offering ourselves to each other, and there continue to be times when this is not easy, when the timing isn't right, when we hurt each other. It takes a lifetime to learn all the varied ways of love, including intercourse. Love-making is like a Bach fugue; you can't go to the piano and play a fugue the first time you hold your hands out over the keys.

When love is not possession, but participation, then it is part of that co-creation which is our human calling, and which implies such risk that it is often rejected.

John of Kronstadt, a Russian priest of the nineteenth century, counseled his penitents to take their sins of omission and commission, when they get too heavy, and hang them on the cross. I find this extremely helpful, and particularly during the summer when the larger family gathers together and I often cook for a minimum of twelve. We had four summers when we were four generations under one roof—something unusual in this day of small, nuclear families, and something which calls for enormous acceptance and humor from everybody. Sometimes when I hang on the cross something which is too heavy for me, I think of it as being rather like the laundry lines under our apple trees, when I have changed all the sheets in the house. The wind blows through them, the sun shines on them, and when I fold them and bring them in in the evening they smell clean and pure.

If I could not hang my sins on the cross I might tend to withdraw, to refuse responsibility because I might fail. If I could not hang my sins on the cross, Hugh and I probably wouldn't still be married. And I would certainly never write a book.

When Hugh criticizes my writing, no matter how just the criticism, I fight him. He has learned that if he makes a criticism and I say calmly, "Thank you, I see what you mean," then I have no intention of doing anything about it. But when—as usually happens—I defend the work hotly, when I lose my temper, when I accuse him of wanting to "just cut it all," he knows that I have taken what he has said seriously, and that I will do something about it, even if it means six more months of hard work.

I withdraw from him completely at first, feeling abused and misunderstood. I take the dog and go for a long, furious walk. And then my subconscious creative mind—the dark side of Mercury—gets to work, and when I return I am ready to go back to the typewriter—if not to my husband. By the time I have written a few pages the knowledge that all this unwanted work is going to make for a much better book has me so excited that by dinnertime I'm ready to cook a good dinner and give Hugh a grateful kiss.

I've learned something else about family and failure and promises: when a promise is broken, the promise still remains. In one way or another, we are all unfaithful to each other, and physical unfaithfulness is not the worst kind there is. We do break our most solemn promises, and sometimes we break them when we don't even realize it. If a marriage has to be the pearly-pink perfection suggested by commercials for coffee or canned spaghetti sauce or laundry detergents, it is never going to work. A young woman asked me in amazement, "You mean it's all right to quarrel after you're married?" I can look at the long years of my marriage with gratitude, and hope for many more, only when I accept our failures.

If our love for each other really is participatory, then all other human relationships nourish it; it is inclusive, never exclusive. If a friendship makes me love Hugh more, then I can trust that friendship. If it thrusts itself between us, then it should be cut out, and quickly. I've had that happen several times, so I know whereof I speak. Sometimes I have realized myself that a friendship was a destructive one. Sometimes Hugh has said, "I don't think so and so is good for you," and I've resented it, defensively, refused to do anything, and ultimately realized that he was right. It works, of course, both ways.

On the other hand, we both have rich, deep, abiding friendships which have nourished our marriage and helped it grow. Friendship has become more and more a lost art in a society which feels that in order for a relationship to be fulfilled it must end in bed. A true friendship is always amoureuse; it is part of my human sexuality; each encounter with a friend is a time of creation. I see this most clearly in my professional life. My relationship with my editor has got to be amorous. This doesn't mean sexual indulgence, though I don't think that either editor or writer can find the other physically repugnant. It does mean something happening on that non-empirical level, in the mediating band between nightside and sunside. Two editors, reading a manuscript of mine, may make exactly the same comments or suggestions, but with one of them no response whatsoever is evoked in me, whereas with the other, something happens which sets all my little writing wheels and cogs turning. It is not a matter of intellect alone, of an editor knowing what should be done to make a book better; many editors are qualified to do that. But with only a few is the spark set off in me, so that I know what must be done to make a manuscript come alive.

Not long ago the editor with whom I had done eleven books retired, and I started to work with a new one, and this was not unlike the beginning of a love affair for which I had great expectations, and in which I am rejoicing as they are fulfilled; but it is not in any way an act of unfaithfulness in my marriage, any more than is my husband's relations with the women he works with on stage and on television —not that such relations cannot be destructive; I've seen them be so —but in my definition of marriage they should be nourishing rather than devouring.

LOVERS APART

In what, love, does fidelity consist?
I will be true to you, of course.
My body's needs I can resist,
Come back to you without remorse;

And you, behind the footlight's lure,
Kissing an actress on the stage,
Will leave her presence there, I'm sure,
As I my people on the page.

And yet—I love you, darling, yet
I sat with someone at a table
And gloried in our minds that met
As sometimes strangers' minds are able

To leap the bounds of time and space
And find, in sharing wine and bread
And light in one another's face
And in the words that each has said,

An intercourse so intimate
It shook me deeply to the core.
I said good night, for it was late;
We parted at my hotel door

And I went in, turned down the bed
And took my bath and thought of you

Leaving the theatre with light tread
And going off, as you should do,

To rest, relax, and eat and talk—
And I lie there and wonder who
Will wander with you as you walk
And what you both will say and do. . . .

We may not love in emptiness;
We married in a peopled place;
The vows we made enrich and bless
The smile on every stranger's face,

And all the years that we have spent
Give me the joy that makes me able
To love and laugh with sacrament
Across a strange and distant table.

No matter where I am, you are,
We two are one and bread is broken
And laughter shared both near and far
Deepens the promises once spoken

And strengthens our fidelity
Although I cannot tell you how,
But I rejoice in mystery
And rest upon our marriage vow.

There's not as much risk of failure with an editor as in a marriage, but risk there is. A couple of times I've plunged into the risk, and the amoureuse-ness has been abortive rather than creative, and the book has never come properly to term. But the risk must be taken if the book is to be born at all. There are writers who do not need editorial help; I am not one of them. I seldom show more than the beginnings of a book before I have a complete rough draft, but then I need help. And to ask for help involves risk, and the danger of failure.

When I look back on the first years of Hugh's and my enormous risk of marriage, I marvel that we lasted. Certainly in my ignorance I did everything wrong. I drenched Hugh with my love, gave him all of me in great, overwhelming waves. I, in my turn, had a few things to put up with. However, in our naïveté we unknowingly did one thing which was right, and which I recently found superbly expressed by Rilke: "It is a question in marriage not of creating a quick community of spirit by tearing down and destroying all boundaries, but rather a good marriage is that in which each appoints the other guardian of his solitude, and shows him this confidence, the greatest in his power to bestow. A togetherness between two people is an impossibility, and where it seems . . . to exist it is a narrowing . . . which robs either one . . . or both of his fullest freedom or development.''

Somehow or other, Hugh and I have managed to be guardians of each other's spaces—most of the time—and because of this the spaces between us are not chasms, but creative solitudes. When we blunder, then the spaces are horrendous and solitude turns into the most painful kind of loneliness; but then a willing acceptance can turn the loneliness back into solitude.

Marriage as defined by Madison Avenue, Hollywood, and TV, would seem to include permanance, whereas, paradoxically, Christian marriage is built on impermanence. Like everything else on this earth it will come to an end; one of us will die, and in our society we think of death as failure, as the ultimate failure. And in worldly terms it is. No wonder we tend to extol the amoeba. Live forever, amoeba. Mortal, you will die. That's cold, stark fact, and there's nothing romantic about it. Death is the enemy, the last enemy to be defeated, and it is not I—or any scientist—who will defeat it. The defeat of death was prefigured in the Resurrection, and what that means not one of us will know in terms of provable fact while we are in this life. But until we stop thinking of death as failure, we will never have either a theology of death or an understanding of Christian marriage.

Sometimes it seems that the Church has forgotten this in its rush to conform to the world. Everything is being made easy for us. Everything is permissible. Divorce and remarriage are almost as unimportant as they are in the secular world, where marriage is a legal contract made before a justice of the peace and not a covenant made before God. I understand casual divorce where the mighty and terrible promises have not been made in the sight of God. And I also understand that sometimes even when the promises are made in good faith, the marriage which follows is not marriage, never has been, or no longer is, and I am glad that the Church is looking on such marriages with more compassion than it used to in the legalistic days. But compassion is not the same thing as permissiveness, and the pendulum, as usual, has swung too far, and no one seems to notice that the sexual permissiveness in the Church hasn't made a happier people of God. Where little is demanded of the people, the pews become emptier each year. All of us, like our children, want standards upheld for us. If I am not expected to grow and deepen in faithful and chaste love, I'm less likely to be able to stand firm when the tempter comes and tells me it's really all right to go out to dinner and probably to bed with the attractive man who sits next to me on the plane; it really won't do anything to my marriage.

In a sense Hugh and I have an 'open marriage,' but it has never involved playing around and making light of our promises. I am free to leave him for a week or more to lecture at universities, to teach at writers' conferences, conduct retreats, just as he is free to go away from me for weeks at a time with a play or to make a movie. We have a theory that one reason our marriage has lasted so long is that we never eat breakfast together. Hugh likes to emerge slowly in the morning, breakfast, newspaper, crossword puzzle, shave, shower; whereas I, once I have managed the heavy athletic feat of getting my feet out of bed and onto the floor, am ready to talk. So I roll into my clothes, fill my thermos with coffee, call Timothy, and set off for the Cathedral library.

A decade ago I wasn't getting enough writing done at my bedroom desk, what with children still at home and a husband apt to be around the house during the day, so I asked Canon Tallis if it was all right if I wrote in the then almost unused library at the Cathedral. My first few weeks there were marvelously productive, and just as I came to the point where I needed to get my penned pages onto the typewriter, the young librarian got called on jury duty, and was quite upset about abandoning his post. I looked longingly at his electric typewriter and told him I'd be glad to keep the place open for him as long as I could use the typewriter. I had a blissful two weeks, and when he came back it was only briefly, and I became librarian by default. I have no training whatsoever as a librarian, but I am very happy in the beautiful paneled room which is used far more now than it was, so that I need an assistant to do the library work while I get on with my writing. I've been prolific during my years there, and have made an extraordinary number of friends.

My dog is welcome to come with me, and he stays dutifully under the desk, only his black nose showing. I have a little radio set for a classical music station, WNCN, and after the eleven o'clock news I call Hugh, briefly, just to check in. When I come home in the late afternoon I check in again, go over the mail, and then head for the piano for an hour and a half. After that we are together, and really together, for the evening, talking and having a drink while I get dinner. It is a free relationship, but it is built on promises. Like every other couple we break our promises one way or another, but we take the breaking of the promises seriously; the fact that the promise has been broken does not make us permissive about breaking it again; instead, we try to mend. We have used an extraordinary amount of glue.

Written words about marriage inevitably come from the mind, from the sunside of Mercury; whereas I know, with nightside, with heart informing mind, that the largest part of marriage and love abides in the mediating zone, in the non-empirical area of our identities. With my conscious mind and with my body I can think about the freedom a promise brings, the joy an explosion of passion. But there's more to it than that.

> Because you're not what I would have you be
> I blind myself to who, in truth, you are.
> Seeking mirage where desert blooms, I mar
> Your you. Love, I would like to see
> Past all delusion to reality.
> Then would I see God's image in your face,
> His hand in yours, and in your eyes his grace.
> Because I'm not what I would have me be
> I idolize two Ones who are not any place,
> Not you, not me, and so they never touch.
> Reality would burn. I do not like it much.
> And yet in you, in me, I find a trace
> Of love which struggles to break through
> The hidden lovely truth of me, of you.

My love for my husband and his for me is in that unknown, underwater area of ourselves where our separations become something new and strange, merge and penetrate like the drops of water in the sea. But we do not lose our solitudes, or our particularity, and we become more than we could alone. This is mystery. I cannot explain it. But I have learned that it makes up for our clashes, our differences in temperament, our angers, our withdrawals, our failures to understand.

No long-term marriage is made easily, and there have been times when I've been so angry or so hurt that I thought my love would never recover. And then, in the midst of near despair, something has happened beneath the surface. A bright little flashing fish of hope has flicked silver fins and the water is bright and suddenly I am returned to a state of love again—till next time. I've learned that there will always be a next time, and that I will submerge in darkness and misery, but that I won't stay submerged. And each time something has been learned under the waters; something has been gained; and a new kind of love has grown. The best I can ask for is that this love, which has been built on countless failures, will continue to grow. I can say no more than that this is mystery, and gift, and that somehow or other, through grace, our failures can be redeemed and blessed.

On Valentine's Day, for a saint most misunderstood

He was a strange old man
given to solitude on the forest,
eating acorns and locusts.
When he saw a young virgin
he ceased baying at the moon,
lay down, and put his head in her lap.

He helped the sun rise every morning
and pulled the ocean high on the shore
at each full moon. He knew that love
is like a sword. He felt its pain.
His blood fell on the snow and turned to roses
and so he was, of all saints, most misunderstood.

His eyes are flame, and their look sears.
We pretend he's someone else to avoid burning.
I would go into the forest, silent and alone.
If I find him, will he dry my tears?

5... Lion and Lamb

LENT. Strange bleak season in the Church year; strange bleak season in the part of the world in which I live. February—how right the Romans were to make it the shortest month of the year. And March. In March I am ready for spring, and spring is not here. When I went to Smith College from Charleston, South Carolina, I could not understand why March was still winter; in Charleston, spring was at its height. In Northampton the sky was clamped whitely over a frozen earth. Ice crackled in the puddles along the paths; snow piled greyly in shady corners.

I am too eager for spring. Around Crosswicks the sere fields need their blanket of snow to prepare the ground for growing. In my heart I am too eager for Easter. But, like the winter fields, my heart needs the snows of Lent. I used to make up lists as Lent approached, lists of small things to give up. But then it occurred to me that if what I was giving up was something bad, it should be given up once and for all, and not just for forty days and forty nights. There is a value to giving up something which is in itself good, as an offering of love. But now I feel that I want to do something positive, rather than something negative, for these wintry weeks. The horror of starvation all over the world makes a moderate diet obligatory at all seasons of the year.

Perhaps what I am supposed to do about Lent is to think about some things I have put off thinking about. The Beatitudes, for instance. They have seemed to make demands on me that I'm not sure I want made. But I have a hunch that if I stop being afraid of the Beatitudes and consider them seriously, I may discover a way of life which will not only be simpler than life usually is in New York City in the late nineteen-seventies, but which will also be more free than life normally is for a middle-class American.

As I glance superficially at these extraordinary directions they seem absurd when set against the United States of America at the end of the twentieth century. Perhaps they were more possible in the smaller and simpler world of two thousand years ago.

But were Nineveh and Tyre that much different from Manhattan and Dallas? Or Sodom and Gomorrah from Chicago and Kansas City?

The days grow longer, the cold grows stronger. According to the new liturgical year in my Church we no longer have the three weeks of preparation for Lent dividing the joy of the Epiphany season from the journey into the darkness of Lent, and I miss them because it appears out of step with the needs of the world, which seem to cry out for a return to the austere observance of Lent. It's not that I want us to go in for breast beating and navel gazing, but I do find the lack of penitence in both the Roman Catholic and the Anglican proposed liturgies extraordinary. Here the world's in the worst mess we've been in for generations, and we no longer get down on our knees and say, I'm sorry. Help!

It's not that I want us to get stuck in that position or to grovel. My mother used to want to say the General Confession from the Book of Common Prayer, and that was fine, but I didn't want her to stop there. After the Confession I wanted her to go on to the Thanksgiving. But I agree with her that the Confession must come before we can rejoice.

Rejoice and be happy—what does it mean? Each one of the Beatitudes begins with *Blessed,* and translated from the Greek, *blessed* means *happy.* In my French Bible blessed is *heureux.* (*Creed* is *symbole* and I find this helpful too.) Sometimes I think that we have forgotten how to be truly happy, we are so conditioned to look for instant gratification. Thus we confuse happiness with transitory pleasures, with self-indulgence. How, in fact, can we live happily when we are surrounded on all sides by so much pain and misery? War and alarums of war, earthquake, flood, drought. Crime is rising; anger and frustration burst into violence, and violence itself becomes a perverse form of gratification. What is this blessedness, this promised happiness? What, if we follow the directions given us in the Beatitudes, is expected of us?—not a general 'us,' but each one of us in all our particularity.

If it is worth being expected of, then something unique, something different, is asked of each of us.

Jesus wanted the rich young man as a disciple; he probably wanted him as one of the twelve. He loved him, and so he asked everything of him. And the rich young man—as so often happens with the very rich—could not respond to the demand.

With Zaccheus it was different. Zaccheus was a small man, so small that he couldn't even see Jesus through the crowd until he climbed up into a tree. What Jesus asked of Zaccheus was what Zaccheus was capable of giving. Maybe it's easier for those who have less, to give what they have, than for those who have much.

Most of us, I suspect, fall somewhere between the rich young man and Zaccheus, and we have to find out for ourselves where we are.

We live in a day of false expectations, false expectations of ourselves, of others. People I know who are professed non-Christians are horrified because their Christian friends behave in what they consider a non-Christian way. It strikes me as rather ironic coming from people who usually affirm their atheism, and who assert that man does not need God in this enlightened age of technocracy; man is perfectable of his own effort; give us enough education, enough technique, and we can cope with everything on our own; virtue and moral judgment are acquirable characteristics. So I am not quite sure what it is they are looking for in Christians, although they are right that most of us, most of the time, behave in a non-Christian way, in that our light too often burns dim and we are not recognized by our love for each other.

I remember one night at the dinner table when two college students asked, rather condescendingly, if I really needed God in order to be happy (blessed). And I said, "Yes. I do. I cannot do it on my own." Simply acknowledging my lack of ability to be in control of the vast technological complex in which my life is set helps free me from its steel net.

Okay, they agreed. So we know we can't control traffic jams and sanitation-department strikes and flu epidemics, but certainly you can't believe in heaven, can you? All that pie-in-the-sky stuff?

Certainly not pie-in-the-sky. Whoever dreamed that one up didn't have much imagination. But the Beatitudes tell me that *Blessed are the poor in spirit: for theirs is the kingdom of heaven.* That's the very first one. I may hold off on heaven till the last of the Beatitudes because it's going to take a steady look at all of them to get me ready. All I know for now is that wherever God is, heaven is, and if I don't have glimpses of it here and now, I'm not going to know it anywhere else.

But of course I have heaven dreams:

> *Perhaps*
> *   after death*
> *the strange timelessness, matterlessness,*
> *   absolute differentness*
> *   of eternity*
> *will be shot through*
> *like a starry night*
> *with islands of familiar and beautiful*
> *joys.*
>
> *For I should like*
> *to spend a star*
> *sitting beside Grandpa Bach*
> *at the organ, learning, at last, to play*
> *   the C minor fugue as he, essentially,*
> *   heard it burst into creation;*
>
> *and another star*
> *   of moor and mist, and through the shadows*
> *   the cold muzzle of the dog against my hand,*
> *   and walk with Emily. We would not need*
> *   to talk, nor ever go back to the damp*
> *   of Haworth parsonage for tea;*
>
> *I should like to eat a golden meal*
> *   with my brothers Gregory and Basil*
> *   and my sister Macrina. We would raise*
> *   our voices and laugh and be a little drunk*
> *   with love and joy;*
>
> *I should like a theatre star*
> *   and Will yelling, "No! No! That's not*
> *   how I wrote it! But perhaps 'tis better*
> *   that way, 'To be or not to be.' All right,*
> *   then, let it stand!"*

And I should like
another table
—yes, Plato, please come, and you, too,
Socrates, for this is the essential table
of which all other tables are only
flickering shadows on the wall.
This is the heavenly banquet
(Oh, come)
the eternal convivium

the sky blazes with stars

And you, my friends? Will you come, too?
We cannot go alone,

Perhaps, then, star-dazzled,
we will understand that we have seen him
and all the stars will burst with glory
and we, too, in this ultimate explosion
of matter
and time
will know what it is

to be

perhaps

Relying on that glorious cloud of witnesses to attend to heaven, I want to concentrate on blessing, and on being poor in spirit. I'm coming to a wider understanding of blessing than the old one which implied that if you were virtuous and good, God would bless you by giving you an abundance of material things. Even in the Book of Job this attitude prevails, for Job ends up with more wives and more sons and more cattle than he had before.

But the happiness offered us by the Beatitudes is not material; it is more spiritual than physical, internal than external; and there is an implication which I find very exciting that the circle of blessing is completed only when man blesses God, that God's blessing does not return to him empty. This completing of the circle is difficult for adults to comprehend, but is understood intuitively by children. Our youngest child, when he was a little boy, used to have intimate, leisurely, and long conversations with God. Bedtime was my most special and privileged time with my children; we read aloud; we sang; and then we had prayers, and although I knew that the prayers were often extended to inordinate lengths in order to prolong bedtime, that was all right, too. It's not a bad thing to extend conversation with God, no matter what the reason.

This little boy's conversations with God were spontaneous, loving, and sometimes dictatorial. Many of them I recorded in my journal, so that I would not forget them—such as the prayer one rainy autumn evening when he paused in his God-blesses and said, "O God, I love to listen to the rain; I love to listen to you talk." Another evening he paused again and said severely, "And God: remember to be the Lord." This was during one of the many times when the adults had huddled by the radio during a world crisis; but it took a four-year-old to remind me in my own praying that God is the Lord who is in charge of the universe no matter what we do to mess it up.

And one night this little boy, when he had asked God to bless family and friends and animals, said, "And God! God bless you, too."

But we outgrow this spontaneity and forget the completeness of the circle of blessing. Once again we have come to think of happiness as material prosperity, as affluence. This is the consumer mentality, and is how Madison Avenue would have us think. When we have been turned into consumers we are lowered from being men and women, thinking human beings. Far too often we fall for the not-very-subtle temptation: the more we consume, the happier (more blessed) we will be: more cornflakes, Tang, Preparation-H, automobiles, washing machines, aspirin, Exedrin, Drano, Tide, Bufferin—but it gives us headaches, not happiness. Happiness comes to the poor in spirit.

Who do I know who is poor in spirit? Have I ever, myself, been poor in spirit? What do I have that I can give up, in order to become poor in spirit?

I once talked at length to a Roman Catholic nun about her vows, and the things these vows made her renounce, that she might be poor in spirit. She could understand, she said, her vow of poverty, giving up the material things of the world. She could even understand her vow of obedience, giving up her own will. But, she said, "if sex is good, why should we give it up? We used to be taught that sex is bad, and now we're taught that sex is good, so why should we give it up?"

She, an Irish Roman Catholic, was completely hung up on all our distortions of the Puritan ethic. In my marriage I am certainly not required to be celibate, but I am required to be chaste. Chaste love is participatory and knows, I am convinced, far greater physical joy than possessive, or unchaste love, where either or both partners are using the other.

Chastity for a monastic does include celibacy, and my first understanding of celibacy as a positive, rather than a negative, quality came during the Second World War.

It's easy to be smug about what is going on in another country from the safe distance of one's own, and, like everybody else, I found myself violently condemning the behavior of the Germans to the Jews. But even in the act of condemning I would stop short and ask myself, What would I do if I were an ordinary citizen living in Berlin instead of New York? How strong would my moral convictions be? How far would my courage carry me? If I knew everything that Hitler and his cohorts were doing to exterminate all Jews from the face of the earth, Would I have the poverty of spirit to continue being friendly with the Jewish professor in the next apartment?—knowing that this would probably send me to a concentration camp?

At that time I was unmarried. So, yes, I would be free to act according to my belief in what was right, and probably die for it— *if* I had the courage, the poverty of spirit.

But if I were married and had children? Would I have the same freedom? Would I have the right to endanger their lives for what I believed was right? I didn't know the answer then and I don't know it now; I only know that there is no easy, unequivocal answer. I did learn that celibacy gives a freedom to take mortal risk which is not as easily open to those with families.

I haven't often been tested on poverty of spirit. It was easier to be poor in spirit in the early days of the years of our Lord when all Christians were daily tested in their beliefs. Once Christianity became acceptable, and even mandatory, it lost the early poverty of spirit which sustained it when any group gathered together for bread and wine in his Name had to have one ear open for the knock on the door.

But don't we ever have opportunities for poverty of spirit, we middle-class, comfortable Americans?

We do, though what is asked of us is not as spectacular or as dangerous as what was asked of the first Christians. But it is our response to the small things which conditions our response to the large. If I am unable to be poor in spirit in the small tests, I will be equally unable in the great.

There's one time I'm sure about, though I didn't know it while it was going on. It was while our children were little and we were living year round in Crosswicks, and earning our bread and butter—and not much else—running the General Store in the center of the village.

Hugh's parents' golden wedding anniversary came in late August, and the year of this great occasion we left our butcher and the post-mistress in charge of the store, and flew to Tulsa, Oklahoma, for a week of family gathering and festivities. We were to stay with Hugh's parents, and the big old house was going to be stretched to the limits with our family; with Hugh's sister and brother-in-law, with their two children; and his brother and sister-in-law.

I knew to my rue that I would not have been my mother-in-law's choice of a wife for her beloved baby boy. Hugh had, without consultation, chosen to marry a young woman living alone in Greenwich Village in New York, a 'bachelor girl' who had already had two books published and was working in the theatre. Added to which, we had been married quietly, without what was in those days considered a proper wedding, and although we were married in church it was in an Episcopal church with the oddly un-Protestant name of St. Chrysostom's, and this was probably the worst blow of all to my devout Baptist mother-in-law.

It is easier for daughters-in-law to get on with fathers-in-law. I adored my distinguished father-in-law, known to many who admired him as "Old Judge Franklin," or "Uncle Ben." He had white hair and fine-boned features and it was apparent that Hugh was going to look very much like him as he grew older. I had no trouble in loving and being loved by this gentle man.

But with my mother-in-law I felt inadequate. She already knew that I could not iron a man's shirt so that it would be fit to wear. I was clumsy and inept as a housekeeper. I knew that I could not begin to come up to her requirements for a wife for her baby, and most of the qualities which had drawn Hugh to me were the very ones she approved of least. And so I tended to be awkward and defensive.

When we set off for Tulsa I had decided within myself that I was going to do everything possible to make this a happy time for my parents-in-law, both of them. After all, a golden anniversary is a special occasion. So, from the moment we arrived, I really knocked myself out to be pleasant and helpful. I enjoyed my sister-in-law, and we drank countless cups of coffee over breakfast as we planned the rest of the meals for the day. I may not be able to iron a man's shirt, but I'm a good cook, and cooking is the one part of housekeeping I actively enjoy.

Our children were having a marvelous time playing with the numerous children on the block. We hardly had to think about them, whereas at home playmates had to be fetched and carried, and this freedom to run out to find someone to play with, without pre-planning, was delightful and new. The older children took care of our three-year-old son, so I was free to cook and do dishes and make beds and kaffee-klatsch.

It was an eminently successful week. The great day came and went and I was deeply moved by the joy of these two old people who had lived together for fifty years, and whose love for each other was the brightest gift of that golden day.

When we were on the plane on the way home I suddenly realized that I had been intensely happy all week. Somehow or other I had been given the grace to get out of my own way; all my activities had been unselfconscious; and so, all during that week, I had been given the gift of poverty of spirit without even realizing it.

And there in Tulsa, in a world in which I felt myself to be inadequate and inept, I was given a glimpse of the Kingdom of Heaven.

I am slow to understand the obvious. I have been saying the Lord's Prayer for lo these many years, and only recently did the words *thy Kingdom come on earth as it is in Heaven* click in my mind so that I understood that whenever, somehow or other, we manage to do God's will, there is the Kingdom of Heaven, right here and now.

So I am taught by the first of the Beatitudes and move on to the second: *Blessed are they that mourn: for they shall be comforted.*

Everything in the secular world tries to keep us from the essential comfort of mourning. Even *comfort* has been diluted to mean coziness, rather than comfort, with strength.

My English boarding school trained me to feel that any show of emotion is bad form; no matter what has happened, we must keep a stiff upper lip. Tears, from either the male or the female of the species, are to be repressed.

When my father died, my last year in boarding school, I was true to this training. After all, I was president of my class and president of Student Council. I had a position to uphold, and uphold it I did. I was much too brave to shed tears.

It was a long time before I could write the following lines, on the anniversary of my father's death:

Boarding school: someone cried jubilantly,
"There's a letter for you! Didn't you see it?"

The letter was from my mother. My father
was in the hospital with pneumonia.
This was the autumn before the miracle drugs were discovered.
In any case, his lungs were already half eaten away from mustard gas.

I did not tell anyone. I tried to pray. Perhaps I knew how better then
*   than now.*
I only whispered God's name; then, Father; then, God.

In the evenings we did our lessons in a basement room with many desks,
and windows looking out on the Charleston street.
Little black boys with wildly painted faces and bobbing jack-o'lanterns
peered in on us and shrieked, and their laughter
is all I remember of Hallowe'en.

I sent Father a poem, knowing it would not reach him in time.

The next afternoon the headmistress sent for me; my father was very ill.
I was to take the train right after the evening meal.
It was the night when the Head Girl was to say grace. How odd
that I should remember it, and that all that seemed important
was that my voice be steady.

One of the teachers took me to the train.
I tried to read Jane Eyre.

When my parents had put me on the train for school
my last words as I climbed up the high step onto the train were to
my father:
"Be good." I remember: the last words, and my father standing
on the station platform in a rain-darkened trench coat, and the rain
beating on the dirty glass of the station roof
so that we saw each other only darkly.

I tried to read Jane Eyre *and to pray to the rhythm of the wheels:*
Please, God, do whatever is best for Father. Please, God, do whatever
is best
please
God

My two Godmothers met me. I asked, "How is Father?"
It took the whole drive home before they told me.
I was taken to see my father in the manner of the times.
I did not know him.
I closed my eyes and stood there
seeing him better, then.

My mother and I talked quite calmly
about things like toothpaste.
I remember that. I did not cry.
It was thought that I did not care.

I was a human being and a young one.
We cannot always cry at the right time
and who is to say which time is right?

I did not cry till three years later
when I first fell, most inappropriately,
in love.
But I began, after the tears,
to know my father.

When we are grown up enough
compassed about with so great a cloud of witnesses
that we are not afraid of tears
then at last
we can say
Father
I love you
Father.

It would have been better for both Mother and me if we had been able to break down, to hold each other and weep out our grief. Perhaps Mother was able to cry when she sent me back to school— I was home only a few days, and I was uncomfortably grateful to escape back to the familiar structure of boarding-school life where I was expected to be controlled and brave and could thus repress the grief with which eventually I had to come to terms. Because of this escape into repression, I went through a very dark period which might have been avoided had my training allowed me to grieve at the appropriate time.

Odd: my training was nominally Christian; my boarding schools were Anglican, and in the English school there was daily Morning and Evening Prayer from the Book of Common Prayer. So why was I discouraged from natural grief? My grief was for myself, for my mother, not for my father. Father had been ill and in pain for a long time. Father, I somehow knew, was all right. But Mother's life, and mine, had been totally disrupted. Mother no longer had the delightful companion with whom she had traveled all over the world for nearly thirty years. I no longer had the father whose intellect and honor I totally trusted.

So perhaps it was not strange, when I went to college the following autumn, that I was through with the organized religious establishment. It really hadn't given me any help in time of crisis.

Freshman year at college was all right. Everything was new. I enjoyed my studies and the intellectual stimulation with which I was surrounded. I made casual friends. But I do not think that I felt anything. Mother and I spent the summer following freshman year at a rented cottage on the beach, for the old beach house which was so important to me had had to be sold after Father's death. It was a good summer. I worked on a novel, and walked for hours on the beach at night with the companion who is still my friend of the right hand, or canoed with her in the dark lagoons, rejoicing in her knowledge of the flora and fauna of the subtropics. It was a happy summer but there was a seed of unease under the happiness.

Sophomore year came and I was doing well at college, though I had warnings which I did not understand and so could not heed. But I remember one or two of them. As a newly elected class officer I had to make a long list of phone calls, and as I stood there by the phone in the dorm hall, I thought to myself, —I am calling all these people, and that means that I am real.

An even stronger warning came during my daily hour in one of the piano practice rooms. I was working on a Mozart sonata and it became a compulsion with me that I play it through without striking a false note. I had to play it through without making a mistake or I would die.

I must have been in a deep depression for some time before I realized what was happening. My panic fear of death alternated with a state of deadly despair when I would sit and stare into nothing and think nothing and feel nothing. On the surface I was functional, and nobody noticed anything.

I knew nothing about psychiatrists, despite the fact that I was taking a psychology course, and it never occurred to me to go anywhere to ask for help. After all, my Establishment training had taught me to Be Brave, and Do It Myself. I had not yet come across Dean Inge's marvelous saying: God promised to make you free. He never promised to make you independent.

I'm not sure what got me out of the dark pit. Writing helped. I moved, that year, into a new vein in my work, writing more out of my own experience than I ever had before, and becoming conscious of style and structure. And I fell most inappropriately in love, and loving and being loved freed me to weep. At last I was able to shed the tears which I had been repressing for so long. By springtime when I went to my practice room in Sage Hall I no longer felt the bony hand of death at my throat if I made a mistake in the Mozart sonata, and I had emerged from that black, killing depression I can never forget. And I was no longer ashamed of legitimate tears—never tears used as blackmail, or tears of self-pity, but tears when it is proper for a human being to cry.

I'm a little better about mourning, now, though not enough. There never seems to be a right time to cry, and then emotion builds up, and suddenly something inappropriate will cause it to overflow, and there I am with tears uncontrollably welling up at the wrong time and in the wrong place.

I pray for courage to mourn so that I may be strengthened. There is much to mourn, for we feel grief not only for the physical death of one we love or admire. I mourn for the loss of dreams and the presence of nightmare. On a small freighter, passing the Statue of Liberty ('with her crown of thorns,' a friend of mine commented), I mourned the loss of the dream which was responsible for the presence of that great lady. When I was a little girl I loved hearing of all the French children saving their pennies; the Statue of Liberty was dreamed of and paid for by children who were enthralled by the idea of a country which welcomed all the poor of the world and gave them opportunities which could not be found anywhere else.

Until I can mourn the loss of a dream I cannot be comforted enough to have vision for a fresh one. I have not often mourned well, and here again my children teach me. Hugh says that when I have finished a book I can no longer separate what is imaginary in it and what is fact, and he's largely right. There is a brief sequence in *Meet the Austins* which came from experience, but for a few years we had a statistically horrendous number of deaths to mourn, and I'm not sure whose this was—but Rob's prayer is exactly as it was in real life.

The voice is Vicky's, and I am Vicky, far more than Mrs. Austin, who is a much better mother than I could ever hope to be.

"When Mother closed the book, we turned out the lights and said prayers. We have a couple of family prayers and Our Father and then we each say our own God Bless. Rob is very personal about his God Bless. He puts in anything he feels like, and Mother and Daddy had to scold Suzy to stop her from teasing him about it. Last Christmas, for instance, in the middle of his God Bless, he said, 'Oh, God bless Santa Claus, and bless you, too, God.' " (See what I mean?) "So I guess that night we were all waiting for him to say something about Uncle Hal. I was afraid maybe he wouldn't, and I wanted him to, badly.

" 'God bless Mother and Daddy and John and Vicky and Suzy,' he said, 'and Mr. Rochester and Colette and Grandfather and all the cats and Uncle Douglas and Aunt Elena and Uncle Hal and . . .' and then he stopped and said, 'and all the cats and Uncle Douglas and Aunt Elena and Uncle Hal,' and then he stopped again and said, 'and especially Uncle Hal, God, and make his plane have taken him to another planet to live so he's all right because you can do that, God, John says you can, and we all want him to be all right because we love him, and God bless me and make me a good boy.' "

At the age of four he had gone through the acceptance of grief; it was not easy for him to keep Uncle Hal in his prayers that night, with sudden death having taken Uncle Hal out of his grasp; it would have been easier to have left him out of the prayer entirely, and I was afraid he was going to. But he had the courage to mourn and be comforted, and so I was comforted, too.

The following conversation also is a literal reproduction of an actual one.

"Rob slowly got out of my bed. He stood up on the foot of it and said to Mother, 'Do you ever cry?'

" 'Of course, Rob,' Mother said. 'I cry just like anybody else.'

" 'But I never see you cry,' Rob said.

" 'Mothers have to try not to cry,' Mother said. 'Now run along to your own room.' "

I suppose Mothers do have to try not to cry. But never to say that they don't cry. Would it have been better or worse for the children if I had cried in front of them at this death? I don't know. They did know that it mattered to me, though. I didn't try to hide that. And as always whenever anything big happened to us, good or bad, I piled everybody and the dogs into the car and drove up to the top of Mohawk Mountain, four miles away, to watch the stars come out and talk. I hope that it helped the children. I know that it helped me.

Blessed are the meek: for they shall inherit the earth.

The meek? Meekness is not a quality we value much nowadays. People of my generation think of Mr. Milquetoast, and I just checked with a high-school senior and she laughed and said yes, that's her idea of meekness. It goes along with being a coward, and if you turn the other cheek it's because you don't dare fight back, not because you're strong enough to have the courage to turn and let someone hit you again.

Is this what the Beatitudes are talking about? I looked up *meek* in a theological dictionary, and all it had was *meek vs pride,* but I found that in itself helpful.

It was pride which caused the fall of man, that *hubris* which was the tragic flaw in all the heroes in Greek drama. And in Elizabethan and Jacobean drama, too. Faust in Western literature has become the prototype of the prideful man, and fascinated Goethe as much as he did Marlowe or Boito or. . . . Shakespeare understood *hubris* with the mind in the heart. Macbeth, Mark Antony, Prince Hal—all are potentially warrior saints who are felled by pride.

So if *pride,* usurping the prerogatives of the gods, is the opposite of *meek,* that begins to give me a better idea of what meekness is.

One with no pride would therefore be meek, and I can only think of one man who rejected all the temptations of pride, and that is Jesus of Nazareth. So he was meek, then.

My theology about Jesus of Nazareth and Jesus the risen Christ is always wobbly, but I discover that I have no problem at all with Jesus and meekness. He was just as meek when he took a whip and drove the money changers out of the temple as when he turned the other cheek. And certainly his ultimate turning of the other cheek was his acceptance of the cross.

I keep turning back in my mind to Satan and the temptations, because each temptation implied more than it actually said. It wasn't only because Jesus himself was hungry that Satan tempted him to turn the stones into bread. There's also the implication, 'Come along, turn these stones into bread and you can feed all the poor of the earth. . . . Nonsense, when you come right down to it, man does live by bread alone. Feed 'em and you've got 'em.' True, as the Grand Inquisitor made clear. But Jesus said the poor are always with us. We may not like it, but that's what he said. Not that the poor are to be ignored, nor did he ignore them, but he wasn't out to win them by magic tricks.

So Satan tried again, innuendoes subtle under the words. "Well, then, just throw yourself down from this great height. You know the angels will hold you up lest you hurt your foot against a stone—one of those stones you so foolishly refused to turn into bread. But just jump! What a spectacle that will be for the mob! They'll adore it—and you."

But that kind of adulation had long since been rejected by Jesus. It was Simon the Magus who fell for it—and from it. And a few others who have been more impressed by the magician than by the priest.

"Oh, well, then, just worship me," Satan cajoles, "and I will give you all the glories of the world, right now, without any waiting, without any suffering, without any cross."

And Jesus still said, No.

Worshipping Satan is more like worshipping ourselves than anything else, and Jesus never confused himself with the Father. It was always, 'Not I, but the Father.' There was no *hubris* in Jesus, and if we want to know what meekness is, we must look to him.

And to his mother. I wish we weren't so afraid to love the most holy birth-giver, as the Orthodox call her. It takes great courage to be truly meek, and the best description of meekness I know is the first four lines of the Magnificat.

My soul doth magnify the Lord, and my spirit hath rejoiced in God my Saviour.
For he hath regarded the lowliness of his handmaiden.
For behold, from henceforth all generations shall call me blessed.
For he that is mighty hath magnified me; and holy is his Name.

It's not nearly as meek and mighty in the new translations. I don't want my meekness watered down.

And how am I, myself, to be meek? Meekness is something else which is not a do-it-yourself activity. Meekness is so wild that most of us don't have the courage for it and certainly would not ask for it willingly.

> *Who shoved me out into the night?*
> *What wind blew out the quavering light?*
> *Is it my breath, undone with fright?*
> *   This is the Kingdom of the Beast.*
> *   For which will I provide the feast?*
>
> *Who once was daft, with fear am dafter.*
> *Who went before? Who will come after?*
> *Who in this darkness sends me laughter?*
> *   I cannot pray, but I am prayed,*
> *   The prey prepared, bedecked, arrayed.*
>
> *The dark is sound against my ear,*
> *Is loud with clatter of my fear.*
> *I hear soft footsteps padding near.*
> *   I, who have fed, will be the eaten,*
> *   Whose dinner will I sour or sweeten?*
>
> *This is not hell, nor say I damn.*
> *I know not who nor why I am*
> *But I am walking with a lamb*
> *   And all the tears that ever were*
> *   Are gently dried on his soft fur,*
>
> *And tears that never could be shed*
> *Are held within that tender head.*
> *Tears quicken now that once were dead.*
> *   O little lamb, how you do weep*
> *   For all the strayed and stricken sheep.*
>
> *Your living fur against my hand*
> *You guide me in this unseen land,*
> *And still I do not understand.*

The darkness deepens more and more
Till it is shattered by a roar.

Lamb, stop! Don't leave me here alone
For this wild beast to call his own,
To kill, to shatter, flesh and bone.
    Against the dark I whine and cower.
    I fear the lion. I dread his hour.

Here is the slap of unsheathed paws.
I feel the tearing of his claws,
Am shaken in his mighty jaws.
    This dark is like a falcon's hood
    Where is my flesh and where my blood?

The lamb has turned to lion, wild,
With nothing tender, gentle, mild,
Yet once again I am a child,
    A babe newborn, a fresh creation,
    Flooded with joy, swept by elation.

Those powerful jaws have snapped the tether,
Have freed me to the wind and weather.
O Lion, let us run together,
    Free, willing now to be untame,
    Lion, you are light: joy is in flame.

It is only when the lion has me in his jaws that I am shaken into the courage to be meek.

I knew meekness when John, friend and doctor, dropped my newborn son between my breasts and said, "Madeleine, here is your son," and this after nearly forty-eight hours of work. I knew meekness half an hour later when the placenta wouldn't come and I began to hemorrhage and spent the next hours fighting for my life. I remember thinking, "Hugh will have to marry Gloria to take care of the children," and immediately I thought meekly, "No! I am going to take care of my own children! I am going to be Hugh's wife! I have more books to write!" And then all thoughts had to stop and all concentration had to go into breathing, simply breathing, because I knew that as long as I could breathe I was still alive. The foot of the bed was raised into shock position yet I knew exactly what was going on. I tried to concentrate on nothing but keeping one breath following the one before as the doctors struggled to get a needle for a transfusion into veins which kept collapsing on them. And I kept on meekly breathing. A fresh doctor was called in, one who wasn't exhausted with the struggle of holding, by hand, the uterus closed in order to stanch the flow of blood. The needle found a vein which would hold it, and life-giving blood began to move in my veins, and I meekly kept on breathing, for my babies, for my husband, for my work, and the breathing itself was prayer, please God, please God, please God . . .

And the pain was bad, bad, and I kept on breathing and saying Please God . . .

And after several hours I was all right, and my son was brought to me and put in my arms and my soul magnified the Lord . . .

It strikes me how each Beatitude leads into the next. Poverty of spirit gives us the humble courage to mourn, which in turn frees us to be meek.

But what's this about inheriting the earth? Would we even want it? When God in his strangeness has allowed us to make such an incredible mess of it?

But an inheritance is nothing we ask for or earn or deserve. It is something we are given by the testator, and we can either accept or betray the responsibility.

> We need not wait for God
> The animals do judge
> Of air and sea and grass
> Accusing with their eyes
> Waiting here en masse
> They cry out with their blood
> The whale caught in surprise
> By oil slick's killing sludge
> The cow with poisoned milk
> The elephant's muted roar
> At radioactive food
> The tiger's mangy hide
> The silkworm's broken silk
> (The animals do judge)
> The dead gulls on the shore
> Mists of insecticide
> Killing all spore and sperm
> Eagle and owl have died
> Caterpillar and worm
> The snakes drag in the mud

Fallen the lion's pride
Butterfly wings are bruised
They cry out with their blood
Cain! Killer! We are blamed
By beast and bird condemned
By fish and fowl accused
We need not wait for God
The animals do judge

Adam and Eve stopped being responsible stewards of the earth when they were tempted by Satan to eat of the fruit of the tree of the knowledge of good and evil, 'and ye shall be as gods.'

Our mythic ancestors crashed on the tragic flaw of *hubris* and so they were no longer meek.

We are very blessed that it is the meek who are to inherit the earth, for they can be trusted with it.

Blessed are they which do hunger and thirst after righteousness: for they shall be filled.

The planet earth is filled with starving people.

What are we hungry for?

What are we thirsty for?

When I was in boarding school, one of the very youngest girls stole a watch. She was eight years old. Her parents were divorced. Her father was trying to forget this not very mute reminder of his broken marriage. Her mother flitted from pleasure spot to pleasure spot. There was no room in her frenetic life for a child.

So the little girl stole a watch she didn't want or need, because she was so hungry for love that she had to reach out, blindly, for something, anything, to assuage her hunger.

We're all hungry for something. Uncontrolled overeating usually masks an unacknowledged hunger. We have to know what we are hungry for before we can hunger and thirst after righteousness. Man does not live by bread alone, but bread does matter; it is not easy to hunger and thirst after righteousness with a belly bloated from starvation and bones bent with rickets.

What is *righteousness,* anyhow? Like *meek,* it is a word which has lost most of its original power. I'm afraid it gives rise in me to pictures of gaunt women with thin, repressed lips, who know absolutely what is right and what is wrong, and certainly anything which is fun is wrong.

But that's self-righteousness, and no one ever said, 'Happy are the self-righteous.'

Since it helped me to understand meekness when I looked to Jesus, I look to him again to try to avoid all our distortions of righteousness. What do I see?

I see a man compassionate and gentle with women in a day when this was extraordinary. I remember that the first miracle was turning water into wine at an Oriental wedding feast, and this kind of wild party would definitely be disapproved of by our self-righteous friend. His power is so great that more than once he brings the dead back to life, and yet he feels the power drain from him when the hem of his garment is grasped by the woman with the issue of blood. He has a robust sense of humor, and small children love him.

Righteousness begins to reveal itself as that strength which is so secure that it can show itself as gentleness, and the only people who have this kind of righteousness are those who are integrated and do not suppress the dark side of themselves.

After the baptism there was no question in Jesus's mind as to who he was, and it was this self-knowledge which enabled him to see through the snares and delusions of the temptations. Most of us don't have that certainty, and so we are hungry and thirsty for the wrong things.

It is only when I know myself as a child of God by adoption and grace, a child of a God so loving that he notes the fall of every sparrow, calls all of the stars in all of the galaxies by name, and counts the very hairs on every head, that I am free to accept all of myself, the dark and the bright, and so become free to hunger and thirst after righteousness—and righteousness, ultimately, is a person.

And in this person, righteousness includes the strength of forgiveness—a righteous person has a forgiving heart. The ancient Hebrew understood the word *righteousness* to include judgment, not the cold judgment of blind justice, but a judgment which must be tempered with mercy if it is to be righteous. Heaven knows, the best of us, in looking toward our own judgment, pray that justice will include clemency and compassion. I cannot think of any instance where I could throw the first stone.

'Forgive us our trespasses (or debts or sins or whatever) as we forgive those who trespass against us' means exactly what it says. As we forgive, so shall we be forgiven.

If I am to hope to hunger and thirst after righteousness, then my heart as well as my will must know forgiveness. There are still things I cannot remember without an upsurge of pain, which means that I have not yet completely forgiven, no matter what my intellectual self has said. Deep wounds must heal from the inside out, and this may take a long time, but I must be very careful to do nothing to slow or hinder the healing. Until the memory of a hurt no longer pains me, I have not forgiven the hurter.

When I am angry with husband, children, friend, it is impossible to hunger and thirst after righteousness. This doesn't mean that we are never to get angry—Jesus got very angry on occasion; we mustn't stay locked in anger, but must move on out to forgiveness and reconciliation—and suddenly we'll find that we have been filled.

Righteousness leads directly into *Blessed are the merciful: for they shall obtain mercy.*

But mercy goes further than that forgiveness taught us in the Lord's Prayer. The human being is given the ability to forgive, but that capacity of mercy which not only forgives but also removes the sin is more than human.

The English language, despite what we have done to it with all our jargons, is still extraordinarily rich and powerful in quality, though not in quantity, of words. Both the Greeks and the Hebrews used many words where we have been satisfied with one. As there are many words for our one *love,* so with *mercy.* The Hebrew *chesed* is seen over and over again in the Psalms, and Coverdale frequently translates it as *loving kindness,* that continued forbearance shown by God even when his chosen people are slow to keep his commandments and swift to turn to foreign gods.

Another Hebrew word for mercy is *rachamim,* which has to do with tender compassion, the care of the shepherd for the stray lamb, the pity shown to the weak and helpless. And there is *chaninah,* a joyful, generous mercy, loving and kind.

So mercy, as all the other Beatitudes, is a Christ-like word, and I must look for understanding of it in the small and daily events of my own living, because if I do not recognize it in little things I will not see it in the great.

Again my children teach me. One time, shortly after we had moved back to the city and our children were still young—seven, ten, and twelve—we spanked our son for something the younger of his sisters had done. I don't remember what it was; he was spanked because his father thought he was lying, rather than for any misdeed, and that is not the point of this memory, which is a happy one, so happy that it was easy to find the place where I had recorded it in my journal:

Bion was spanked this afternoon for something Maria had done. And when Maria heard about it when she came home from Scouts she was upset, truly upset that Bion had been punished for something he hadn't done. So we ran to the subway to go down to judo class where Bion was with Hugh, to clear everything up. Hugh had been terribly upset when he spanked Bion, as he thought Bion was lying to him. And I was so proud of Maria for owning up, and for being concerned. And the wonderful thing was how happy and loving *both* Maria and Bion were all evening. We had a hilarious dinner, playing buzz (the math game), which we had such a wonderful time with last night, and laughing almost as hard over it tonight. Funny how something like that can serve to clear the air.

It was the laughter and joy of that evening which is proof of the mercy which mediated between sunside and nightside. I can conceive of forgiveness without this hilarity, but not mercy, which is the step beyond and leads to joy.

O HILARITAS

According to Newton
the intrinsic property of matter on which weight depends is
mass.
But mass and weight vary according to gravity
(It is not a laughing matter).
On earth a mass of 6 kilograms has a weight of 6 kilograms.
On the moon a mass of 6 kilograms has a weight of 1 kilogram.
An object's inertia (the force required to accelerate it)
depends entirely on its mass.
And so with me.
I depend entirely on a crumb of bread
a sip of wine;

it is the mass that matters
that makes matter.
In free fall, like the earth around the sun,
I am weightless
and so move only if I have mass.
Thanks be to the creator
who has given himself
that we may be.

If I look at the Beatitudes not only as though each were a description of Jesus, but also as a definition, they shine in a powerful and brilliant light, so that light and darkness are suddenly alike. He is poor in spirit as we are seldom able to be, because we are seldom that spontaneous. He mourns with them that mourn and dances with them that rejoice and is criticized for both. He is meek, that lamb who is also lion. He hungers and thirsts, as we do, and offers himself to assuage our hunger and thirst, and so we are filled. He is merciful, with a compassion and joy beyond forgiving. There is the power of life and death in his mercy, and it is good to remember this each time we receive the power of his mercy in the bread and wine.

It is only this extraordinary unstrained quality of mercy which helps me to make any sense out of *Blessed are the pure in heart: for they shall see God.*

This is a rough one. We all know that no one can see God and live, it's all through the Bible. And it isn't only a Judaeo-Christian idea—it's in Greek and Roman mythology: in fact, it's a basic presupposition of humankind.

When Semele insisted on seeing Zeus in all his glory she was immediately incinerated. The human being is charred to ash by the glory of the living God. So who has seen God and lived? Who was that pure in heart?

Well, here I come another cropper. The first person who comes to my mind is Jacob, and Jacob does not fit any normal definition of the pure in heart. Jacob was really pretty much of a stinker, cheating his brother Esau, tricking his blind and dying father to get a blessing which did not belong to him.

But he recognized God when he wrestled with him, and he limped forever after. And that limp is important, for the point the Old Testament writer is making by emphasizing Jacob's thigh is that anyone who has seen the living God and survived is marked by this experience and is recognized forever after by the mark.

The early Christians were recognized by the rest of the world, for they bore the mark of the wound of love, and the sign of this love is light, by which they were recognized and for which they lay down their lives. There's a chorus of a song which goes, "You can tell we are Christians by our love."

Can we? Are we wounded enough to be recognized as Christians?

In a church in New Jersey I saw this poster made by the teenagers: *If you were arrested as a Christian would there be enough evidence against you to convict you?*

That arrow really shot me right through the heart.

But I was severely questioned by a young man, a song writer, on this very subject. Oh, sure, he said bitterly, you can recognize Christians by their love for one another because they don't love anybody else.

There's a good deal of truth in this accusation, but of course that kind of self-love isn't love at all, and it isn't Christian, either. But if I am to love others, and not only my own kind as he pointed out, then I must first accept that I am loved; this is the necessary prelude for my acceptance of myself. Then am I able to love those close to me, parents, husband, children, friends. Only then am I free to move out and love those less lovable to me, to love my enemy.

When this young man was a boy he had read *A Wrinkle in Time,* which he said he still rereads occasionally. So I said, "Okay, remember when Meg has to go back to Camazotz to rescue Charles Wallace from the power of It, the naked brain, she knows that if she could love It, her love would defeat It. And she can't do it, so she turns to Charles Wallace because she *can* love her little brother, and that love is strong enough to defeat the cold intellectual power if It. I came to this ending from my own experience, because there was someone I knew I ought to love, and with every effort of will I tried to love and I couldn't do it. But I found that if I turned away completely, and thought about those I could love, my husband, my three children, then I could *get back into love,* and then I could turn with love to the person I had such difficulties with."

And later I said, "But in *A Wind in the Door* Meg has to make the next step into mature love; she has to learn to love Mr. Jenkins, and Mr. Jenkins is not an easy person to love."

We love wherever we can love, and the power of that love spreads until the circumference of the circle of love grows wider and wider. At least that has been my own experience, even though I know to my rue that the circumference of my love is still much too small.

It's too small for all of us; I'm not just breast beating. The circle grows slowly and painfully even with the saints, and so does purity of heart. Who can possibly be pure of heart in this impure world?

Peter. Peter recognized Jesus as the Messiah, the Christ. And Jesus said, "Flesh and blood has not told you this." So purity of heart is not a virtue, it is a gift, and Peter, bumbling, noisy Peter, was given the gift of purity, the ability to see God. And after this he betrayed the God he had seen, he ran from him, he denied him, he was not there when they crucified his Lord. But he believed in the Resurrection, and his confession of Jesus as Messiah was the rock on which the Church was founded, and in the end he lay down his life for what he had seen and known.

The fact that Peter could see God, and thus be pure in heart despite all his faults and flaws, is a great comfort, because it tells me that this purity, like every single one of the Beatitudes, is available to each of us, as sheer gift of grace, if we are willing to be vulnerable.

But Peter saw God two thousand years ago, when the second person of the Trinity came to his Creation as a man, when his footsteps were left in the dust, when the light of his smile lit the sky with the brilliance of the sun. What about now, two thousand years later, when his presence among us has been gone for so long? Who can be pure in heart and see God now?

It is one of the burdens of living in a fallen world that each generation has its war. For Hugh and me it is World War II, and in one of the stories coming from this war I find my image of that purity of heart which allows a human being to see God and live.

This story concerns a Lutheran pastor in Germany who could not reconcile his religion with the Third Reich, which pretended to protect the religious establishment as long as those who belonged to it were pure Aryan (forget that Jesus was a Jew) and were willing to *heil Hitler*. This pastor had met with Hitler, who liked him, and wanted to give him preferment. But the choice was as cut and dried for the pastor as it was for those first Christians when they were asked to burn a pinch of incense to the divinity of the emperor. And he did not have celibacy to make his choice easier. He had a wife and children and he loved his family and he did not take lightly his responsibility to them.

But he could not betray everything he believed, everything that he stood for in his ministry; he could not burn that pinch of incense.

He and his wife and children were sent to a concentration camp, and the wife and children died there. Like Anne Frank's father, he was the only one left.

When it was all over, when Hitler's megalomaniac kingdom had fallen, and the world was trying to put itself back together and return to everyday living, it was remembered that he had seen Hitler. Someone asked him curiously, "What did Hitler look like?"

He replied quietly, "Like Jesus Christ."

And that is what it is like to be pure in heart and to see God.

I'm not anywhere nearly there. I don't know if I'll ever get there, where I can see through my own sin and sham to the image of God in the lowest of his creatures. Like Meg, I do have to start where I *can* love. But that is at least a start.

Blessed are the peacemakers: for they shall be called the children of God.

Never have we needed peacemakers more. There is a peculiar horror in turning on radio or TV for the news and hearing about Christians fighting Moslems, or Catholics fighting Protestants, or Jews fighting Arabs.

If I continue to struggle to think of the Beatitudes as a description of Jesus, it is bound to affect my understanding of peace, because Jesus, the peacemaker, the Son of God, said that he came not to bring peace, but a sword. And the Hebrew word *shalom*—peace—is not a passive word like the Greek *eirēnē,* a primarily negative word denoting the absence of war, but a positive word, *shalom,* the peace which comes after the last battle.

Do we have to think about war before we can think about being peacemakers? A teenager wrote to me about one of my books and then added, "We've been studying the Crusades in school. *Can* there be such a thing as a Holy War? Can a Christian kill?"

It was not an easy letter to answer, nor did I answer it to my satisfaction. Offensive war, never. That's easy. But defensive? Could we, in conscience, Christian conscience, have refused to enter World War II? Could we have stood by and let Hitler take over our friends and neighbors and accomplish his mission of exterminating all Jews? We couldn't, my generation, or at least so it seemed to us. And we had to take on our American selves some of the responsibility for all that caused Hitler and his rise to power. We felt deep in our hearts that the only way to be peacemakers was to fight the Nazis and then cry, Shalom!

Several young men who were close to me were killed in that war, and if we had learned enough to know that there is no such thing as a war to end war, at least they died believing their cause was just, and something in me will not let me say that they died in vain.

But I have to look directly at the fact that the Hitler Jugend believed in the justness of their cause, too. They were saving the world. It's confusing, this trying to think about war, and it makes me understand with deep pain that, despite the bite of that apple, a great deal of the time we do not know what is good and what is evil. We cannot tell our left hand from our right.

I was sorting these thoughts out one morning, and began outlining them to my friend Tallis.

He looked down his nose at me. "Don't be so cosmic."

"Am I being cosmic?"

"Yes. Don't be."

When I tend to go cosmic it is often because it is easier to be cosmic than to be particular. The small, overlooked particulars which are symbols of such things as being peacemakers are usually to be found in our everyday lives. Of course we'd rather have something more dramatic and spectacular, so we tend not to see the peacemakers in our own path, or the opportunities for peacemaking which are presented us each day.

When I need to think particularly rather than cosmically, I turn as always to my family, this time once again to the little boy whose sister hurried to the judo studio the day he had been punished for something she had done.

The judo lessons came about not because of the dangers of living on the Upper West Side of Manhattan, but because of the school bus in our small New England village. When Bion was in first grade the school bus stopped at the bottom of the hill, nearly a mile from our house. The two other boys who got off at the same stop were both older and bigger, and when there was nothing better to do, they jumped on the little first-grader and roughed him up.

Hugh asked, "Why don't you fight them back?"

Bion answered reasonably, "There are two of them, Daddy, and they're bigger than I am."

So when we moved to New York in the middle of the next school year, he had judo lessons. He enjoyed judo, and he was good at it.

One Saturday he took the bus down Broadway to spend the day with a friend. As he was walking the long block between Broadway and West End Avenue, three boys came up to him and demanded his money. All he had was his bus fare, which he handed over. He then went on to his friend's, and in the late afternoon borrowed the bus fare to come home.

He told us about it at dinner, and Hugh said, "Why didn't you use your judo on them?"

"For fifteen cents, Daddy? I might have hurt them."

He was, and is, a peacemaker.

So are many of the people I pass each day on the rough streets of the Upper West Side. I remember one time when we were setting off for Crosswicks for the first weekend in the spring, and Hugh went to the liquor store to see if he could have a carton in which to pack some things. But the cartons had just been picked up, so the proprietor of the liquor store went next door to the pharmacy to see if there was a box there. There wasn't, but the pharmacist went to the laundromat to see if there was one there. . . .

Peacemaking. Peacemaking on Upper Broadway, illumined by this quick generosity of all the shopkeepers on the block knocking themselves out to find an empty carton.

It's there for me to see, as long as I recognize it. And I must recognize, too, the opportunities for being a peacemaker which are daily offered me. Nothing dramatic or spectacular, but lots of little things, and the smallness does not make them less opportunities.

Just on the walk between our apartment and the Cathedral library, for instance; it's a crowded time of day, when I take off in the morning a little after eight o'clock, with mobs of people going to work, sleepy, unready for the damp cold in winter, the humid heat in summer. Each morning I walk past a large supermarket. Across the sidewalk is a metal slide, sloping from a huge delivery truck to a side entrance of the market. There is a small gap in the slide, just large enough to let one person pass through at a time. A man in the truck sends heavy cartons down the slide, and they are lifted over the gap by another man who stands trying to do his job of getting the truck unloaded while people coming from both directions are trying to get through the gap. My dog and I are among them. The man struggles to get the cartons across the gap and onto the lower section of the slide under conditions which are, to put it mildly, frustrating.

One winter the man with this thankless job was large and strong-looking, but older than a man ought to be who has to lift heavy cartons. His skin, which had once been coffee-with-cream, was tinged with grey. His expression was dour, and who can blame him? Most people, hurrying to jobs which are no more than drudgery, thought only of getting through the bottleneck which was impeding their way, a reaction which is no more than natural. But my job is real work, and real work is play, not drudgery. I walk through the dirty and crowded streets to a place of trees and grass and beauty, and within this place to a gracious, book-filled room where I am free to write, and this is joy.

So, one morning as the dog and I slid through the bottleneck, I smiled and said, "Good morning."

I got no response. Naturally. The sour look did not soften. Why should it? It was stubbornness which made me persist in saying "Good morning," or "Thank you," day after day.

One day he smiled back.

One day he smiled first.

Not much in the way of peacemaking, is it? But it is what is offered me each morning. And, as my grandmother was fond of reminding me, little drops of water and little grains of sand make the mighty ocean and the pleasant land.

The way of peacemaking given us may be something so small that it seems hardly worth doing, but it is these small offerings which build our reflexes for the larger ones. The ways of peacemaking given middle-class Americans like me are far less spectacular than—for instance—those given the group of Protestant and Roman Catholic women in Northern Ireland who daily risk their lives to cross the battle lines and pray with each other, but the grace to brave such danger has been built on the foundation of the small responses—even things as small as not wanting to hurt the boys who took your bus fare, or everybody on the block trying to find a carton, or smiling at the dour man who now smiles, too—it may not seem like much; it is not much; but it is what is given at the present moment, and it is what ultimately provides the grace for the greater tests.

When we are given the grace to be peacemakers even in these little, unimpressive ways, then we are children of God, children by adoption and grace, but children nevertheless, who are bold to call him Father, Abba. So we children are helped to become peacemakers, and one day we will truly be able to cry, Shalom!

6... The Noes of God

LENT HAS GONE BY too quickly. Holy Week is here and I have to start thinking about Good Friday; God's Friday; and there is the last Beatitude waiting for my attention, and so I feel that it is somehow appropriate to work it into my Holy Week thinking: *Blessed are they which are persecuted for righteousness sake: for theirs is the Kingdom of Heaven.*

Tallis tells me that the Eastern Orthodox Church emphasizes Easter, whereas the Western Church emphasizes Good Friday, but I have never been able to think of one without the other. As it takes both male and female to make mankind, so it takes both Good Friday and Easter to make Christianity.

On Palm Sunday in the Cathedral the congregation participates in acting out the Gospel, and we are the mob, and I choke as I shout out, *His blood be on us, and on our children. Crucify him! Crucify him!* I choke not because it is something I would never under any circumstances say, but because just as I do not know what I would have done had I been an ordinary German under Hitler's regime, neither do I know what I would have done had I been caught up in that mob. I might well have cried, *Crucify him!* and been convinced that this was the right thing to do.

An even more deeply moving service is on Maundy Thursday when, after the bread and wine has been given and received, one by one the candles are snuffed out. Then everything is taken away. The altar is stripped down and the naked marble has wine poured into the five "wounds" and washed with water. Finally the seven great hanging lamps are, with difficulty, lowered by the sacristan who pulls them down by a long pole with a hook on the end. As he gets each one down he blows it out.

Darkness. Emptiness. There is nothing left.

That is how it must have been for the disciples. For his friends. Dark. Empty.

He was dead. All their hopes were shattered. No one knew there was going to be a resurrection. Their hearts were heavy and without hope. He was just a minor political agitator after all, instead of what he said he was. On Good Friday no one thought about Easter, because Easter hadn't happened yet, and no one could dream of such an impossible possibility.

Perhaps, we call Good Friday good because it was what made Easter possible. But why wasn't there any other way? Does it always take failure in man's terms to make success in God's?

One of my young married students has suffered all her life because she was taught in her Church that she was born so sinful that the only way the wrath of God the Father could be appeased enough for him to forgive all her horrible sinfulness was for God the Son to die in agony on the cross. Without his suffering, the Father would remain angry forever with all his Creation.

Many of us have had at least part of that horror thrust on us at one time or other in our childhood. For many reasons I never went to Sunday School, so I was spared having a lot of peculiar teaching to unlearn. It's only lately that I've discovered that it was no less a person than St. Anselm who saw the atonement in terms of appeasement of an angry God, from which follows immediately the heresy that Jesus came to save us from God the Father.

The quality which has always amazed and rejoiced me about God is his constant loving concern for his Creation. Even when we are most disobediant to the laws of love he still cares; he is slow to anger and quick to forgive—far quicker to forgive than his human creatures, such as Jonah, who is intensely irritated by the Father's compassion. This loving concern is apparent all through the Old Testament, preparing us for the ultimate concern shown in the New where he actually comes to us as one of us.

If he is truly one of us, wholly man as well as wholly God, then his death is inevitable. All men must die. All created matter ultimately comes to an end.

But Jesus as wholly man at the same time that he is wholly God is as impossible as St. Paul's conception of a spiritual body. But on these two absolute contradictions I build my faith.

We still want corroboration of scientific proof behind what we believe. But if something can be proved, then we don't need faith in order to believe in it. I don't need faith to believe in any of the lab experiments we did in high-school chemistry; they are in the realm of provable fact. And when we depend too much on provable fact we blunt and diminish the human talent for faith.

Little worth believing in is scientifically provable. In literal terms, God can neither be proved nor disproved. That the result of living according to the Beatitudes is happiness does not lie in the realm of provable fact; yet when I look at the people I know whose faces are alight with joy, no matter how terrible their outward circumstances, I can see in them poverty of spirit, the comfort of mourning, purity of heart—all those characteristics which, put together, are a description of Jesus of Nazareth:

who died on a cross, publicly, between two thieves, on Good Friday. A failure. In worldly terms, a complete washout, the original non-achiever.

That, too, is part of the blessing we are offered if we call him Lord. Death.

I doubt if it is given to the human being to understand completely the blessed passion and precious death, the mighty resurrection and glorious ascension of our Lord Jesus Christ. I know that I do not understand. But I also know that it has nothing to do with the angry, unforgiving God who so upset my young friend. If the basic definition of sin is lack of love (that love without which all men are dead in the sight of God, as Cranmer wrote in one of his collects), then an inability to forgive is lack of love, and if God is unable to forgive us then he is lacking in love, and so he is not God. At least, he is not the God who makes glad my heart.

So why the crucifixion, then, if it was not to appease the anger of God?

When Christ, the second person of the Trinity, became, in Jesus, wholly man, he had to experience death for us, just as he had to experience being born, and breathing, and eating, and eliminating, and sleeping, just like all mankind. But why on the cross? Why despised and rejected by the majority of the Jews, his people, forsaken by most of his friends? Why a total failure?

And here again I bump headlong into God's failure vs. man's success, and man's success is worth nothing, in comparison with the glorious failure of God.

Experience is painfully teaching me that what seems a NO to man from man's point of view, is often the essential prelude to a far greater YES. The Noes which have been said to me may be as small and inconsequential as the opportunities given me for peacemaking, but they are mine. During the two years when *A Wrinkle in Time* was consistently being rejected by publisher after publisher, I often went out alone at night and walked down the dirt road on which Cross-wicks faces, and shouted at God; 'Why don't you let it get accepted? Why are you letting me have all these rejection slips? You know it's a good book! I wrote it for you! So why doesn't anybody see it?'

But when *Wrinkle* was finally published, it was exactly the right moment for it, and if it had been published two years earlier it might well have dropped into a black pit of oblivion.

Another No which was the prelude to a Yes came way back when I was working in the theatre. I knew early that I was to be general understudy and have a couple of walk-on roles in Eva LeGallienne's and Margaret Webster's production of Chekhov's *The Cherry Orchard.* A young actor in whom I was intensely interested, and who had already made a name for himself, was being considered for the role of Petya Trofimov, the student who is Chekhov's mouthpiece, and I was certain that my friend was going to get the job and my love life was going to be assured. When I went to the first rehearsal he was not there. Instead, I saw a tall thin young man with black hair and great blue eyes who was introduced to me as Hugh Franklin, and I was not pleased.

I think it was after the second rehearsal that Hugh asked me out for a bite to eat; this was at three in the afternoon. It was three in the morning when I unlocked the door to my apartment in the Village. I cannot imagine what the past thirty-plus years, the greater part of my life, would have been, had Hugh not played Petya.

But of course the real example which makes all our little stories pale is seen in the life of Jesus of Nazareth. He begged in agony that he might be spared the cross, and his father said No to him, and this No was the essential prelude to the Yes of the Resurrection. This No was necessary for the defeat of death. In dying, as a mortal, Jesus defeated the power of death. Death is often brutal, but death does not win. The sting has been removed. The victory of the grave is turned to defeat.

So Good Friday is good because it is the defeat of death.

In a Good Friday sermon Alan talked about the human desire to play God. We all have it. The trouble is that we want to play at God rather than be like God. We forget that playing God, if we take it seriously, involves a love so great that it accepts the cross.

It is difficult for us to hear, and even when we hear, it is difficult for us to understand.

The disciples heard, but they didn't understand, otherwise they might not all—all except John—except the women—have run away from the horror of Good Friday.

Blessed are they which are persecuted for righteousness' sake: for theirs is the kingdom of Heaven.

We aren't persecuted very much nowadays, we Christians, at least not overtly. But in point of fact there is a good bit of sub-rosa persecution, ridiculing if not reviling. In children's books death and sex used to be taboo. Now death and sex are 'in,' and Christianity is the new taboo; other religions are appreciated, Buddhism, Hinduism, the pre-Christian Druidism; Christianity is not tolerated. And not only in children's literature. It has been made taboo by those who do not understand it and who are terrified by its wider and wilder implications, and so take refuge in sarcasm and supercilious arrogance: of course we intelligent people don't need God and we certainly aren't interested in the cross. Only those poor creatures who aren't strong enough to manage on their own go in for the false promises of religion.

On the other hand, self-sufficient intellectuals who can't stand Christianity are far too often given a vicious travesty of what Christianity is about by the various Christian establishments. If I want to find a Christian, I look not to the ecclesiastical success as much as to the lame, the halt, the blind, who come to church, because only for us do the promises have any meaning.

One time in London, after I had come from the Holy Mysteries, I wrote:

How very odd it seems, dear Lord,
That when I go to seek your Word
In varied towns at home, abroad,
I'm in the company of the absurd.

The others who come, as I do,
Starving for need of sacrament,
Who sit beside me in the pew,
Are both in mind and body bent.

I kneel beside the old, unfit,
The young, the lonely stumbling few,
And I myself, with little wit,
Hunger and thirst, my God, for you.

I share communion with the halt,
The lame, the blind, oppressed, depressed.
We have, it seems, a common fault
In coming to you to be blessed.

And my fit friends, intelligent,
Heap on my shoulders a strange guilt.
Are only fools and sinners meant
To come unto you to be filled?

Among the witless and absurd
I flee to find you and to share
With eyes and ears and lips your Word.
I pray, my God. God, hear my prayer.

From city streets and lanes we come.
I slip unto you like a thief
To be with you, at peace, at home,
Lord, I believe. Oh, help my unbelief.

Perhaps we must accept our brokenness and not try to repress it before we can affirm the goodness of Good Friday, and all that it promises. We are all broken, we human creatures, and to pretend we're not is to inhibit healing. It is people who consider themselves whole who tell me that the Christian promises are false, but as I look at these 'whole' people I see that they are in fact less 'whole' than some who admit their brokenness.

Are these promises by which I live false ones? If so, I want to discard them immediately. But I don't think that they are. Perhaps they are called false by the people who, underneath, are afraid they are only too true: Good Friday. The Cross. Death. Judgment.

I'm afraid, too. I think we all are. But we are given the grace to move beyond the fear because this is not all of the promise.

Those who look down condescendingly on us struggling Christians call the rest of this promise pie-in-the-sky and hope to demolish it by ridicule. The blessedness of being persecuted does indeed promise us heaven, and we're not very good about heaven. The problem with all that is promised the Christian, and it's all spelled out very clearly in the Beatitudes, is that it's too good to be believed. It has nothing whatsoever to do with the world of provable fact and technology-turned-into-technocracy. And much of the time the Christian establishment is no help to us hungry sheep. I've been shocked at the number of clergymen of all denominations who either ignore the Resurrection or deny it—thereby relegating Jesus Christ to the status of merely a good rabbi—in which case he was wrong about himself, the disciples were wrong about him, Paul was wrong about him, and we've been worshipping a false god for nearly two thousand years.

Often we have indeed been worshipping false gods. The Christian establishment does not always remain true to its Lord. Like the stiff-necked Hebrews we, too, turn aside to our own equivalent of the altars of Baal. I was utterly appalled by a book endorsed officially by the Episcopal Church for use in high-school age Sunday School classes which equated belief in the Resurrection and our own everlasting life as 'no better than superstitious belief in ghosts.'

I stand with Paul here. When we deny the Resurrection, we are denying Christianity. We are no longer the Church; no wonder the secular world is horrified by us.

It is not easy to have the courage to stand up and publicly be counted as Christians, when we know that our Christianity is going to be misunderstood and reviled. It is not easy to stand firm in our faith in heaven, our faith that Good Friday is good because it was not the end of the story, but was followed by the glory of Easter.

Christians are often accused by the secular world of being so hooked on heaven that we consider what is happening in this world unimportant, that we couldn't care less about battlefields and slums and insane asylums; we ignore the poor; we turn our backs on racial injustice; we do not even consider the plight of the lame, the halt, the blind. Throughout the past two thousand years there has far too often been more than a modicum of truth in this accusation, because a great deal of the time Christians are simply not Christian at all.

But if we look at the record of concern for poverty and weakness and suffering, that of the atheist is by and large worse than that of the believer, because if you take seriously the glorious promise that God created all of us to live forever, then what we do here and now matters far more than if this life were all, and at the end of our mortal span we're snuffed out like a candle—so why not eat, drink, and be merry, for tomorrow we die.

If we look back throughout history, the record shows quite clearly that societies where man is god have far less concern for human life than those which believe in God's loving concern for every iota of his creation. Alexander the Great, Tiberius, Hitler/Mussolini were big on causes and small on people. I could list some Americans in my lifetime, but because they are in my lifetime, more water needs to flow under the bridge before I can see with any objectivity.

The Church that went along with Hitler was not the Church. The Church was in the concentration camps. To a Christian, no human being is expendable, and we cannot justify trampling on people now by promising them pie-in-the-sky by-and-by. When this is tried, it is simply not Christian. Our record is horribly smudged, and not for a minute would I pretend that it isn't.

If at death we are to be judged on this life, then what we do here and now matters enormously. It may be of ultimate import whether or not we give a thirsty child a cup of cool water, whether or not we feed the hungry stranger who comes to our door. St. John of the Cross said, "In the evening of life we shall be judged on love." So if, when we die, Christ looks on us with love in his eyes, and we are able to respond with love, then we know heaven. But if he looks at us with love and we respond with fear or hate or indifference, then we know hell. If I have denied bread to one hungry stranger I could have fed, that slice of pie is going to taste bitter indeed.

We can't consider heaven as a result of the cross without considering the other possibility, hell, and we're as bad about hell as we are about heaven.

In the Western Church, we jump directly from Good Friday to Easter Day, with Saturday a vague blank in between. But in the Eastern Church, Great and Holy Saturday is one of the most important days in the year.

Where was Jesus on that extraordinary day between the darkness of Good Friday and the brilliance of Easter Sunday? He was down in hell. And what was he doing there? He was harrowing hell, or to put it in simpler words, he was ministering to the damned.

Christian graphic art has often tended to make my affirmation of Jesus Christ as Lord almost impossible, for far too often he is depicted as a tubercular goy, effeminate and self-pitying. The first 'religious' picture I saw which excited me and stretched and enlarged my faith was a small black and white photograph of the fresco over the altar of the Church of the Chora in Istanbul; a few years ago it was my privilege to visit Istanbul and see this fresco for myself.

The Church of the Chora is now a museum, but when we went there on a chill morning with the smell of the first snow in the air, it was empty. As we stepped over the threshold we came face to face with a slightly more than life-size mosaic of the head of Christ, looking at us with a gaze of indescribable power. It was a fierce face, nothing weak about it, and I knew that if this man had turned such a look on me and told me to take up my bed and walk, I would not have dared not to obey. And whatever he told me to do, I would have been able to do.

The mosaic was preparation for the fresco over the altar. I stood there, trembling with joy, as I looked at this magnificent painting of the harrowing of hell. In the center is the figure of Jesus striding through hell, a figure of immense virility and power. With one strong hand he is grasping Adam, with the other, Eve, and wresting them out of the power of hell. The gates to hell, which he has trampled down and destroyed forever, are in cross-form, the same cross on which he died.

GREAT AND HOLY SATURDAY

Death and damnation began with my body still my own,
began when I was ousted from my place,
and many creatures still were left unnamed.
Gone are some, now, extinct, and nameless,
as though they had never been.
In hell I feel their anxious breath, see their accusing eyes.
My guilt is heavier than was the weight of flesh.

I bear the waste of time spent in recriminations
("You should not have. . . ." "But you told me. . . ." "Nay, it was you
who. . . .").
And yet I knew my wife, and this was good.
But all good turned to guilt. Our first-born
killed his brother. Only Seth gave us no grief.
I grew old, and was afraid; afraid to die, even knowing
that death had come, and been endured, when we
were forced to leave our home, the one and only home a human man
has ever known. The rest is exile.
Death, when it came, was no more than a dim
continuation of the exile. I was hardly less a shadow
than I had been on earth, and centuries
passed no more slowly than a single day.

I was not prepared to be enfleshed again,
reconciled, if not contented, with my shadow self.
I had seen the birth of children with all its blood and pain
and had no wish ever to be born again.

The sound, when it came, was louder than thunder,
louder than the falling of a mountain,
louder than the tidal wave crashing down the city walls,
stone splitting, falling, smashing.
The light was brutal against my shaded eyes,
blinding me with brilliance. I was thousands
of years unaccustomed to the glory.
Then came the wrench of bone where bone had long been dust.
The shocking rise of dry bones, the burning fleshing,
the surge of blood through artery and vein
was pain as I had never known that pain could be.
My anguished scream was silenced as my hand was held
in a grip of such authority I could not even try to pull away.
The crossed gates were trampled by his powerful feet
and I was wrenched through the chasm
as through the eye of the hurricane.
And then—O God—he crushed me
in his fierce embrace. Flesh entered flesh;
bone, bone. Thus did I die, at last.
Thus was I born.
Two Adams became one.
And in the glory Adam was.
Nay, Adam is.

My young friend who was taught that she was so sinful the only
way an angry God could be persuaded to forgive her was by Jesus

dying for her, was also taught that part of the joy of the blessed in heaven is watching the torture of the damned in hell. A strange idea of joy. But it is a belief limited not only to the more rigid sects. I know a number of highly sensitive and intelligent people in my own communion who consider as a heresy my faith that God's loving concern for his creation will outlast all our willfulness and pride. No matter how many eons it takes, he will not rest until all of creation, including Satan, is reconciled to him, until there is no creature who cannot return his look of love with a joyful response of love.

Origen held this belief and was ultimately pronounced a heretic. Gregory of Nyssa, affirming the same loving God, was made a saint. Some people feel it to be heresy because it appears to deny man his freedom to refuse to love God. But this, it seems to me, denies God his freedom to go on loving us beyond all our willfulness and pride. If the Word of God is the light of the world, and this light cannot be put out, ultimately it will brighten all the dark corners of our hearts and we will be able to see, and seeing, will be given the grace to respond with love—and of our own free will.

The Church has always taught that we must pay for our sins, that we shall be judged and punished according to our sinfulness. But I cannot believe that God wants punishment to go on interminably any more than does a loving parent. The entire purpose of loving punishment is to teach, and it lasts only as long as is needed for the lesson. And the lesson is always love.

It may take more years than we can count before Nero—for instance—has learned enough love to be able to look with joy into the loving eyes of a Christ who enfleshed himself for a time on earth as a Jew, but Nero's punishments, no matter how terrible they may be, are lessons in love, and that love is greater than all his sick hate.

We will be quicker to respond with love, under judgment, if we have learned to respond with love, now. Every response of love gives us a glimpse on earth of the Kingdom of Heaven, that brilliant Easter which is born from the dark womb of Good Friday. We cannot repress or deny the darkness, the sinister and mysterious side of love. Without it, Easter, too, is only a fragment of a whole.

On every occasion when we are enabled to do the Lord's will, now, here on earth, we know the Kingdom. I knew it, for instance, during the week of my parents-in-law's golden anniversary. I know it when

I am smiled at by the dour man unloading groceries on Broadway. I know it whan I cook dinner for family and friends, and we are gathered around the table, extraordinary unity in diversity, and are given a foretaste of the Heavenly Banquet, and glimpse the meaning of the cross which leads to life. Then we understand the total failure of God which showed itself by a love so deep that he does indeed die with us and for us and our sins. This dying for us is part of what my young friend was taught, but the next step is left out by her teachers: this dying is something we all must experience; we all die for each other, for if we are children of God, nothing can be left out. When the gates of hell are trampled down, they suddenly become the welcoming door to heaven.

What a good day is this Friday. There is no coming to birth without pain, and out of the pain of this day are we born into the new life of Easter.

7... The Icon Tree

EASTER: that day which follows the harrowing of hell of Great and Holy Saturday; Easter, which turns a terrible Friday into Good Friday. It is almost too brilliant for me to contemplate; it is like looking directly into the sun; I am burned and blinded by life.

Easter completes the circle of blessing, and the joy of the completion remains, despite all the attempts of the powers of darkness to turn it into cursing.

A graduate student wrote to ask if my Christianity affects my novels, and I replied that it is the other way around. My writing affects my Christianity. In a way one might say that my stories keep converting me back to Christianity, from which I am constantly tempted to stray because the circle of blessing seems frayed and close to breaking, and my faith is so frail and flawed that I fall away over and over again from my God. There are times when I feel that he has withdrawn from me, and I have often given him cause; but Easter is always the answer to *My God, my God, why hast thou forsaken me!*

Easter is the most brilliant of all blessings, and all through the Bible, in both Old and New Testaments, comes the message of blessing, and that it is the vocation of the People of God to bless as well as be blessed, and to turn away wrath with a soft answer—a softness which is not flabby, but which has the power of meekness.

That is the point which is most important to me in the story of Balaam and his ass, and perhaps because I loved this story as a child, I responded to it with particular affection when I returned to it as an adult.

One of the best pieces of advice I had from Mary Ellen Chase, that superb teacher I was privileged to study with in college, was that anybody who was seriously considering writing as a profession must be completely familiar with the King James translation of the Bible, because the power of this great translation is the rock on which the English language stands.

So, as a young woman, I turned to the Bible for purely literary reasons. But I discovered that the Bible is a great deal more alive than the Church establishment seemed to be. It is a repository of joy and piety and history and humor and storytelling and great characters, and my writer's mind was nourished. I stayed with the Book all through the years when I kept my back turned on the Establishment.

One of the first messages that struck me is that the Bible is not a moral tract. It may contain all that is necessary for salvation, but the glory of Easter is not a result of self-righteousness. Not long ago I gave a talk to a group of students studying for advanced degrees in education. During the question and answer period one of them asked me about the moral precepts in my stories, and the question alarmed me, because a novel should not be a moral tract, it should be a story. Moralism and moral values are by no means the same thing, but with the slurring of language the two have come pretty close. So I said, somewhat dubiously, because this was a secular lecture to a general audience and I was afraid of being misunderstood, that my point of view about life was going to show under the story, because that's inevitable, but I never consciously write about moral precepts, and I do not like moralism, which is another form of do-it-yourself-ism. And I tried to explain that people who think themselves capable of setting up rigid moral standards are playing dictator, like the occasional prideful people who attempt to get *Winnie-the-Pooh* taken out of the library because they thinks it's immoral.

Other questions came in then, but I went on thinking about it, afraid that some of the students thought that I was advocating immorality. Finally I ventured to mention the Bible. The Bible is not a moral tract and it is not about moral people. Look at them! ordinary human beings, full of flaws, sins, humanness, but found by God. God called Abraham, an old man past his productive years, to be the father of a nation. Jacob, whose behavior was shabby, to say the least, wrestled with an angel. And Rahab was a harlot and Jesus was gentle with a woman taken in adultery.

If a calling committee today were looking for someone to take over
an important parish, they'd pass over such people as being completely
unqualified. And Paul of Tarsus would certainly never have made it,
with his particular list of credentials, such as helping at the stoning
of Stephen. But God always calls unqualified people. In cold reality,
no one is qualified; but God, whose ways are not our ways, seems to
choose those least qualified, people who well may have come from
slums and battlefields and insane asylums. If he had chosen great
kings, successful and wealthy merchants, wise men with their knowledge of the stars, it would be easy to think that these people, of their
own virtue and understanding, accomplished on their own the blessing which God asked them to complete.

And Jesus chose his disciples with the same recklessness as his
father; he chose them not in the Sanhedrin, not in the high places of
the wealthy; he found them as they were fishing, collecting taxes,
going about the ordinary business of life.

The men and women called by God to do his work would never
have passed a test in moral virtues. David's getting Bathsheba by
conniving to have her husband killed in battle was a totally immoral
act. Nathan the Prophet made this quite clear to his king, and David
repented. Everything that happened to the shepherd boy who became
a king was a lesson, loud and clear, that the blessing is always God's.
And what happened after David repented? He sang.

> *Your altar smelled of the slaughterhouse.*
> *The innocent eyes of men and beasts*
> *Lost in confusion of laws and vows*
> *Was the high price paid to you for feasts.*
> *They had to be men of iron, your priests.*
>
> *And so did I, born but to sing,*
> *To tend the lambs and not to kill.*
> *Why, my Lord, did you have to bring*
> *Me down from the safety of my hill*
> *Into the danger of your will?*
>
> *I learned to fight, I learned to sin;*
> *I battled heathen, fought with lust;*
> *When you were on my side I'd win.*
> *My appetites I could not trust.*
> *I only knew your wrath was just.*

> *What I desired I went and stole.*
> *I had to fight against my son.*
> *You bound my wounds and made me whole*
> *Despite the wrong that I had done.*
> *I turned from you and tried to run.*
>
> *You took me, also, by the hair*
> *And brought me back before your altar.*
> *You terrified me with your care.*
> *Against your rage I could but falter.*
> *You changed me, but refused to alter.*
>
> *So I grew old, but there remained*
> *Within me still the singing boy.*
> *I stripped and sang. My wife complained,*
> *Yet all my ill did I destroy*
> *Dancing before you in our joy.*
>
> *O God, my God, is it not meet*
> *That I should sing and shout and roar,*
> *Leap to your ark with loving feet?*
> *I praise thee, hallow, and adore*
> *And play before thee evermore.*

And so would I, my Lord.

But at that lecture one of the students, still hung up on moralism, said, "But you're looking for something in your books, you can't deny that." "Of course I'm looking for something. But I'm not looking for morals, I'm looking for truth." Probably in searching for the truth of love I'll discover something about morals, though I'm not sure. The older I get and the more I learn, the less qualified I become to make correct moral judgments; that may not stop me from having to make them—an event must be assessed before it can be blessed—but I have learned with hindsight that with all the good will in the world I may be wrong, and it is only by offering my judgments to God that they can be redeemed and blessed.

Slow am I as always to recognize what is right in front of me. Of course: all I'm fumbling on about moralism has already been said for me by Paul. Moralism belongs to the old law and the old covenant. Jesus Christ in his life, death, and resurrection oveturned the laws of moralism. *Christ hath redeemed us from the curse of the law, being made a curse for us.* That's not very acceptable language, but it does help to put my fragments together.

It is difficult to bless and not to curse when one's control of a situation is taken away. I witness daily the cursing which is the result of impotence. My threshold of anger is much lower than it used to be. Small annoyances provoke much too strong a reaction of irritation. I may not curse, but blessings do not come to my lips as often as I would like.

The doors of many of the neighborhood shops around our apartment are no longer open to welcome the customer. One has to be buzzed in, because there have been so many shopkeepers shot or stabbed that it has become necessary to live in this sadly realistic climate of suspicion, which increases my own feelings of impotence. When Hugh is late coming home from theatre or television studio I pace about nervously, fearful that he may have been mugged. And the very muggers themselves are reacting irrationally to an impotence and frustration far greater than mine, so it is no wonder that they respond with a curse.

But our television commercials, our political speeches, our 'how-to' and 'do-it-yourself' books would seem to offer us a world in which, if we only eat a low carbohydrate and low cholesterol diet, or buy a new combination washing machine and outdoor barbecue, we will be in charge of our lives.

We aren't, and most of us know we aren't, and that isn't easy to accept.

If we have so little control over the world in which we live, can our lives, and the lives of those we love, have any meaning?

Easter affirms meaning, even though it's not possible for finite brokenness to define the meaning of infinite wholeness. The acceptance of this not-knowing is nothing new; rather, technocracy has refused to accept what the anonymous author of *The Cloud of Unknowing* understood and expressed for us so beautifully.

It is only when I am not afraid to recognize my own brokenness, to say, "Turn us again, Lord God of hosts, cause thy face to shine and we shall be whole"—that the broken bones may begin to heal, and to rejoice. Without this *phos hilaron,* this joyous light, we fight against our impotence, in our spiritual lives, our intellectual lives, a large portion of our physical lives.

But in the small events of daily living we are given the grace to condition our responses to frustrations. It's something like driving a car. If you're driving along a highway and a car comes at you from a side road, and you have to think what you ought to do, you're not likely to avoid an accident. In an emergency you don't have time to stop and think. You act before thought, on your conditioned reflexes.

So it is with all of life. If our usual response to an annoying situation is a curse, we're likely to meet emergencies with a curse. In the little events of daily living we have the opportunity to condition our reflexes, which are built up out of ordinary things. And we learn to bless first of all by being blessed. My reflexes of blessing have been conditioned by my parents, my husband, my children, my friends.

Blessing is an attitude toward all of life, transcending and moving beyond words. When family and friends gather around the table to break bread together, this is a blessing. When we harden our hearts against anyone, this is a cursing. Sometimes a person, or a group of people, do or say something so terrible that we can neither bless nor curse. They are anathema. We put them outside the city walls, not out of revenge, not out of hate, but because they have gone beyond anything we fragile human beings can cope with. So we say, Here, God, I'm sorry. This is more than I can handle. Please take care of it. Your ways are not our ways. You know what to do. Please.

But sometimes I am confronted with a situation which demands a response of either blessing or cursing, and from me. I cannot refuse to meet the emergency by turning aside. And I have cause to remember Balaam, who was ordered by King Balak to go and curse the children of Israel. Rather reluctantly he saddled his ass and went to do the king's bidding, and his ass stopped in the middle of the road, because she saw something Balaam didn't see; she saw the angel of the Lord standing in the path, and she refused to allow Balaam to go on. And in the end Balaam heeded the ass, and he blessed the children of Israel, blessed instead of cursed.

Blessing is no easier for me than it was for Balaam, and there was a Friday after Easter, two years ago, when I was put to the test.

When we open our house in the country in the spring we know that it will still be winter on our hill; Crosswicks is a good three weeks behind New York, where the Cathedral Close is bursting with blossom, and the cement islands which run down the middle of Broadway are astonishing with the glory of magnolia blooms. At Crosswicks the forsythia will show no bud, though if I bring it indoors it will take only a day or so before it bursts into gold. The house, even with the furnace running, will not be quite warm enough, and we'll huddle around the fire and rush upstairs to bed to plunge beneath the covers. Things which were part of the burden when we lived in Crosswicks year round are fun when it's only on a weekend basis.

I look forward with intense anticipation to the first weekend in the country. Each year the city gets more difficult. Each year the world seems in a worse mess than it was the year before. Our own country is still in trouble, and this trouble is reflected in the city and on the Cathedral Close. I need to get away and find perspective.

On that particular Friday after Easter it had been a bad week in the world, a bad week in the country, a bad week on the Close. I looked forward to the peace and quiet of the first weekend the way, as a small child, I had anticipated Christmas. When we got up to Crosswicks it was still light, one of those rare blue-and-gold afternoons when the sky shimmers with radiance. Hugh said to me, "I bet you're going right to the brook."

"Would you mind?"

"Go ahead, but don't stay too long."

So I called Timothy from sniffing the rock garden and set off across the big field and over the stone wall. Easter was late that year, and the trees were beginning to put forth tiny gold shoots which in another couple of weeks would be green leaves. Some of the budding maples were pale pink, and the beech trees were almost lavender. I could feel myself unwinding from the tensions of the past weeks. I felt surrounded by blessing.

I have several favorite places where I like to sit and think. Probably the most favorite is a large rock above the brook. Directly in front of the rock is an old maple tree. When the trees are fully leafed it is always shaded, and on the hottest day it is cool there. I knew that now the brook would be rushing, filled with clear, icy water from melting snow.

The summer before, I had gone with Josephine and Alan and the two little girls to a fair at Regina Laudis Monastery in Bethlehem, Conn. I have a good friend among the Sisters there, and that afternoon she gave me a small, laminated icon of a medieval Mother and Child, and a little cross. I had put these on the trunk of the big maple, and in the late afternoon it was my habit to go to my thinking rock and say my prayers and then, with the icon tree as my focus, to try to move beyond the words of prayer to the prayer of the heart.

So that spring afternoon I headed straight for the rock and the icon tree. But as I started down the tiny path through the trees which leads to the rock, I felt that something was wrong. I quickened my steps and when I had climbed up on the rock I saw. Someone had shot the icon at close range. It was split in four parts. There was a bullet hole through the face of the holy child. The cross had been pulled from its ring; only the broken ring still clung to the nail.

I felt an incredible wave of hate flood over me. I was literally nauseated. What had been done had been done deliberately; it was not an accident; it was a purposeful blasphemy, an act of cursing.

I was beyond any response of either blessing or cursing. But I knew that I couldn't go home until I had been washed clean of the hate. The very trees around the rock seemed to draw back in horror and apology because they had not been able to stop the intruder.

Feeling sick and cold I called Timothy and walked and walked.

Seeking perspective in a hate-torn world,
Leaving, for respite brief, the choking city,
I turn to trees, new leaves not quite unfurled,
A windswept blue-pure sky for pity.
Across a pasture, over a stone wall,
Past berry brambles and an unused field,
Listening for leaf sound and the brook's clear call,
Turning down path by bush and tree concealed,
Forgetting human sin and nature's fall
I seek perfection in the cool green still.
Small trees with new spring growth are tall.
Here is no sign of human hate or ill.
   Unexpecting any pain or shock
   I turn to climb upon my thinking rock.

The rock stands high above the snow-full brook.
Behind the rock an old tree breaks the sky,
And on the tree where bird and beast may look
An icon and a cross are hanging high.
So strong are they, placed lovingly together,
I need have little fear for their protection
Through wind and snow and bitter wintry weather.
They speak to me of joy and Resurrection
And here my self-will stills, my heart beats slow.

God's presence in his world is bright and strong.
Upon the rock I climb, and then—No! No!
The sky is dark and here is hate and wrong.
*   O God! Make it not be! Oh, make it not!*
*   The icon: target for a rifle's shot.*

A wave of dark blasts cold across my face.
My stomach heaves with nausea at the dirt
Of hate in this pure green and loving place.
The trees pull back and cower in their hurt.
Rooted, they could not stop the vicious gun
Fired straight at God's birth-giver and her child.
There's only death in this. It's no one's fun
To blaspheme love. A shot has made a wild
Distortion of the young and ancient face.
I give the broken fragments to the brook
And let the water lap them with its grace.
And then I sit upon the rock and look
*   At the great gouge in the tree's wood.*
*   Evil obscures all peace and love and good.*

My dog knew that something had upset me. He kept close as we walked, instead of tearing off in great loops. We kept walking until I had come to the point where I could simply turn over to God whoever had shot the icon and the cross. This person was beyond my puny human ability to understand. I could not add to the curse by cursing. But I did not know how to bless. I went back to the house and told Hugh what had happened. The next day I carried tools and took the remains of the icon off the tree and gave them to the brook. I took away the small nail with the broken loop. Then I sat on the rock and looked at the gouge in the tree's wood. What I describe in the next sonnet did not happen that day, but it did happen, and redeemed the act of hate, and made the tree far more of an icon for me than it was before.

As I sit looking at the shot-at tree
The rough wound opens and grows strange and deep
Within the wood, till suddenly I see
A galaxy aswirl with flame. I do not sleep
And yet I see a trillion stars speed light
In ever-singing dance within the hole
Surrounded by the tree. Each leaf's alight
With flame. And then a burning living coal

> *Drops hissing in the brook, and all the suns*
> *Burst outward in their joy, and the shot child,*
> *Like the great and flaming tree, runs*
> *With fire and water, and alive and wild*
>   *Gentle and strong, becomes the wounded tree.*
>   *Lord God! The icon's here, alive and free.*

Balak sent Balaam to curse the children of Israel, and the ass saw an angel of God and sat down under Balaam and refused to move, and the curse was turned to a blessing.

I don't understand and I don't need to understand.

Bless the Lord, O my soul, I cry with the psalmist whose songs after all these thousands of years still sing so poignantly for us. O bless his Holy Name, and may he bless each one of us and teach us to bless one another.

Throughout these pages there has been an affirmation, explicit as well as implicit, of my faith in the promise of Easter, of the Resurrection, not only of the Lord Jesus Christ but of us all; the Resurrection not as panacea or placebo for those who cannot cope without medication, or as the soporific of the masses (Simone Weil said that revolution, and not religion, is the soporific of the masses), but as the reality which lights the day.

The experience with the icon tree was a *symbole* of resurrection for me, an affirmation which helps me to respond with a blessing where otherwise I might curse.

There are too many books which affirm resurrection now and can't quite believe in resurrection after death. Resurrection now is indeed important for resurrection then, but resurrection now means little if after death there is nothing but ashes to ashes and dust to dust. The God who redeemed the icon tree for me will not create creatures able to ask questions only to be snuffed out before they can answer them. There is no pragmatic reason why any of my questions should be answered, why this little life should not be all; but the joyful God of love who shouted the galaxies into existence is not going to abandon any iota of his creation. So the icon tree is for me a *symbole* of God's concern, forever and always and unto ages of ages, for all of us, every single one of us, no matter what we think or believe or deny.

So let there be no question: I believe in the resurrection of Jesus of Nazareth as Jesus the Christ, and the resurrection of the body of all creatures great and small, not the literal resurrection of this tired body, this broken self, but the body as it was meant to be, the fragmented self made new; so that at the end of time all Creation will be One. Well: maybe I don't exactly believe it, but I know it, and knowing is what matters.

ALL THAT MATTERS

Nothing.
Out of nothing
out of the void
(what?
where?)
God created.

Out of
nothing
which is
what?
But it is
not a what
or a where
or an opposite
of something
or anything.
Nothing is
nothing
we can know.
Does it matter
that matter's mind
must not mind
not knowing
nothing
doubly negatively
or in any way
positively
not.

O Mind
that alone knows
nothing
O Word
that speaks
to matter
that

speaks matter
from the unspoken:
that you mind
is all that matters.

And this minding makes my lack of faith no matter, for I know; I know resurrection, and that is all that matters.

The strange turning of what seemed to be a horrendous No to a glorious Yes is always the message of Easter. The destroyed icon and the wounded tree are a poignant symbol of the risen Christ. The gouge in the tree is beginning to heal, but I will always know that it is there, and it is living witness that love is stronger than hate. Already things have happened which have put this knowledge to the test, and sometimes I have been where I could not go to the rock and see the tangible assurance of the tree's tall strong trunk. But I can turn in my mind's eye and see it, can image the whole chain of events from the cruel destruction of death to the brilliance of new life.

I need to hold on to that bright promise.

8... The Blue Balloon

THERE IS a theory that Jesus of Nazareth, like many other extraordinary men who have walked this planet, was in reality a visitor from the stars, a man of a higher race than we terrans, who came to help us out of the muddle we were making of our world and then, his mission accomplished (or failed, depending on your point of view), got into his space ship and ascended into the heavens and returned to his own galaxy.

The idea of extraterrestrials coming to visit their lower brethren does not seem to me particularly farfetched (after all, I both read and write science fiction), but it doesn't work with my theory of incarnation. It's simply a modern variation of an old heresy, that Jesus wasn't really man. He came and lived with us and shared our lives with magnificent compassion and generosity, but he wasn't really one of us. He went through the motions of death, but being an immortal he didn't really die, he only seemed to.

Throughout the centuries we have teetered back and forth on this paradox of Jesus as wholly man and wholly God, and too often for comfort have found it too difficult to believe. We emphasize either the divinity or the humanity, to the weakening of the other.

One evening Tallis and I were talking, after teaching a class together. One of the students had been defining God, and everybody agreed that this is impossible. But I said afterwards to Tallis, "*We* can't define God, but didn't God define himself for us, in Jesus Christ?"

He replied, "That's all very well, as long as you remember Kierkegaard's saying that Jesus came to us and looked like us and ate like us and talked like us, and the disguise was so perfect that we believed that he was just like one of us."

I hesitate to disagree with either Kierkegaard or Tallis, but this bothered me so much that I blundered on. "But Jesus *was* us: isn't that the whole point? Jesus is us; and it's we who aren't us, and haven't been, not since Adam and Eve."

And I still think that's true. The second Adam was what the first Adam was, what we were *all* meant to be: spontaneous, free, aware, unafraid to love, without *hubris:* whole. Not as we are, fragmented, inhibited, sunside and darkside in collision instead of collaboration, so that we are afraid of all that we might find in the sinister world of the subconscious, are suspicious of intuition, and close our doors to the knocking of the Spirit.

> *Go away. You can't come in. I'm shutting the door.*
> *I'm afraid of you. I'm not sure who you are anymore.*
> *I'm closing the door. I'm staying safe and alone.*
> *Batter against it all you like. This house is built on stone.*
> *You can't come in. I've shuttered the windows tight.*
> *You never say who you are. If it's You, then it's all right,*
> *But you might be the other, the beautiful prince of this world*
> *Who makes my heart leap with his cohorts and banners unfurled.*
> *I could be unfaithful with him without any trouble*
> *If I opened the door. He could easily pass for your double.*
> *I've buried my talents. If I put them to use*
> *I could hurt or be hurt, be abused or abuse.*
> *I wish you'd stop blowing. My whole house is shaken.*
> *I'll hide under the covers. Be gone when I waken.*
>
> *What's that light at the windows, that blast at the door?*
> *The shutters are burning, there's fire on the floor.*
> *Go away. I don't know you. My clothes are aflame,*
> *My tongue is on fire, you are crying my name;*
> *I hear your wild voice through the holocaust's din.*
> *My house is burned up.*
> > *What?*
> > *Oh, welcome! Come in!*

It's not easy to understand the fire of the spirit which burns and does not consume, to keep our door open so that we are helped to understand a God so loving that he can actually be one of us, and still be God.

The idea of a Jesus who really wasn't one of us after all is easier to believe in than the technical impossibility which I daily struggle to believe, the extraordinary paradox which is all that makes the universe bearable. Jesus of Nazareth was wholly man as well as wholly God. He did die. For our sakes he suffered everything we suffer, even doubt. And then he broke the powers of death and returned briefly to quite a few people—not everybody, but enough so that his presence was noted—though he was never recognized on sight. And then, after a time, he ascended, whatever that means.

What it means in terms of physical, provable fact, I cannot know. Whatever really happened has been lost in the mists of two thousand years. I do know that it has something to do with love, the kind of open, joyful, giving love I fail in daily, and struggle daily to understand.

I know it's not like that sunny Sunday afternoon
when we went to the zoo; evening came too soon
and we were back on the crowded city street
still full of pleasure from the afternoon's treat,
and our little girl clutched in her fingers a blue balloon.

It bobbed above our heads. Suddenly there came a cry,
a howl of absolute loss. We looked on high
and there we saw the balloon, ascending,
turning and twirling, higher and higher, blending
into the smoky blue of the city sky.

We wiped the eyes, blew the little nose, consoled the tears,
did not, of course, offer a new balloon, instead were silly,
   waggled our ears,
turned sobs to laughter, accepted loss, and hurried
home for dinner. This day is not like that. And yet they must
   have tarried,
looking up into the sky the day he left them, full of loss and fears.

He had come back to them, was with them, and then was lost
again, or so perhaps it seemed, the table left without the host.
The disciples did not understand all that he had said,
that comfort would be sent, there would be wine and bread.
Lost and abandoned (where is my blue balloon?) they did not comprehend
   until the day of Pentecost.

Even after he told them, his followers did not hear and see:
"What is this that he saith unto us? A little while and ye

Shall not see me, and again a little while, and ye shall. . . . when?
  tomorrow?
We do not understand." Lord, nor do I, and share thus in their
  sorrow
at the same time that the Spirit sets my sorrow free
to turn to love, and teaches me through pain to know
that love will dwell in me and I in love only if I let love go.

So the Ascension is freed to move into the realm of myth.

It doesn't bother me when people talk condescendingly about the Christian myth, because it is in myth that sunside and night-side collaborate and give us our glimpses of truth. But when I use the word *myth* I bump headlong into semantic problems, because myth, to many people, is a lie. Despite the fact that during the last decade myth has been rediscovered as a vehicle of truth, there are still those who cannot help thinking of it as something which is false. We give children the Greek and Roman myths, the Norse or Celtic myths, and expect them to be outgrown, as though they are only for children and not to be taken seriously by realistic adults. If I speak of the Christian myth it is assumed not only that I am certainly not a fundamentalist, but that I am an intellectual who does not need God and can speak with proper condescension of the rather silly stories which should be outgrown at puberty. But I am far closer to the fundamentalist than the atheist when I speak of myth as truth.

The rediscovery of myth hasn't helped, because what does his Satanic Majesty do when the sons of Adam stumble upon something which would further the coming of the Kingdom and destroy the Prince of this World? He infiltrates, and so myth becomes part of the jargon, and jargon has no power.

Nonetheless, myth is the closest approximation to truth available to the finite human being. And the truth of myth is not limited by time or place. A myth tells of that which was true, is true, and will be true. If we will allow it, myth will integrate intellect and intuition, night and day; our warring opposites are reconciled, male and female, spirit and flesh, desire and will, pain and joy, life and death.

God became man, was born of a woman, and we would have liked to keep this man-child with us forever; and that kind of possessiveness leads to disaster; as most parents know.

When I wrote the following lines I thought of them as being in Mary's voice, but they might just as well be in mine—or any parent's.

> *Now we may love the child.*
> *Now he is ours,*
> *this tiny thing,*
> *utterly vulnerable and dependent*
> *on the circle of our love.*
> *Now we may hold him,*
> *feeling with gentle hands*
> *the perfection of his tender skin*
> *from the soft crown of his head*
> *to the sweet soles of his merrily kicking feet.*
> *His fingers softly curl*
> *around one finger of the grownup hand.*
> *Now we may hold.*
> *Now may I feel his hungry sucking at my breast*
> *as I give him my own life.*
> *Now may my husband toss him in the air*
> *and catch him in his sure and steady hands*
> *laughing with laughter as quick and pure*
> *as the baby's own.*
> *Now may I rock him softly to his sleep,*
> *rock and sing,*
> *sing and hold.*
> *This moment of time is here,*
> *has happened, is:*
> *rejoice!*
>
> *Child,*
> *give me the courage*
> *for the time*
> *when I must open my arms*
> *and let you go.*

I looked at my last baby lying in his cradle, knowing that he was the last child I would bear, for I nearly didn't survive his birth; looked, touched, listened, with an incredible awareness I might not have had if I had been able to expect to bear more children. As each change came, I had to let the infant-that-was go, go forever. When he was seven months old I weaned him, as part of that essential letting go, letting him move on to child, little boy, young man. . . . Love, and let go. Love, and let go.

It's always pain, this letting go, and yet it leads to joy, and a kind of lightness which is almost physical.

> *Pride is heavy.*
> *It weighs.*
> *It is a fatness of spirit,*
> *an overindulgence in self.*
> *This gluttony is earthbound,*
> *cannot be lifted up.*
> *Help me to fast,*
> *to lose this weight.*
> *Otherwise, O Light one,*
> *how can I rejoice in your*
> *Ascension?*

We tend to be heavy, we middle Americans, heavy in all ways. More than half the world is starving, and we go on crash diets to try to take off weight. Nor are we jolly fat people. Affluence tends to bring with it a stupor, a flatulence of spirit. It is difficult to laugh freely as long as we are clutching all that we have accumulated and are afraid to lose.

One day in early spring Pat and I drove up to Crosswicks. There was snow on the ground; I made Pat put on boots and a heavy coat and trek with me across the fields to the brook. I strayed from the path several times, fell, laughing, into snowdrifts, from which she had to pull me, but at last we reached the brook, which was rushing noisily, at its fullest from melting snow. And Pat looked at it and then said in a bemused voice, "It's not polluted!"

Pat is a physician who is Chief of Health for a large Southern city. Part of her job is understanding problems of pollution, overconsumption. This was three years before the oil crisis, but she had already seen that it was coming, and told me so. Standing there on the rock bridge over the brook I asked her, "Are we going to be able to save planet earth?"

She replied calmly, "No. Not unless we're willing to make drastic changes in our standard of living. Not unless we're willing to go back to being as cold in winter as our grandparents were, and as hot in summer."

That is even more true now than it was then. But we are loath to let go all the creature comforts which are the result of the distortion of the American dream. The idea of the recovery of the real dream is an exciting one. My family and I do try to live simply, and the simpler our lives, the freer. Not that I enjoy being hot in summer, sitting at the typewriter with the sweat trickling down my back and the inside of my legs. In late afternoon with the sun pouring onto my desk it is often so hot that I cannot stay in my workroom. But there's always a moderately cool place somewhere. The leaf-protected rock at the brook is always cool.

We eat largely out of Hugh's magnificent vegetable garden, and we are indeed blessed in having the space for it. I freeze vegetables all summer long, so that the garden feeds us for much of the winter.

When we lived in the house year round we got used to putting on more clothes when it got cold, as the English do, rather than turning up the heat. But I'd better be careful not to get sentimental about being hot in summer and cold in winter, as our forebears were. The old, the ill, the weak, did not survive the excessive temperatures of either winter or summer. And we have become delicate, with our thermostats set to keep us at a constant temperature of around 70° year round. Pat told me that college football coaches discovered the hard way that they had better warn their athletes not to take a summer job in any kind of air-conditioned office, but to work outdoors in the heat of the sun. When the body becomes accustomed to a constant temperature, our inner thermostats lose the ability to adjust, and so a young man who has spent the summer sitting at a desk in an air-conditioned office drops dead on the playing field on a hot autumn day, because his body's thermostat can't cope.

I console myself when I'm wet with heat in summer, shivering with cold in winter, that I'm helping my body's thermostat to become functional once more.

I would like to travel light on this journey of life, to get rid of the encumbrances I acquire each day. Worse than physical acquisitions are spiritual ones, small grudges, jealousies, hurt feelings. I am helped by the fact that nursing a grudge gives me no pleasure; I cannot bear to go to bed angry; I am compelled by an inner drive to 'make up,' to reconcile, to restore relations. It doesn't always work, of course. It does take two, and there are people who not only cannot make an apology; they cannot accept one. Once when this happened to me, Tallis said, "You've done what you had to do. That's all you have to worry about. Let it go." Letting go, again.

I once had an acquaintance who was a far more regular church-goer than I, rose early to go to Holy Communion each morning before he went to work, and yet hated all Orientals. Whenever an Oriental priest celebrated communion, he refused to receive the bread and wine.

I knelt behind him in a small chapel on a morning when a Japanese priest, one of my friends, was the celebrant, and I knew that this man would not touch the Body and Blood because it was held by yellow hands. And I was outraged.

I am not in love and charity with this man, I thought, and therefore, according to the rubrics, I should not go up to the altar. And yet I knew that my only hope of love and charity was to go forward and receive the elements.

He did not know that he, himself, was acting wholly without love and charity. Something within him obviously justified this abominable reaction, so that at the next Eucharist, if it was presided over by somebody he recognized as priest, as he was unable to recognize the Japanese priest, he would hold out his hands and receive in love and humility.

He does not know what he is doing. He does not know.

Surely within me there is an equal blindness, something that I do not recognize in myself, that I justify without even realizing it.

All right, brother. Let us be forgiven together, then. I will hold out my hands for both of us today, and do you for me tomorrow morning when I will be asleep while you trudge through the dirty streets to church. It is all right for me to be outraged by what you are doing here in the presence of God, as long as it does not set me apart from you.

It was heavy, heavy for a while there. I put on several hundred pounds in a few minutes, and now they are gone, at least for a while. My spiritual scales fluctuate wildly. They are always on the heavy side, but there are days when I am able to travel light, and these days show me the way.

The most difficult thing to let go is my *self,* that self which, coddled and cozened, becomes smaller as it becomes heavier. I don't understand how and why I come to *be* only as I lose myself, but I know from long experience that this is so.

9... Whispers

THE HOLY SPIRIT, the third person of the Trinity, is the easiest of this not-at-all-easy concept for me to understand. Any artist, great or small, knows moments when something more than he takes over, and he moves into a kind of 'overdrive,' where he works as ordinarily he cannot work. When he is through, there is a sense of exhilaration, exhaustion, and joy. All our best work comes in this fashion, and it is humbling and exciting.

After *A Wrinkle in Time* was finally published, it was pointed out to me that the villain, a naked disembodied brain, was called "It," because It stands for Intellectual truth as opposed to a truth which involves the whole of us, heart as well as mind. That acronym had never occurred to me. I chose the name It intuitively, because an IT does not have a heart or soul. And I did not understand consciously at the time of writing that the intellect, when it is not informed by the heart, is evil.

But a further proof that my books know more than I do came later, again with this same book, when my husband's television wife, Ruth Warwick, who plays Phoebe Tyler in *All My Children,* was on the *Today Show* with Ed Mitchell, who was one of the second group of astronauts actually to walk on the moon. His present job is to explain scientific concepts of space to laymen. And, he told Ruth, he finds this very difficult to do; scientific concepts of space are not easy to understand. So he uses a book, a book which he said can get these concepts across far better than he is able to. "It's supposed to be a children's book," he said, "but it really isn't. It's called *A Wrinkle in Time.*" "Oh, yes," said Ruth, "my husband's wife wrote it."

So my book knows more about physics than I do, and I find this very exciting. I did, indeed, study physics while I was writing *Wrinkle,* but I've never taken a course in physics, and surely I could not have learned enough, reading on my own, to make my book useful to an astronaut.

It was not until I was nearly forty that I discovered that higher math is easier than lower math. Lower math lost me way down in the grades when I was informed that three multiplied by zero = zero. Now, I understand that if I have nothing, and I multiply it by three, three somethings are not suddenly going to appear. But if I *have* three apples, and I multiply them by zero, nobody has been able to explain to my satisfaction why they are going to vanish—and yet this is what lower math would have us believe.

It was not until I discovered higher math that I understood 0 × 3 = 0. First of all, I had to accept that arithmetic is simply an agreed-upon fiction which makes life easier. Secondly, I realized that 0 × 3 = 0 is a philosophical rather than an arithmetical problem, and I worked this out in writing *The Other Side of the Sun.* But I have a hunch I understood it already, with my intuition, while I was working on *Wrinkle;* any kind of hate which would annihilate, any kind of lust for power which makes people expendable, is an example of three multiplied by zero equals zero.

When I talk about my books knowing more than I do, I am not referring to something magic. Nor is it an easy way out which eliminates the hard work of putting together a story. Writing a book is work; it involves discipline, and writing when I don't feel like writing. Robert Louis Stevenson said that writing is ten percent inspiration, and ninety percent perspiration. The inspiration doesn't come before the perspiration; it's usually the other way around. Inspiration comes during work, not before it. The hardest part of the morning is the first half hour or so when I will put off for as long as possible the actual work on whatever book I'm currently writing. I'll sharpen pencils I don't intend to use; I'll check over my black felt pens, with which I write when I'm not near a typewriter; I'll even change the typewriter ribbon; anything to put off the moment of plunging in. But after I've dipped my toes in the cold water for long enough, I hold my breath and jump in. And once I'm in, if it is a day of grace (and it often isn't), then something will happen, and just what that something is remains, for me, a mystery. But it is involved in servanthood, my servanthood, in a day when service is considered degrading.

I am convinced that each work of art, be it a great work of genius or something very small, has its own life, and it will come to the artist, the composer or the writer or the painter, and say, "Here I am: compose me; or write me; or paint me"; and the job of the artist is to serve the work. I have never served a work as I would like to, but I do try, with each book, to serve to the best of my ability, and this attempt at serving is the greatest privilege and the greatest joy that I know.

At its highest, the relationship between the artist and the work shifts, and artist and work collaborate. In my own way I have known such moments—I think all artists know them, because it has nothing to do with the degree of talent. And, just as in my tiny efforts at peacemaking I must not reject the small things which are given me in my daily life, so I must not worry about comparisons between great and small. I used to irritate my children by frequently quoting Marlowe: "Comparisons are odious."

As I understand the gift of the spirit in art, so I understand prayer, and there is very little difference for me between praying and writing. At their best, both become completely unselfconscious activities; the self-conscious, fragmented person is totally thrown away and integrated in work, and for the moments of such work, be it prayer or writing, I know wholeness, and sunside and nightside are no longer divided.

> *Whence comes this rush of wind?*
> *I stand at the earth's rim*
> *and feel it streaming by*
> *my hair, my eyes, my lips.*
> *I shall be blown clean off.*
> *I cannot stand the cold.*
>
> *Earth shrinks. The day recedes.*
> *The stars rush in, their fire*
> *blown wild as they race by.*
> *This wind's strange, harsh embrace*
> *holds me against the earth,*
> *batters me with its power.*

My bones are turned to ice.
I am not here   nor there
but caught in this great breath.
Its rhythm cracks my ribs.
Blown out   I am expelled
Breathed in   I am inspired

The wind broods where it will
across the water's face.
The flowing sea of sky
moves to the wind's demand.

The stars stretch fiery tongues
until this mortal frame
is seared to bone, to ash,
and yet, newborn, it lives.

Joy blazes through the night.
Wind, water, fire, are light.

One of the holiest of archbishops, Father Anthony Bloom likens the Holy Spirit to a shy and gentle bird who must be approached quietly and slowly, lest he be frightened and fly away.

Whereas Alan likens the Holy Spirit to a ravening hawk, and while both similes hold truth, when I have been aware of the Spirit at the time (rather than later, by hindsight) my experiences have been more hawklike than dovelike. But considerable violence is needed to pull my fragments together, to join sunside and nightside; it's a rather wildly athletic act to place the mind in the heart, and a lot of muscles get pulled.

And, of course, whenever we become whole, Satan moves in to fragment us again. There's a renewed awareness of the gifts of the Spirit nowadays, but Alan reminded me that not all spirits abroad are the Holy Spirit.

We have forgotten the warning in the Letter to the Ephesians, where the people of the Church at Ephesus are warned that "we wrestle not against flesh and blood, but against principalities, against powers, against the rulers of the darkness of this world, against spiritual wickedness in high places." When we limit ourselves to the rational world of provable fact, a warning like this tends to sound like something out of science fiction rather than the Bible, but as I look at the world around me, in the city, as I listen to the news, the warning seems like anything but fiction, and I read on gratefully as Paul continues, "Wherefore take unto you the whole armour of God, that ye may be able to withstand in the evil day."

In his letter to the People in Rome, Paul talks reassuringly about the help of the Holy Spirit in this battle against the dark spirits, "for we know that the whole creation groaneth and travaileth in pain together until now. And not only they, but ourselves also, which have the firstfruits of the Spirit, even we ourselves groan within ourselves. . . . Likewise the Spirit also helpeth our infirmities: for we know not what we should pray for as we ought: but the Spirit itself maketh intercession for us with groanings which cannot be uttered."

Paul's language is strong, too strong for many of us. We'd like the joys of the Spirit without any of the groaning. But any spirit which promises us easy ecstasy is not the Holy Spirit. Indeed, one of the quickest ways to make sure that the spirit is not the Holy One is to be convinced, at the moment of inspiration, that it *is.*

If I am conscious of writing well as I am writing, those pages usually end in the wastepaper basket. If I am conscious of praying well, I am probably not praying at all. These are gifts which we know only afterwards, with anamnesis.

Trouble always comes whenever we begin to take credit for any of the gifts of the Spirit, be they gifts of prayer, tongues, prophecy, art, science. This can be as fatally true in the secular world as in the religious—but one of the greatest victories of the Enemy has been the separation of sacred and secular, and placing them in opposition. All of creation is sacred, despite everything we have done to abase and abuse it. Healing used to be looked on as a sacred calling, and surely the Hippocratic oath is a prayer. Modern medicine suffers, despite all its advances, because it has almost completely forgotten that healing is a gift as well as a science. I want my doctor to have every possible amount of training, but this training will not make him a great doctor unless he has the gift as well.

We need to recover and reverence vocation in this time of confusion between healing and curing. We have forgotten the Spirit.

I believe in prayer, and I believe in miracle, because I have seen enough evidence, pragmatically and scientifically documented, to satisfy the coldest scientist. But it is not the proof which has convinced

me. It is far greater and more exciting than proof.
  As the woman with the issue of blood knew:

> *When I pushed through the crowd,*
> *jostled, bumped, elbowed by the curious*
> *who wanted to see what everyone else*
> *was so excited about,*
> *all I could think of was my pain*
> *and that perhaps if I could touch him,*
> *this man who worked miracles,*
> *cured diseases,*
> *even those as foul as mine,*
> *I might find relief.*
> *I was tired from hurting,*
> *exhausted, revolted by my body,*
> *unfit for any man, and yet not let loose*
> *from desire and need. I wanted to rest,*
> *to sleep without pain or filthiness or torment.*
> *I don't really know why*
> *I thought he could help me*
> *when all the doctors*
> *with all their knowledge*
> *had left me still drained*
> *and bereft of all that makes*
> *a woman's life worth living.*
> *Well: I'd seen him with some children*
> *and his laughter was quick and merry*
> *and reminded me of when I was young and well,*
> *though he looked tired; and he was as old as I am.*
> *Then there was that leper,*
> *but lepers have been cured before—*
>
> *No, it wasn't the leper,*
> *or the man cured of palsy,*
> *or any of the other stories of miracles,*
> *or at any rate that was the least of it;*
> *I had been promised miracles too often.*
> *I saw him ahead of me in the crowd*
> *and there was something in his glance*
> *and in the way his hand rested briefly*
> *on the matted head of a small boy*
> *who was getting in everybody's way,*
> *and I knew that if only I could get to him,*
> *not to bother him, you understand,*
> *not to interrupt, or to ask him for anything,*

not even his attention,
just to get to him and touch him . . .

I didn't think he'd mind, and he needn't even know.
I pushed through the crowd
and it seemed that they were deliberately
trying to keep me from him.
I stumbled and fell and someone stepped
on my hand and I cried out
and nobody heard. I crawled to my feet
and pushed on and at last I was close,
so close I could reach out
and touch with my fingers
the hem of his garment.

Have you ever been near
when lightning struck?
I was, once, when I was very small
and a summer storm came without warning
and lightning split the tree
under which I had been playing
and I was flung right across the courtyard.
That's how it was.
Only this time I was not the child
but the tree
and the lightning filled me.
He asked, "Who touched me?"
and people dragged me away, roughly,
and the men around him were angry at me.

"Who touched me?" he asked.
I said, "I did, Lord,"
So that he might have the lightning back
which I had taken from him when I touched
his garment's hem.
He looked at me and I knew then
that only he and I knew about the lightning.
He was tired and emptied
but he was not angry.
He looked at me
and the lightning returned to him again,
though not from me, and he smiled at me
and I knew that I was healed.
Then the crowd came between us
and he moved on, taking the lightning with him,
perhaps to strike again.

The woman with the issue of blood was both cured and healed, and that is easy to understand, but curing and healing are not always the same thing.

It is always all right to pray for healing. It is also all right to pray for curing as long as we are willing to accept that this may not be God's will, and as long as we are willing to accept God's will rather than our own. Above the lintel of a church in New England are carved these words:

REMEMBER, NO IS AN ANSWER.

But we don't like Noes; and sometimes we like the Noes of God less than any other No. This is a problem prayer groups must face. I believe in the power of prayer to heal, and in the power to cure as well as heal—for curing and healing are like mind and heart when they are separated. One young man told me of being called home from college to see his father in the hospital. His father had been ill for a long time, and he was warned that this was probably the end, and he was rebellious and angry. His father was in his early fifties, an active and brilliant man. It was not time for death. But when my friend got to the hospital and saw his father, his anger ebbed. He told me later, "I find this very difficult to explain, but I knew that my father was healed. I told this to my sister, and she said, 'But Dad's dying, the doctor says so.' And I tried to tell her that that didn't make any difference. I knew that Dad was dying, that death was very close, but I also knew that Dad was healed. And so it was all right."

That was a profound lesson, and few of us learn it so young. I think I learned, in nightside, at any rate, something of this lesson at the time of Father's dying; and when I was asking God, "Do whatever is right, do whatever is right for Father," what I was asking for was healing for this brave man.

I have witnessed the healing which is more profound than curing, several times in my adult life. There was one young girl, a few years ago, who came frequently to the Cathedral, borrowed books from the library, found on the Close the kind of accepting community she was seeking. She was a pretty girl, with soft blue-black hair, and matching blue-black eyes with long, fringed lashes, too pretty for her own good. She wasn't very bright; not retarded, but just not quite up to making any kind of adult decision. She leaned too heavily on a few of us, and we tried, as best we could, to help her be her own self. Until she was stricken with an acute and especially painful form of cancer. The symptoms had been there for over a year, but she had tried to pretend to herself that if she didn't look at them they'd go away, and when she finally told someone, and was taken to the doctor, the disease was so far gone that there was nothing to do but put her in the hospital and hope that the end would be swift.

One time when I went to visit her she clung to me and repeated over and over again, "I'll be all right as long as you don't leave me alone."

I don't think that anyone prayed that Bethie be cured. But we all knew that she had no tolerance whatsoever for pain, and that she was not equipped to bear the pain which we were told was an inevitable part of her form of cancer. So we prayed that she not have more pain than she could endure.

Bethie herself had no faith in her own prayers, and absolute faith in the prayers of half a dozen or so of us.

She was able to leave the hospital. She came back to the Cathedral, where she was given odd jobs. For about six months she worked happily in her adopted family, and took aspirin for what she called her arthritis; the doctors told us that cancer was so deep in her bones by this time that morphine shouldn't have been able to cut the agony. When she went back to the hospital, she was only there a few days before she died, and someone was with her all the time, and the prayers never stopped, and the pain never got too bad to be relieved.

As far as I am concerned, that is miracle, corroborated by the doctors. Bethie wasn't cured. She died. But she was healed.

There's a lot about this kind of healing that I don't understand. The gift of intercessory prayer is not mine, though that does not let me off from praying for others. I know that when I prayed for Bethie, I hurt. I don't think it was physical pain, but it was pain. During her dying I would wake up at night and pray for her, and this praying hurt. I knew that there were others praying for her, too, and that they, too, were probably hurting, and hurting worse than I. In some way all of us together took Bethie's pain. I doubt if one of us could have done it alone; it would have been too much—though sometimes we are required to bear what is too much and we are given the strength to bear it. And what we bear is not, I think, pain by substitution, about which I am wary. I think of the stern face of the Christ in the mosaic in Istanbul, and know that when and if I am required to take such a burden without help, I will be given strength to do it; it will not be my strength, but it will be available for me.

One of my favorite cousins had, at one period, excruciating back pain, and she had an old friend with the gift of healing in her hands who used to come and massage her back. The old woman would knead gently, and then she would take her hands and rub them, hard, against the carved posts of the bed, and Lacy asked her why she kept on doing this.

"Why, Miss Lacy, I take the pain from your back, and I have to put it somewhere, and it's not going to hurt the bedpost, so I put it there."

That explains something to me, but it's still in the realm of mystery and miracle—not magic, definitely not magic, which has to do with man, but with miracle, which has to do with God.

And it helps, when we are praying for others, if we have some understanding of what we are praying about. I can pray better about pain, because I have had severe pain. Whether this is my ill fortune or my good, it does help to enlarge my capacity for compassion for those in pain.

One compassionate and deeply loving Russian Orthodox priest said that he was often baffled when asked to intercede for those who were ill, because their suffering did so much good for their souls. This sounds callous, but it isn't. I'm sure he wouldn't have hesitated to pray for Bethie. I think that it has something to do with my theology of failure, and the Noes of God, and that out of the events in life which seem most negative, positive joys are born.

When I was nine or ten I had my first attack of iritis, a little-known disease which causes an inflammation of the iris. When I had a second attack the following year, the doctor told my mother, in my hearing, that if I had a third attack, I would go blind. So the shadow of blindness has always loomed over me. But it has also caused me to see far more than I might have otherwise. This visual awareness is an extraordinarily positive joy.

Medicine knows more about iritis than it used to. I have had more than a dozen attacks, and although each one sends me into momentary panic, I have come out of it and, again, am more intensely and joyously aware of everything I see than I was before.

A few years ago the effects of iritis caused secondary glaucoma.

This complication was compounded by the fact that the eye drops which are essential for the control of glaucoma irritate iritis, and the medication for iritis increases the high pressure of glaucoma. A vicious circle. A terrifying circle. I was very much afraid. My eyes' reaction to the eye drops was not good. I knew that these were essential if my sight were not to be destroyed by glaucoma, but they gave me a constant headache, and acute photophobia; I, who so much loved the light, could see nothing when facing directly into light.

This threat has been with me for so long that its very familiarity was a help. Like Bethie, I did not pray for myself. It was not so much that I had no faith in my own prayers, as that intuition told me to leave God alone about this, and let others do the praying. I did not hesitate to ask for prayers. I went running to my confessor. I asked him for (at the very least) courage. I told him that I was incapable of being brave for myself, but that I could be brave for those who expected me to be.

Now, five years later, I know that his prayers, the prayers of a number of Sisters, both Anglican and Roman Catholic, of friends, of companions, of all kinds of people with the gift of intercessory prayer, are responsible for the fact that these two incompatible eye diseases have kept at least a kind of truce. I may not see as well as I used to, and I am, as always, myopic, and can't see two feet in front of my nose without my glasses, but I SEE. I see to revise my own manuscripts. I see the faces of those I love. I see sunsets and mountains and babies and rain and daffodils and snow and oceans and storms and daybreaks.

One winter a young English priest came to stay at the Cathedral for a semester of sabbatical leave. He was taking one or two courses, and he did most of his studying in the pleasant Cathedral library. Obviously we did a good bit of talking: about his life in England; about the girl he hoped to marry; about the failures of the established Church on both sides of the ocean; about his studies; about a paper he was writing on intercessory prayer. I told him about Bethie.

One day he pointed at something far across the Close, and when I couldn't see it, he was concerned. I made light of it, but a couple of days later he asked me if I would be willing to accept healing for my vision.

"Ewen, of course I would, but I'm really all right, you know. Lots of people can't see things as far off as you can."

But he said that he was well aware that there was more to it than that. Wouldn't I like to be able to go outdoors without dark glasses? to drive a car again? Wouldn't I like to be able to see as well as I once used to?

Again I told him that of course I would, but that I already knew healing, that the very fact that I saw, that I was still visually functional, was miracle, and miracle enough.

"But could you accept healing?"

"Of course I could. But I can also accept it if this is not what God wants for me. I've learned a lot from having to accept a few limitations on my rugged independence."

I had also been through days of painful rebellion and struggle, and had worked through to at least a kind of acceptance, largely during several days spent alone on retreat at the House of the Redeemer, where the Sisters lovingly protected my silence, fed me, and shared their Offices with me. I did not at that time tell them that I had come to do battle with panic, but they helped me without words, and I worked out my fear and rage in silence and prayer, and when silence and prayer were too much for me, in writing reams of poetry. Perhaps the most useful was one I called

ABRAHAM'S CHILD*

Towards afternoon the train pulled into the station.
The light came grey and cold through the dirty glass panes
*   of the terminal roof,*
and the passengers on the platform blew upon their hands and stamped
*   their feet,*
and their breath came out like smoke.
In the comfortable compartment I leaned back against the
*   red plush of the seat*
and looked out the window. All the signs were in a language
*   I could not read.*
I got out my passport and held it, waiting in readiness.
My papers were in order and the train was warm.
The conductor slid open the door to the compartment and said to me,
"This is the last stop on this train. You will have to get out."
I held out my passport. "No, no, my journey's barely half over,"

*From L'Engle, *Lines Scribbled on an Envelope*, copyright © 1969. Reprinted with permission of Farrar, Straus & Giroux.

and I told him the cities through which the train was going
to pass.
He handed me back my passport and said again, "You will have
to get out,"
and he took me by the arms and led me from the train. His hands
were so strong
my arms cried out in pain. On the platform it was cold.
"But I don't know where I am!" I cried, "or where I am going."
"Follow me," he said. "I have been sent to show you."
Through the glass of the station roof I could see the sun was
going down
and a horror of great darkness fell upon me.
"Come," the conductor said. "This is the way you are to go."
And he led me past the passengers waiting on the platform
and past the foreign signs and a burning lamp in this strange
land
where I was a stranger. He led me to a train with no lights,
and broken windows,
and a pale wisp of smoke lifting from a rusty engine, and said,
"Get in. This is your train."
I fell upon my face and laughed and said, "But this train isn't
going anywhere."
And he said, "Get in," so I got in, and through a hole in the roof
I saw the stars.
He said, "You may sit down," and I sat on a wooden bench
and he put my satchel on the rack over my head. "I must have
your passport."
I gave it to him. "Where are we going?" I asked. The train was
cold.
"The way will be shown," he said, and closed the compartment
door.
I heard a puff of steam. The old engine began to pull the dark
car
and we ventured out into the night.

It was not that I did not believe in prayer in general, or in Ewen's prayers in particular, because I did. Of course I wanted to drive again, to be able to go out into the bright sunlight without pain. I don't know why something in me was bothered by Ewen's questions. It's partly prickly pride if anybody notices any curtailment of my independence. But it was more than that. Ewen and I had become friends. I really didn't mind his knowing my visual limitations.

He persisted. "But you wouldn't reject healing?"

"Of course not. I don't have any masochist or martyr complexes. I just want you to understand that the fact that my eyes are still seeing is already the result of prayer. I already know miracle. I expected to be blind long before now, and I am not. My marvelous present eye doctor doesn't cluck gloomily like the last one and give me dour warnings. He just tells me he'll keep me going, and I believe him. I see, Ewen. I see you. God has already said Yes in all kinds of ways."

But his loving heart wanted me to see perfectly. One unusually quiet morning when almost everybody on the Close was tied up with a big conference, we locked the library door and prayed. It was a beautiful and healing experience. We prayed for each other. The sound of tongues was limpid and lovely. I shall never forget that morning. And I was healed.

Not my eyes. For a few days nothing changed. Then, shortly after Ewen's brief sabbatical was up and he had returned to England, I became radically allergic to my eye drops, an allergy which manifested itself by a black headache. I lost the rest of that spring and summer to pain. My doctors tested me for everything, from brain tumors on down, to make sure that the eye problems were not masking another cause for the headache. The pain was so severe that I was unable to write, and usually I can write my way through anything. I managed to stay on my feet, to cook the meals. But I was anything but whole, and it seemed particularly ironic that this should have happened almost immediately after the beautiful morning of prayer with Ewen when I had felt so strongly the presence of the Spirit.

Ewen had said to me, "I don't think God can want anybody not to be whole. Of course he wants your eyes to be perfect." And I thought of the Orthodox priest who found it difficult to pray for his people who were ill and in pain, and I said, "I think God wants us to be whole, too. But maybe sometimes the only way he can make us whole is to teach us things we can learn only by being not whole." And I remembered reading *The Limitations of Science,* by J. W. N. Sullivan, the only book which made sense to me during my dark agnostic period, and the book he wrote on Beethoven, in which he said that Beethoven's deafness was necessary for his full genius. As I think over Beethoven's work chronologically, this seems to be indisputable. How amazing to think that the paeon of joy in the great Ninth Symphony was written when Beethoven was totally shut off from any external sound. And Milton wrote *Paradise Lost* after he was blind.

I don't think that my months of pain had anything to do with Ewen's prayers for my eyes. Ewen is truly 'a beautiful person' (I wish that had not become jargon); he lives his faith; he is dearly loved by his parish and he ministers to each of his lambs with a tender and constant gentleness which leaves me in awe. And I don't think either of us was to 'blame.' It wasn't our 'fault.' I do think that there were things I had to learn from those bad months. One of my friends, a wise and compassionate woman, was so distressed by my pain one afternoon when she dropped in to see me that she asked, "If it's going to go on like this, wouldn't you rather be blind?" And my immediate response was, "No!" Anything, anything to be able to keep on seeing those I love, the world around me.

That was one of the times I learned enough about pain to be able to be compassionate about pain in others. I learned more than I had known before about Hugh's loving patience. I learned to stay on my feet even when tears were constantly close to the surface, and too often overflowed—always at the worst possible moment. I learned what real friendship means, and what it is to be let down by those I had expected to hold me up. I undoubtedly learned a lot of things I'm not even aware of yet. I think some of what I learned in this still not quite conscious area has to do with the gifts of the Spirit. Certainly, as St. Paul said, more important than speaking in tongues is interpreting tongues, is understanding each other, as did those early Christians of all races and tongues on that first Pentecost.

If I speak with the tongues of men and angels and have not charity I am hollow, unreal.

Meanwhile, my doctor experimented with eye drops and found some on which I was quite comfortable for about a year. Then, on the night before I was to fly West to teach at a writers conference, my eyes declared a new allergy, and I taught through the conference weeping copiously!

Experiments again, and now a glorious miracle! I am on brand-new eye drops which are hardly properly on the market and to which my eyes are almost completely tolerant. I walk through many days without headache for the first time in over five years. When it is cloudy and there is no glare facing me, I even know once again the joy of driving our car along familiar roads. This may be a miracle of science, but as far as I am concerned it is sheer miracle of grace, and I know that Ewen's continuing prayers are part of it, and the prayers of other friends and companions along the way. Please don't stop!

But somehow we have all, all of us, lost something since the tongues of fire descended on those first Christians. We've fallen headlong into every mistake they made, despite all of Paul's warnings. That outspoken man was loud and clear in his condemnation of anyone who felt special and singled-out by any gift of the Spirit.

Something has been forgotten, forgotten for two thousand years, or maybe it's far, far longer than that; we're not very good about chronology. We've forgotten something of ultimate importance, something I ought to remember, I do remember, no, it's only the faintest of echoes, only the sad susurration of whispers:

It was there once; we could hear the melody; we knew the words; we understood the language:

I listen for the dim whisper, funneled down the ages, of the dark parables of the old prophets telling the people of God that God is One and God is All, and whenever we make any part of his creation into God, or think of any of his people as divine, or think that we can do anything of our own power and virtue rather than his, we sin. But the voices are faint, and we heed them as little now as the ancient Jews did then.

> *The children at the party*
> *sit in a circle playing games,*
> *rhythm games, singing games, clapping games,*
> *and finally the whispering game:*
> *the little girl in the white organdy dress and blue sash*
> *whispers a sentence to the little boy in grey flannel shorts*
> *and he in turn whispers it to the little girl on his right* `
> *and so it goes all the way around the circle*
> *round and round*
> *as the earth whirls round the sun*
> *and the sun swings in the great circle of the galaxy*
> > *he is risen*
> > *we thought he was the one who*
> > *we thought it was he*
> > *he is risen*
> > *he is exactly like us but sinless*
> > *not like us then*

sinful
he is risen
three in one
and one in three
and the great hawk cracks the sky
he in us
we in him
bread and wine
ashes to ashes
and
dust to dust
he is risen
is he

And the sentence returns to the little girl
and she says the nonsense words aloud
and everybody laughs and no one understands.

The whispers are no more than echoes and we forget there is something to be heard. We forget that there are two sides to Mercury. We sit in the brilliant sunshine of intellect and don't even know that we are not whole.

It is not popular to be willing to admit to sin. The churches are still deleting *miserable offenders* from the General Confession. There appears to be a general misconception that if we admit to sin, then we are wallowing in it, like hippopotamuses in mud. Maybe some people are.

But freedom and lightness follow when I say "I'm sorry" and am forgiven.

It is equally unpopular to say "I can't do it myself." The misconception here is that this means a whining attitude and an unwillingness to try, being a coward under the blows of fate, instead of fighting back. Nor can I blame my favorite scapegoat, Madison Avenue, for this. Again I have to unlearn the 'virtues' I was taught in my Anglican boarding schools. But Jesus of Nazareth always said, 'I don't do this. It is my Father speaking through me.'

Once Alan preached about the necessity for Christian atheism; we must stop worshipping the false gods which have crept into Christianity (all those Anglo-Saxon moral virtues); we must be atheists for Christ's sake. He did not mean, of course, that we are to stop believing in God, God who is One, God who is All, but that we must be certain that it is God we believe in, and not all those false spirits masquerading as the Holy One. We must shun the lovely little idols Satan erects for us, idols much easier to accept than the One God who is so difficult to believe in, whose ways are not our ways, who says No and expects us to understand that this is the prelude to a true Yes, who would make us whole, for whom sunside and nightside are alike, who is willing to be in our hearts and who would ask us to put our minds in our hearts that we may know him there.

But I have trouble with the words *Christian atheism*, which are too likely to recall the God-is-dead-ism of the sixties, an *ism* which was certainly the appropriate response to the activism of those days when man was convinced that man-on-his-own can take care of all the problems of the world, and the help of the Spirit is irrelevant.

I read some of the God-is-dead books, though by no means all, because they dealt with problems which simply did not exist for me, and I disposed of them rather ribaldly by writing: "If God is dead/And man's the Head/We're in a hocus focus./We've all been spliced/To an orphaned Christ/And that's a bogus Logos."

It is impossible for us human beings not to keep coming up with anthropomorphic gods. The righteous Lord of the Old Testament is an analogy of human righteousness as it was understood then. The gods we make today are equally anthropomorphic, God in our own image, because it's inevitable with finite human nature. Occasionally we are given the grace to turn away from our own image and toward God's image in us, and we have the model for this image in Jesus. He may have been fully man, but he was most unlike us, or we are most unlike him, in that his Father was not an anthropomorphic God, but a Being entirely new, so new that we still can't understand the glorious Father Jesus showed us in everything he did and said and was.

If I cannot be a Christian atheist because of the confusion which this term arouses, I can shun Christolotry; I can try to live by *symbole* but *sans idole*, though, being human, I will never entirely succeed. But I can keep on trying, and listening for the whispers of the Spirit.

When I am referred to in secular reviews and articles as a 'practicing Christian,' it usually is not meant as a compliment, and on the rare occasions when it is said with approval, it still makes my hackles rise, and this reaction disturbs me. Why should it make me uneasy to be referred to as what I am struggling to be? If I reply by announcing that I am a Christian atheist, or that I am against Christolotry, not many people are going to understand what that means, either.

It annoys me least and amuses me most when my Christianity is referred to with condescension: 'Poor dear, she sometimes writes quite nicely even though she isn't clever enough to know that only fools believe in God.'

D'accord. I am basically intuitive rather than intellectual (which is probably why the the third person of the Trinity is the least difficult for me), although I don't discard or discount my intellect; nightside alone is as incomplete as sunside alone. I stumbled back into Church after years away, not out of intellectual conviction, but intuitive need. I had learned through sorry experience that I cannot do it alone. I am often so irritated in church that I can manage to sit through the service with a reasonably good grace only by writing poetry or memorizing my favorite Psalms. If I go to services with reasonable regularity it is largely because I believe that if I am attempting to understand what it means to be Christian, this cannot be done in lofty isolation.

I may not want to be associated with much that passes today for Christianity; nevertheless I am part of it, even when I rebel because being Christian is becoming more and more a do-it-yourself activity. I rebel when the Church feels that it has to succeed. My theology of failure is incomprehensible to many, intolerable to some. I am saddened when the very air I breathe throughout Christendom is Pelagian: the Church can take care of all the ills of the world as long as we are morally virtuous and politically liberal. Not that I am against either virtue or liberalism! But I watch in horror as a great liberal, passionately interested in the cause of—shall we say—the leper, very carefully avoids speaking to the leper in his path, in order to get on with the cause. And it occurs to me that Jesus couldn't have cared less about the cause of the leper or the rights of the leper. But when there was a leper in his path he did not walk around him, like the priest walking on the opposite side of the road from the man set upon by thieves, on his way to Jerusalem to preach his famous sermon on compassion. Jesus stopped. And healed. And loved. Not causes, but people.

If I see and rebel against activism in others, it is because I have had to see and rebel against it in myself. We can't see a fault or flaw in others unless we have at least the potential for it in ourselves. I don't want us to sit back smugly and serve ourselves, and ignore the suffering around us, but neither do I want us to fall into those temptations which Jesus saw for what they were, and had the meekness to reject. And I remember again that it was the Spirit who led Jesus to be tempted. The Spirit, too, sees through the snare of avoiding pain by taking up causes. It was the Spirit who gave St. Francis the stamina to return day after day to the stench and ugliness of the leper house, to minister to the lepers—not as a group, not as a cause, but one mutilated person at a time. The people who make up causes are often too revolting to be loved easily, but the Spirit will give us the strength to love the unlovable if we ask for help.

An intelligent and thoughtful young woman interviewed me for a course she was taking at Columbia. In answer to one of her questions I talked about doing the small things which are daily put into my path to do, such as smiling at the dour man trying to deliver those boxes of groceries down the metal slide, and she said, "Some people would consider that self-serving." Is it? It may be, but if I cannot see the hungry people I pass each day, if I do not smile at the dour man, if I do not feed the stranger who comes to my door, or give a glass of cool water to the thirsty child, then I cannot see the starvation of people in India or South America. Perhaps if I see pictures on the news or in the papers of victims of earthquake, flood, drought, I will write a small check for the cause of world hunger, and I may even refrain from meat on Wednesdays; but as long as I am responding to a cause it will not affect my entire life, my very breathing. It is only when I see hunger or thirst in one human being, it is only when I see discrimination and injustice in all its horrendous particularity as I walk along Broadway, that my very life can be changed. If it was necessary for God to come to us as one of us, then it is only in such particularity that I can understand incarnation. I am not very good about it. I don't pray, give, give up, nearly as much as I should. But a response to a cause will never change my life, nor open my heart to the promptings of the Spirit.

We may be a global village, but instant communication often isolates us from each other rather than uniting us. When I am bombarded on the evening news with earthquake, flood, fire, it is too much for me. There is a mechanism, a safety valve, which cuts off our response to overexposure to suffering.

But when a high-school student comes to me and cries because the two- and three-year-olds on her block are becoming addicted to hard drugs; when the gentle man who cleans the building in which the Cathedral library is located talks to me about his family in Guatemala, rejoicing because they are alive although their house has been destroyed by earthquake; when a goddaughter of mine in Luxembourg writes me about the hungry children of the immigrant Portuguese family with whom she is living, then in this particularity my heart burns within me, and I am more able to learn what it is that I can and ought to do, even if this seems, and is, inadequate.

But neither was Jesus adequate to the situation. He did not feed all the poor, only a few. He did not heal all the lepers, or give sight to all the blind, or drive out all the unclean spirits. Satan wanted him to do all this, but he didn't.

That helps me. If I felt that I had to conquer all the ills of the world I'd likely sit back and do nothing at all. But if my job is to feed one stranger, then the money I give to world relief will be dug down deeper from my pocket than it would if I felt I had to succeed in feeding the entire world.

Even spirituality and meditation and mysticism have become activities with easy success offered. Do such and such and you will have a mystical experience. You may have an experience, but it won't be a mystical one. Such experience cannot be bought.

Evil doesn't bother to infiltrate that which is already evil. Where there is darkness there is no need to snuff out the light. No wonder Satan rushes to churches filled with the sound of tongues—to any church at all. The Tempter has acquired many hard-working followers within the Christian establishment, and often in the name of the Holy Spirit. What better place for him to work than in the Church which is essentially a place for his redemption. I often feel his breath during a church service, am tempted by his sweet, seductive whispers. He is reasonable, never offends my intellect; whereas my Trinitarian God is frequently unreasonable and intellectually offensive—and yet speaks to the whole of me, mind and heart, intellect and intuition, and speaks most clearly to that element in me which accepts the incomprehensible beauty of love: married love; the loves of friendship; to that element in me which participates in music, poetry, painting. Bach's

Toccata and Fugue in C minor will take me a lot further than any number of books on theology.

After I had given a lecture at a very Protestant university, three postgraduate students, all married and with children, approached me, and the spokesman blurted out, "Does your Church mean less and less to you?" I paused, said "Yes," then "No," then, "What is the Church?"

Not the building in which I stand or sit, often uncomfortably, often irritably. Not any denomination of any kind—and the fact that the Body of Christ is broken by denominations is another cause for Satan's pleasure. Why can't we worship in our differing ways and still be One?

I doubt if Christian unity will ever come through paperwork and red tape. The time has come for us to leap across boundaries. I gave the same series of lectures on myth, fantasy, and fairy tale at a Fundamentalist college and a Roman Catholic monastery, and the responses and questions were the same, and that rejoiced my heart. I am comfortable and at home when I sing hymns with my most Protestant friends. One time I was off to Wheaton College, Illinois, a fundamentalist college with extraordinarily high academic standards, and I said to Josephine that I was going to be met in Chicago by my Baptist priest friend; I used this appellation several times before she said, "Mother, what are you saying?" And only then did it strike me that 'Baptist Priest' is an odd combination. And yet this man *is* my 'Baptist priest friend' and one year I sent him an icon for Christmas.

I have lovingly been offered, and received, communion in the Roman Catholic Church, and while this may be irregular, it is the only response of love possible. Last summer the elder daughter of my beloved nanny, Mrs. O, celebrated her golden anniversary as a Sister of Charity, and I was asked to read one of the lessons at the Festival Mass.

As we drove from Crosswicks to the convent in the Bronx, I wondered what I ought to do about receiving. On the way to the church I whispered to one of the Sisters, "Is it all right if I receive?" And she whispered, "Of course, as long as it's all right with you." "It's fine with me." But even without this unofficial permission the problem would have been quickly resolved. I sat up in the chancel with two of the Sisters; two Sisters who dressed completely in secular clothes; so the priests there that afternoon consistently called me Sister, and there was no question, when it came to the bread and wine, that I was to be with all the others gathered there that day, part of the unbroken body.

It's not quite that easy with the Protestant denominations where the communion service is simply a memorial service, a looking back at Maundy Thursday and Jesus's celebration of the Passover. But I have always felt that God is quite capable of taking care of his own table, and that thousands of nonbelievers are not going to rush up to receive the body and blood without any belief in the Real Presence if we have 'open communion.' And even if some do, isn't God still in control of what is going on? And if we believe in the real and very power of the body and blood, may this power itself not make all the difference?

Tallis used to talk about the academic problem of what a priest ought to do if a pious Turk came up to take communion. And one day he was celebrating Mass and a man whom he knew to be a pious Turk did indeed appear at the altar rail. And was given the body and blood. And was there because he had read the Book of Common Prayer and taken seriously all that it had said. And became a far better Christian than most of us born to it. What might have happened had the letter of the law been obeyed and he turned down?

Perhaps we will once again be One when all the hungry sheep have broken down and leapt over the denominational barriers in order to be nourished together, and ultimately the Hierarchies will recognize that unity is already here, and can throw away all thouse millions of miles of red tape.

When I contemplate the problems of intercommunion, especially Roman Catholic/Anglican/Orthodox vis-à-vis those who do not believe in the Real Presence, it occurs to me that these genuine problems about the Lord's Table are once again problems of our own making. If those who are terrified at the idea of the Real Presence in the bread and wine, those who shudderingly call it cannibalism (but we are all in one way or another cannibals; we do nourish each other; all life lives at the expense of other life), if those who staunchly assert that their communion services are purely memorial services—well, then, if they really remember, in the fullest sense of anamnesis, the problem becomes a semantic one. If the mighty acts of God are truly present, then it is human beings who create divisions among each other. It is our nature to do so, but at least we are coming more to realize how futile and wasteful is a divided Christendom, and how we ourselves, far more than those outside the Church, are willfully slowing down the coming of the Kingdom.

Of course anamnesis doesn't always happen during a service, not in any communion or denomination, just as it does not always happen when I am writing. Tallis told me about an Orthodox attitude which I love; it is also enlightening! During an Orthodox service (and these are longer than those we complain about as being too long) no one worshipper there is able to concentrate on what is going on, to exercise anamnesis, at all times. Our minds do wander. During even the most moving of church services, I constantly have to pull my thoughts back into focus. But the Orthodox feel that this does not matter, because all of the time *some one* is concentrating; there is always someone in the Body who is wholly focused on the Holy Mysteries; there is always someone keeping the strong rope of anamnesis unbroken, and so my belief in interdependence deepens, and my wayward heart is turned toward God, God who is One, who is All, and who must be saddened and perhaps amused by all the theological problems we continually manage to create for ourselves.

My tongue has been informed by Anglican thought; my favorite century of English literature is from the mid-sixteen-hundreds to the mid-seventeen-hundreds, and all the literary masters I look up to speak with Anglican voices. I was born an Anglican, and even if I left the Church forever, just as once Hugh left the theatre forever, that tradition flows in my very bloodstream.

I am grateful for our Crosswicks years in the Congregational Church, when Hugh was a deacon and lay preacher, when I directed choir and taught the high-school discussion group. I learned a lot about the priesthood of all believers which is still important to me. So I go to church, not for any legalistic or moralistic reasons, but because I am a hungry sheep who needs to be fed; and for the same reason that I wear a wedding ring: a public witness of a private commitment.

There was one Pentecost Sunday in our village church which I am not likely to forget. I wrote about it later, for some of the young people involved who are close to me:

It is an old church,
two hundred years old,
and that is old for this gawky country
though perhaps young by other standards.
The congregation today (as in most churches)
is sparse.
In the old New England tradition
we amble into our seats
and only a few outsiders
indulge in the impropriety and popery
of bowing their heads in prayer
(nobody would dare kneel).
So of course nobody remembers that this is
the time of the rushing wind and the tongues of fire.
Today is the Sunday when the Young People's Group,
the Pilgrim Fellowship, is going to lead the worship.
They are dressed in jeans, shirts—
the girls as well as the boys—
and someone puts on a record
and in the chancel they dance to the music
separately
(nobody touches anybody else)
and not very well. But it is Their Own Thing,
their response:
two women get up and leave the church.
Then one of the girls goes to the lectern (she brought me a kitten once)
and tells us that they are not there to shock us
but to tell us what is on their minds.
Another girl talks about the importance of individualism;
what she really means is that she cares
about the fall of the sparrow
and the gloriously unutterable value of persons.
But somebody else walks out.
Then a boy (his mother and I were pregnant
together with our sons; I have seen him
learn to walk and talk)
gets up and says he does not believe in God
or life after death
or anything he's been taught in Sunday School.
If there is a God, he says,
we have to find him where we live,
and he finds church when he walks alone
in the woods.
There is a movement in the back of the church
as someone else leaves.

Then our nearest neighbors' boy,
our son's close friend,
talking too fast in his urgency,
cries out against war
and napalm
and job recruiters for Dow Chemical
and killing killing killing
and more people walk out.
Then the young people (still trying) come to
pass the Peace
and they put on another record and sing to it
and they CARE
And someone else leaves

oh stop
oh stop
STOP

This is Pentecost
the wind is blowing
the flames are bright
the Spirit burns

O stop
listen
all you Parthians, Medes, Elamites,
dwellers in Mesopotamia, Judea, Cappadocia,
in Pontus, and Asia, Phrygia and Pamphylia, in Egypt
and in the parts of Libya around Cyrene,
O stop
strangers of Rome, Jews and proselytes, Cretes and
Arabians, dwellers in New England, New York,
Indiana, India, California, Chile,
China, Russia, Africa.

Stop and listen
to these children who speak in your own tongue
the wonderful works of God.

But the tongue is dulled, the whisper blurred. We do not listen to each other. We are more often known by how we quarrel than by how we love each other. I had a horrendous picture of the face we present to the world when I was asked to be the lay Christian on the panel of Christians and Jews where I met the rabbi who performed Peter's mother's funeral.

But the rabbi and I did not become friends that first night. Fortunately it was an ongoing panel, because the first evening was as full of misunderstanding and refusal to listen as that Pentecost Sunday in the Congregational Church. My job, at that initial meeting, was to respond to a keynote speech by a visiting rabbi who had done some work with the World Council of Churches and who had therefore been brought in to lead the discussion.

He talked more about Christianity than he did about Judaism, but the Christianity he held up to the congregation bore no relationship whatsoever to any kind of Christianity I can believe in. But where, where did he get his picture of Christianity? From Christians, that's where. I listened with growing horror. There was nothing I could respond to. Certain words meant one thing to him, another to me, so that it was as though we spoke foreign languages—and the Holy Spirit did not come that first evening to touch our tongues so that we would understand each other. It was an evening of confusion and, on occasion, hostility toward me and the young priest friend who had got me into this—hostility because we represented to the gathered assembly everything the rabbi was saying about Christians.

At the depressing end of the evening I asked if I might be given ten minutes at the beginning of the next session to say something about what Christianity means to me, and was told that I might. Ten minutes to tell a hostile congregation what the Incarnation means to my life! Impossible, of course. All I could do was to try to speak completely honestly, completely vulnerably. I spent all week trying to choose the few words I could use in ten minutes. I was certainly earnest, and perhaps the very earnestness was what broke the ice, because after that we were able to talk to each other as human beings created by the One same God.

Then we were able to start untangling some of the misconceptions. It's easy enough to respond to "All Christians blame the Jews for killing Jesus, and they're still making us pay for it." We talked about the Palm Sunday service at the Cathedral, and the moment that the 'we' or 'us' becomes 'they' or 'them,' we are no longer Christian.

But there were other, subtler misconceptions, and they have been set up by Western Christianity as it has attempted to conform to this world—not to accept it, to be in it, but to conform to it. The visiting rabbi insisted that Christianity is a religion of superstition, rather than reality, and offers its people the psychological satisfactions of mysticism. Psychological satisfaction? I doubt if any of the great mystics received any more psychological satisfaction than we would if we received a hundred volts of electricity. A mystical experience is not a satisfying one. It is burning. It is a ride on the tail of a comet, freezing, searing—for cold can burn even more than fire. It is not psychologically satisfying to have nightside and sunside meet in a blaze of ice and fire, to understand God as utterly distant and unknowable and yet so close that the comfort of the shadow of his wings can be intimately felt. In this rare, almost unbreathable atmosphere, sunside and nightside are resolved in paradox, and the incomprehensible is yet in some measure comprehended in contradiction.

But the visiting rabbi insisted that Christianity is hung up on such psychological highs, while Judaism accepts this world, enjoying the creation of God, meals together, friendship, the beauties of nature. Jews accept the word; Christianity rejects it. Ouch, again.

This visiting rabbi, whose name I have happily forgotten, did not have a stupid or diabolic version of Christianity. It was prepared for him by the Christians he has encountered. But to deny the world, as he suggests Christians do, is to deny the Incarnation. It is quite possible to have an incarnational view of the universe and not be a Christian; all artists are incarnational and not all artists are Christians, for instance. But it is not possible to be a Christian and not have an incarnational view of the universe. Christianity without incarnation is not Christianity.

The rabbi, given his clue by Christians, told us that Christianity is a pleasant religion. It promises the faithful the joys of heaven to make up for the difficulties of life. And he referred to the Eucharist as 'a magical act,' and said that the Jews, instead of turning to magic, face reality.

Magic? Reality? Who can blame the rabbi? I know that I, too, have misconceptions of Christianity. Sharing my thoughts with the members of the panel and, afterwards, with the congregation, helped me to clarify my own thinking, and by the end of the panel the crackling antagonism was gone and we were moving a good deal closer to understanding and acceptance than we would have thought possible the first night. And the women of the Hadassah asked me to come and share thoughts about being a woman.

During the summer, when we are in the country and there is no

Episcopal church nearby, I very much miss what the rabbi considered a *magical act.* I struggled to work out the difference between miracle and magic in *The Other Side of the Sun.*

"Honoria," Aunt Olivia asked, "what is a miracle?"
Aunt Irene said, "Honoria, I'd like some more soldier beans, please."
Aunt Olivia held up her hand. "Wait. Honoria, what's the difference between magic and a miracle? That ought to interest you, Irene."
Honoria stood, holding the silver dish in a linen napkin. "A human being can do magic. God do the miracle. Magic make the person think the power be in hisself. A miracle make him know the power belong to God." She went out to the kitchen.

But there are many people besides Aunt Irene and the rabbi who would like to toss off the Holy Mysteries as magic, and ineffectual magic at that, and it is Christians who have been responsible for this. The teachers from whom I have learned the most have never tried to make God comprehensible to me by intellect alone. The mind must be flexible enough to bend down to the heart; the mediating band must join nightside and sunside. To receive the bread and wine as the real body and blood of the Lord has indeed in some times and some places degenerated to superstitious magic; this can happen to all ritual, particularly at times when man's power seems so sufficient that God's is not needed.

But all power is God's, and God's power is an expression of his joy, and all earthly ritual is afire with the powerful joy of the Resurrection. I do not fully understand the mystery of the Eucharist, but my lack of human understanding makes no difference; I am nourished and strengthened; this is what I know.

Rejoice!
You have just given me the universe,
put it in my hands, held it to my lips,
oh, here on my knees have I been fed
the entire sum of all created matter,
the everything
that came from nothing.
Rejoice!
Who can doubt its power?
Did not this crumb of bread
this sip of wine

burst into life
that thundered across nothing
and became the cause of all our
celebrations?
Oh, the explosion of nothing into something,
into flaming, raging suns and shouting comets
and drops of dew and spiders' webs
into mountains bursting forth with brilliant volcanoes
valleys falling and rising
laughing with joy
earth's cracking, primordial rains flooding
a snowdrop's star, a baby's cry
oh, rejoice!
rejoice and celebrate
eyes to see and ears to hear
fingers to touch
to touch
the body's living warmth
hand stretched to hand
across nothing
making something
celebrate
lips to smile
to kiss
to take the bread and wine
rejoice
flowers   grass   pavements
gutters   garbage cans
old people remembering
babies laughing
mothers singing
fathers celebrating
rejoice
around the table
hold hands
all round
like a ring circling a finger
placed there as a promise
holding the universe together
nothing into something
into joy and love
rejoice
and celebrate!

So I struggle with my theology of failure and the Noes of God. I cannot totally withdraw from the Establishment again, no matter how sad and angry the Establishment may make me. Of course I find it easier to feel God when I go alone at night to walk Timothy on the upper level of Riverside Park and move quietly through the fog or the falling snow; or in summer when I go out with him at night and walk under the glory of the stars. It is easier to feel and see and touch God thus than it is in church, but this private religion is not enough, is destructive when it is all there is; to find God only in a private mysticism is to break off from the Body, to leave the mainland, and ultimately to worship myself more than my Creator.

On the first Pentecost the Holy Spirit came to the Body gathered together, not to separate individuals. But each one of those individuals was essential to the Body, because the Spirit teaches us that our understanding comes through particulars, never through generalities. Here my long years of writing again inform my groping theology. A story must be about particular people; the protagonist must be someone we recognize, and with whom we can identify.

So should it be strange that this is how it has to be with the Incarnation, too? God shows us his nature through what has been called 'the scandal of particularity.' It *is* a scandal to think of God being fully God in Jesus of Nazareth, but there's no other possible way for us to glimpse his love. Generalities get no further in religion than in fiction.

I am helped to understand the Incarnation because Jesus Christ is the protagonist of Creation. This is the shocking aspect of particularity, that he is the hero, and although all of us want to play leads, we are, in fact, only supporting actors. But, as Stanislavsky, the director of the Moscow Art Theatre, said, "There are no small parts. There are only small actors."

I learn my part only as I am guided by the Spirit. And often I understand this guidance through hindsight, anamnesis, understanding something only after it has happened, as the Disciples could look back and understand Good Friday only after the glory of Easter and the joy of Pentecost.

I know the gifts of the Spirit not only when I hear the rippling of tongues but also in the gift of silence, when understanding and joy come without words, in that mediating circle which is beyond and through the limitations of language, any kind of language at all.

I stood with my friend Gillian at the bedside of a woman who was dying, badly, of a brain tumor, and she asked, "Will I ever again be whole?" And Gillian responded, "More whole than you have ever been before." And we held hands and prayed together and there in the midst of human illness and the shadow of death we were touched with tongues of fire. The Spirit does not only come to us when we rejoice; the Spirit comes when we are most beaten, most in need.

The Spirit broods over the waters before the beginning of man's time; speaks through the Prophets; guides Michelangelo's chisel, Shakespeare's pen, Serkin's fingers. I understand and I do not understand; I know and I do not know.

One evening I was up in Tallis's apartment, leafing through an obsolete icon calendar which he had kept for the beauty of the photographs. One of them struck me with that extraordinary arrow of revelation and recognition which is one of the brightest of human joys. In this icon the prophet Elijah is sitting in the desert, and is telling God that it is better for him to die than to live, in much the same angry way as the prophet Jonah.

In the icon a raven has come, as God promised, to feed the prophet. And in the raven's beak is the round white circle of the communion bread: Chronology once more broken apart by *kairos,* by the truth of love.

> *Silence was the one thing we were not prepared for,*
> *we are never prepared for.*
> *Silence is too much like death.*
> *We do not understand it.*
> *Whenever it comes we make up thunders and lightnings*
> *and we call anxiously for the angels to sing for us.*
> *It is all right for Elijah to kill all those false prophets,*
> *though they were comfortingly noisy;*
> *it is all right for him to bring that poor widow's boy*
> *back to life with his own audible breath;*
> *that is only a miracle. We understand miracles.*
> *But he survived God's silence, and that is more extraordinary*
> *than all the sounds of all of Israel's battles rolled into one.*
> *Why is God silent? Why does he not sound for us?*
> *He came silently to birth. Only the angels,*
> *Taking pity on us, sang to make that silence bearable.*

When he came to dwell among us men on earth
only his mother understood the silence,
and when he died she made no sound of weeping.
Why does silence make us shiver with the fear of death?
There was more sound to comfort our ears
when he was hammered to the cross
and cried out through the strangling bonds
and the temple veil was rent and graves burst wide,
than when he was born. I am not sure
that death is silent. But Easter is.
The angels did not sing for us, heralding the glory.
There was no sound to prepare us, no noise of miracle,
no trumpet announcing the death of death—
or was it what we call life? We did not understand
and we ran from the empty tomb and then
he came to us in silence. He did not explain
and at last I knew that only in silence is the word
even when the word itself is silent.

Thus in silence did that strange dark bird
Bring to Elijah in the desert the whole and holy Word.

If I cannot receive the gifts of the Spirit in silence, I will never be able to receive them in any other way. Often I understand that this strange dark bird has been with me only when I am turned again and look back, with anamnesis, and realize that the No of God, when I felt most deserted, was a Spirit-filled No preparing me for a Yes.

Hugh and Alan and Tallis are my teachers, and better teachers no one could hope for. When I go flying off on a tangent, as I so frequently do, one of them will reach out and pull me back. One time I evidently gave a limiting adjective to God in front of Alan. I don't remember what I said, nor what his rebuke; I only know my response, which was to go off and scribble these lines which, a few minutes later, I put into his hand.

LOVE LETTER ADDRESSED TO:

Your immanent eminence
wholly transcendent
permament, in firmament
holy, resplendent
other and aweful

incomprehensible
legal, unlawful
wild, indefensible
eminent immanence
mysterium tremendum
mysterium fascinans
incarnate, trinitarian
being impassible
infinite wisdom
one indivisible
king of the kingdom
logos, word-speaker
star-namer, narrator
man-maker, man-seeker
ex nihil creator
unbegun, unbeginning
complete but unending
wind-weaving, sun-spinning
ruthless, unbending:

Eternal compassion
helpless before you
I, Lord, in my fashion,
love and adore you.

It is a strange love affair I have with this One who breathed his Spirit into me, baptized me with it all those years ago, willy-nilly, who never betrays me, though I am consistently unfaithful to him, like Hosea's wife. Not only do I listen to the wiles of the dragon, I become the dragon, and then I remember Rilke's words:

How should we be able to forget those ancient myths about dragons that at the last minute turn into princesses who are only waiting to see us once beautiful and brave . . . Perhaps everything terrible is in its deepest being something helpless that wants help from us.

I know that when I am most monstrous, I am most in need of love. When my temper flares out of bounds it is usually set off by something unimportant which is on top of a series of events over which I have no control, which have made me helpless, and thus caused me anguish and frustration. I am not lovable when I am enraged, although it is when I most need love.

One of our children when he was two or three years old used to rush at me when he had been naughty, and beat against me, and what he wanted by this monstrous behavior was an affirmation of love. And I would put my arms around him and hold him very tight until the dragon was gone and the loving small boy had returned.

So God does with me. I strike out at him in pain and fear and he holds me under the shadow of his wings. Sometimes he appears to me to be so unreasonable that I think I cannot live with him, but I know that I cannot live without him. He is my lover, father, mother, sister, brother, friend, paramour, companion, my love, my all.

Until I can say this, I cannot understand my theology of failure, or the Noes of God.

MARCH 25TH: THE ANNUNCIATION

To the impossible: Yes!
Enter and penetrate,
O Spirit, come and bless
This hour. The star is late.
Only the absurdity of love
Can break the bonds of hate.

10... Show Me Your Hindquarters and Let Me Hear You Roar

WHAT'S ALL THIS stuff about a Trinitarian God? We're rugged individualists, we Americans, and all this gabble about three in one and one in three is pluralism and not *E pluribus unum,* whatever that used to mean; we don't have to take Latin in school anymore. This Trinity thing is one way of allowing ourselves polytheism instead of monotheism. And it's tied up somewhere with the family as a unit, but nowadays the validity of the family is being questioned, and even by bishops of the Church.

We've come near to discarding the Trinity season as part of the Church calendar, because 3 in 1 and 1 in 3 makes even less sense than $0 \times 3 = 0$ instead of 3. And if we are becoming free to ignore the Trinity, then we can ignore the breakup of the family as a coherent and creative unit. Most families aren't, so why pretend?

Because of the United States industrial patterns, with many middle-class families consistently being uprooted every few years, thus breaking familial community, we've been forced into rationalizing this breaking up by denying the value of parental and grandparental relationships, and calling them manipulative and abnormal, all full of Freudian nastiness. Few children today grow up with easy coming and going between uncles and aunts and grandparents. This is the way things are, and we tend to justify the way things are as good and right, and so the family as the living image of the Trinitarian God becomes denigrated—otherwise old people couldn't be shuffled off to institutions as so many are. Sometimes there is no choice. The 'nuclear' pattern of family life makes it inevitable. But not always. Sometimes it is simply easier. It's not nice to see someone growing old and incontinent. It's easier to put the sight away. So families fall apart, and divorce is made easy, because this is the way of the world, and put Grandma in a home because it's really horrid for the kids to see her sitting there drooling, and last night she wet her bed. . . . The rector was telling me of a place where they're really very kind to them. . . .

The breaking up of families and the cult of youth has encouraged us to dishonor old age and to ignore the Fourth Commandment as being out of date. It was one thing for those nomadic old Hebrews who didn't have the advantage of Senior Citizens' Villages and Old People's Homes and Nursing Homes and all that technocracy has given us, but it has little bearing on the realities of life in the enlightened United States.

If one thinks of Mother as being devourer and emasculator (some are, but not all; mine wasn't), then it's easy to feel one needn't honor her, or if Father is only the image of the paternalistic male chauvinist pig Old Testament God (some are, but not all; mine wasn't), then one needn't honor him, either. It strikes me as being a weaselly way out of responsible and creative (and therefore painful) relations.

I have been tested about this, and in the fire, too, and I've written about this testing in *The Summer of the Great-grandmother,* and I wouldn't have been able to go on honoring my mother had it not been for the support and compassionate help of the entire family. I may not have thought consciously about the Trinity that summer, but in my intuitive subconscious I learned a lot about it.

We've been trying to understand the Trinity in terms of provable fact instead of poetry, and so we stop saying the Creed at many services. But the Creed is not a blueprint for faith; the Creed is a *symbole.* If I have to say the Creed in terms of scientific proof, I cannot say it all. But the Creed, like the Trinity, is best understood in the open language of poetry, of myth, that language in which we participate when we try to express ultimate things.

Athanasius and his friends, hammering out the *Quicunque Vult* in order to defend the Trinitarian God they adored, struggled to move beyond the literal level of daily words and yet make the point, and sometimes blundered into absurdity (as Dorothy Sayers noted): the Father incomprehensible, the Son incomprehensible, the Spirit incomprehensible—the whole thing incomprehensible. Of course it is. That's partly the point of Athanasius's powerful wielding of words as though he were trying to catch hold of the whirlwind. The Trinity is trapped in neither time nor space. *Before Abraham was, I am,* cries the second person. *I will be what I will be,* shouts the first. And through the brilliant flame of the Spirit I know that the Christ on whose name I call was creating galaxies and snowflakes long before there were living beings naming the animals in the Garden.

Perhaps the morning stars still sing together, only we have forgotten the language, as we have forgotten so much else, limiting Christianity to a mere two thousand years. We've known it by that name for even less, but that is our shortsightedness. When God came to us as one of us he was misunderstood and betrayed and part of that misunderstanding and betrayal is our dimming his brilliance because it's too much for our feeble eyes; our limiting his power because we're afraid of the unsheathed lightning; our binding him with ropes of chronology instead of trying to understand his freedom in *kairos.* Not that we've done any of this to the Lord himself, only to our image of the One we worship, and that's bad enough.

We're so dependent on the literal level that many Christians today have never even heard the Athanasian creed because it's just too much for sane modern man come of age. It was all so long ago, when Christianity was first formulating its *symboles* against the early heresies that it seems irrelevant, and we don't even recognize that we're surrounded by the same old heresies today. Satan doesn't need new weapons to confound us as long as the old ones still work.

In the last couple of decades there has been a new interest in community, so perhaps the idea of a Trinitarian God will once again be valid for us.

Unity in diversity has not always been as difficult for the human mind to understand as it is today. In the Psalms, for instance, we often don't know whether the psalmist is talking of himself, or of the community. And for the psalmist there is very little difference. He is who he is because he belongs to the people chosen by God. Without his community, he has no identity.

The same kind of assurance was known by the early Christians. They knew exactly who they were, through their baptisms, and each one literally held the lives of the others in his hand. That doesn't mean that they were identical, all good little Christians exactly alike, any more than my big toe and my elbow are identical, or my eyebrows and my fingernails. But, with all their radical differences, they had to be one body in order to survive; just as our corporeal bodies must be a unity. If my left foot walks in one direction and my right in another, I'm not going to get anywhere—except flat on my face.

My moments of being most complete, most integrated, have come either in complete solitude or when I am being part of a body made up of many people going in the same direction. A vivid example is a great symphony orchestra, where each instrument is completely necessary for the whole; a violin cannot take the place of a trombone, nor cymbals of the harp; and there are even times when the lowly triangle is the focus of the music.

(I love Chaliapin's definition of heaven: "There will be five thousand sopranos, five thousand altos, ten tenors—I don't much like tenors—a thousand baritones, and I will sing bass.")

Where have I known this unity?

In the Holy Mysteries. Yes.

And years ago when I was in the theatre and was privileged to be a small part of bringing a play to life, I remember one evening during rehearsal lying up on the grid and looking down from this great height to the stage and yet being a complete part of all that was being said and done.

And I knew it when we lived in Crosswicks year round and I directed the choir in the village church, knew it not because I was director, but because I was a part of something which became a whole, and was far more beautiful than the sum of its parts, even in midsummer when all of the tenor and bass section had to be out haying and I sang tenor, or bass an octave high.

And I know it around the family table where all of us different and dominant human beings, with all our diversity, are one.

One night after a small dinner party at a friend's house, I wrote for him:

> *Sitting around your table*
> *as we did, able*
> *to laugh, argue, share*

> *bread and wine and companionship, care*
> *about what someone else was saying, even*
> *if we disagreed passionately: Heaven,*
> *we're told, is not unlike this, the banquet celestial,*
> *eternal convivium. So the praegustum terrestrium*
> *partakes—for me, at least—of sacrament.*
> *(Whereas the devil, ever intent*
> *on competition, invented the cocktail party where*
> *one becomes un-named, un-manned, de-personned.) Dare*
> *we come together, then, vulnerable, open, free?*
> *Yes! Around your table we*
> *knew the Holy Spirit, come to bless*
> *the food, the host, the hour, the willing guest.*

And I knew the beauty of community in the birthing of my babies. We human beings are not meant to give birth to our offspring alone, any more than the dolphin, who delivers her babes with the help of midwife dolphins, in community. The need of the mother for support at this incredible moment has too often been forgotten by science, and it is good that once again the father can be present at the birth of his seed and share in this marvelous communal act.

I wish I knew it more often in church, and that I were a less reluctant Christian. The Church is too grownup for me, too reasonable, too limited. One reason nearly half my books are for children is the glorious fact that the minds of children are still open to the living word; in the child, nightside and sunside are not yet separated; fantasy contains truths which cannot be stated in terms of proof. I find that I agree with many college-age kids who are rejecting the adult world—not those with bad cases of Peter Pantheism, but with those who understand that the most grownup of us is not very grownup at all; that the most mature of us is pretty immature; that we still have a vast amount to learn.

The writers I admire most, who mean most to me, who teach me most, are, by and large, dead. One reason that there are not more great novels or plays or poems written today is that writing, like prayer, has become a do-it-yourself activity. Buy a book, take a course, and you will learn to be in control of your pen, manipulate words, and choose what you want to write, and be a success.

That's not the way it is.

A writer grimly controls his work to his peril, manipulates only in great danger (to be in control of your technique is very different from being in control of the work). Slowly, slowly, I am learning to listen to the book, in the same way I try to listen in prayer. If the book tells me to do something completely unexpected, I heed it; the book is usually right. If a book like this present one, a strange kind of book for a storyteller, pushes me to write it, I have no choice except to pay attention. All I can do, as far as activism is concerned, is to write daily, read as much as possible, and keep my vocabulary alive and changing so that I will have an instrument on which to play the book if it does me the honor of coming to me and asking to be written. I have never yet fully served a book. But it is my greatest joy to try.

It takes courage to open oneself vulnerably to the depths of a book. The moment I set words down on a page I become responsible for those words. Letters from readers have forced me to be aware of this responsibility which I would much rather not know about—but there it is, and I had better accept it. A letter from a teenager ran something like this, "I am thinking about becoming a Christian, but one thing worries me. All my friends who are Christians say that only Christians can be saved. What do you think? I'm writing to you because your stories have made me trust you." That's more responsibility than I want. But we're all of us responsible the moment we get out of bed every morning. I wrote that teenager a long letter (we're still corresponding) and I hope that I gave her a glimpse of God's love which is always greater than our continual misinterpretation of it. But I don't know. And that is frightening.

A woman my age wrote me after reading *A Circle of Quiet:* "I didn't know I was allowed to doubt." And several people, after *The Summer of the Great-grandmother:* "It doesn't worry me any more that I am angry at what is happenning." This is a heavy responsibility, but I blunder into pride if I think that it is all mine, any more than the book is all mine.

A professor and novelist, Dr. Caroline Gordon, from whom I have learned an enormous amount, told our class that we do not judge great art; it judges us. Oh, yes, it does. And the judgment of the work of art is quite apart from the moral virtue, or lack of moral virtue, of the artist. God's ways are not our ways, and quite often the most superbly transcendent work comes from artists who deny God and themselves in their daily living. They may be drunkards, sex-ridden, adulterous, but when they are at work they are wholly thrown out of themselves into collaboration with their work. And a work of art is indeed a work. Serkin does not sit down at the piano and play Beethoven's Appassionata Sonata without doing his finger exercises every single day. I think it was Rubinstein who said that if he did not practice for one day he knew it; if he didn't practice for two days his family knew it; and if he didn't practice for three days his public knew it.

Guernica did not spring in an hour to the canvas. *The Brothers Karamazov* wasn't tossed off in a week; it encourages me to remember that Dostoevsky did version after version of his novels.

To turn closer to home and to a less elevated analogy, one of the girls I lived with in Greenwich Village has gone on to be a concert pianist. No matter what the rest of us were doing, she practiced eight hours a day, finger exercises, one tiny phrase over and over again for what seemed forever. She was working on her first New York concert, and I'll never forget Handel's *Harmonious Blacksmith Variations,* or the Brahms Second Piano Concerto, or the Bach *Chromatic Fantasy and Fugue* as they slowly moved to life as she grew with them. If she diligently practiced her music, it also practiced her.

Montaigne says "the work of its own force and fortune can second the workman and surpass him, beyond his own invention and knowledge." I witnessed the truth of this as I saw the great compositions pushing the young pianist. When a work of art does this, the mediating circle integrating sunside and nightside is widened. Prayer, too, of its own force, can take the one at prayer far beyond the wildest imaginings.

I learned something of the force of the work myself during that same period when I went through my first shattering experience of falling in love and having the love turn to ashes. I not only survived, but did a considerable amount of growing up through the writing of my first full-length novel.

I concentrated on my work because it was what saved me. I had, over this broken affair, left the apartment with the other girls, left my entire group of friends, and moved into a tiny apartment of my own, so the noise and confusion was in my own heart. When I was working on that first novel I was genuinely and painfully unhappy. But during the actual writing I was at play; I was completely thrown out of my subjective misery into the joy of creation, so that what might have been a totally destructive experience became instead a creative one, and a freeing one.

I was freed during the writing as my book wrote me, not as I wrote it. And surely this was an experience of that special kind of unity which makes me understand the Trinity. The pages which built up on my writing table were not me, nor was I typewriter and paper; but we were, nevertheless, one. The same kind of collaboration can come when I read a book; the books which matter to me, to which I turn and return, are those which read me. The music I play, or listen to, is that which actively participates with me in harmony or counterpoint. The same thing is true in graphic art. There has to be an amorous interaction between the work of art and the person who is opening himself to it, and surely the relationship within the persons of the Trinity is one of Love, Love so real we can glimpse it only on rare occasions.

Hugh, or any actor, will tell you that the response of the audience can make or break an evening in the theatre; the audience collaborates, quite literally, with the actor.

As I understand the writing of a book, or a poem, so I understand the Eucharist, so I understand the Creed, the *symboles* by which I live. And in joyful moments I know prayer in the same way that I know great painting, or the Bach B Minor Mass. This is not to say that I think worship and prayer are less real than the daily world of provable fact, but that I think they are more real.

We are a generation out of touch with reality: the 'realistic' novels push me further away from the truth of things, rather than bringing me closer. When once I was asked if I wrote anything other than fantasy, I said that I also write adult novels, and the inquirer grinned, "Nowadays the word *adult* in front of novel means porno."

What about using 'the language of the people' in the translations of the liturgy. What people? We speak English today rather than a form of Norman French because Chaucer wrote in the language of the people, but I doubt if the butcher, the baker, the candlestick maker went around saying, "Whan that Arcite to Thebes comen was/Ful ofte a day he swelte and seyde 'Allas!'/For seen his lady shal he never mo."

Shakespeare, too, wrote in the language of the people, but I doubt if many of his contemporaries talked thus: "We are such stuff/As dreams are made on, and our little life/is rounded with a sleep." The only parts of Shakespeare's plays which seem dated are some of the comedy scenes where he has used the language of the lowest common denominator, and such language is quickly dated and then obsolete.

Nor did Cranmer use the language of the people of the street, but the best language he could possibly offer to God. Using limited vocabulary is to deny us our ability to grow in grace, to move from the limited to the transcendent. I'm glad that those who are working on the new Episcopal liturgies have been aware of this; the most recent draft of the Prayer Book is head and shoulders above the others and gives me hope. As our lives have no future if we have no memory, our language has no future and becomes dead if we forget its roots.

Chaucer and Shakespeare both came along at times when the English language was in need of redemption, and we are at another such time, and perhaps our Chaucer or Shakespeare is yet to be born, or it may be that the English language, like Latin, will dwindle and become obsolete. The Bible becomes more difficult to read with each generation, because the translators for King James weren't threatened by limited vocabulary. This holds true for Shakespeare, too. Recently I reread one of his early plays, written before he had moved into his giant stride, and on a notepad I jotted down all the words which I felt to be valid, useful words which are no longer in our vocabulary. There were over one hundred.

But it is not only the English language which is in danger. It is a fear for languages all over the world. After the Second World War the Japanese lost so many actual written characters that college students today cannot read the great Japanese works of literature, because they no longer know the characters used by the classical writers. This destruction of language is a result of war and is always a curtailment of freedom.

In Russia, where the worship of the Trinitarian God in the full beauty of the liturgy is officially discouraged, it would not be easy for a Russian to read the works of Alexander Solzenitsyn even if these works were not forbidden, because so much vocabulary was lost in Russia after the revolution. In one of Solzenitsyn's books his hero spends long hours reading the great Russian dictionary which came out in the 1890s. Solzenitsyn himself has one volume of this two-volume work, and in his novels he is forging the Russian language back into vitality, taking the words of the people of the streets and the words of the great dictionary and pulling the fullness of language out of the shadows and into the light. This is what Dante did in the writing of *The Divine Comedy.* It is what the English language needs if it is to survive as a great tongue. And surely language and liturgy are intertwined.

When Hugh and I went on a trip to Russia I almost didn't get a visa because our travel agent put down my occupation as *writer.* Writers think. Writers ask questions. Writers are dangerous. She finally persuaded 'them' that I write only for very small children and was not a threat. In any dictatorship, writers are among the first to be imprisoned, and vocabulary is quickly diminished and language deteriorates. Writers, if their vocabulary is not leashed, are quick to see injustice, and rouse the people to do something about it. We need words with which to think; kill words and we won't be able to think and we'll be easier to manipulate.

So I worry about the tyranny of language which is incapable of containing mystery. I worry about the weakening of our theology. For the past few years, for instance, I have missed gifts and *creatures* of bread and wine; this says something theologically important to me: the bread and wine, too, are God's creatures; it is an affirmation of the goodness of creation; when our big vegetable garden is first manured in the spring, the rank, life-giving manure is also a gift and creature, a symbol of incarnation.

If we are children by adoption and grace, how can we drop the *we are bold to say* before the Our Father? We are indeed bold to call the Lord of the Universe by the homely name of Abba, Father, and I don't want this dulled for me, so that in my own eyes the magnificence of the one I worship is dwindled and diminished. I want to cry out to him in all his Trinitarian Glory.

But why only three? If he is indeed the maker of the galaxies, isn't three a small number for his persons? Aren't there probably dozens, if not millions? There well may be, but there is for those of us on planet earth a special quality about the number 3—not magic, though it has been made so—but special. After all, we are the third planet from the sun, so it is bound to be a number of particular significance for us.

CATECHUMEN

A very young star: That, too, is a star?

The wind: Yes, Like you. A sun. But older.

STAR: How old?

WIND: About half way.

STAR: What are those objects circling it?

WIND: They are called planets.

STAR: Will I have them, too?

WIND: It is likely.

STAR: Will this be good?

WIND: It can be very good.

STAR: The ones that travel farthest from their sun—

WIND: Yes?

STAR: There is ice, and flame that is frozen, and much wind that is very unlike you.

WIND: It is part of me.

STAR: And it is good?

WIND: It is very good.

STAR: But I am a blaze of fire and flame—

WIND: And for you I blow, too.

STAR: You blow wherever . . .

WIND: I blow where I will.

STAR: That planet—one, two, three—third from the sun—

WIND: One, two, three: Yes. For it there are numbers, and the number is three.

STAR: Those tiny moving creatures?

WIND: They are men.

STAR: Where the sun shines on their planet they cannot see me; they cannot see stars. How strange. Why is that?

WIND: They could see you if they went down deep, deep, into the bottom of a well.

STAR: Will I, too, have a planet with men?

WIND: It is possible.

STAR: Will this be good?

WIND: Now I must ask a question. What is good?

STAR: Good is—God is—Good is—that it *is*. I cannot answer.

WIND: Then watch these men.

STAR: What is that, which is dark where it should be light?
WIND: It is a hill.
STAR: What is that upon the hill?
WIND: It is a tree.
STAR: What is that upon the tree?
WIND: It is a man.
STAR: But I do not understand.
WIND: You need not.
STAR: But I hear this man.
WIND: Yes.
STAR: But I am because he spoke, because he is spoken.
WIND: Yes.
STAR: But he is not like those other men.
WIND: I did not say he was. They are like him.
STAR: I thought that it was dark upon that hill, and now it is so bright that my light is nothing. O Wind, why do I feel pain?
WIND: From the nails.
STAR: It is not my pain.
WIND: Yes, it is yours, because it is his.
STAR: For you, too?
WIND: Creation groans.
STAR: Wind?
WIND: Yes?
STAR: It is over.
WIND: It has begun.

So for us the number is three, and it is enough; it holds the full glory.

"The Church is lowering its standards," I heard someone remark wistfully. In a wakeful period in the wee sma' hours of the night the phrase echoed back to me. What does it mean? And in my mind's eye flashed a vivid picture of a knight on horseback lowering his standard to the dust in defeat.

There are small subtle lowerings as well as the more obvious ones. If we fast now we do it for sociological and ecological reasons; all valid, and important. But we should not forget that fasting is also an aid to the prayer of the heart. It is indeed right and proper to fast in order to give the money thus saved to the starving people of the world, but it is also good to fast as a discipline which opens our hearts to God, and so to our neighbor.

If I am to show my love of God through love of neighbor, through walking a second mile with a stranger, through cutting my cloak in half in order to share it with the coatless, then I am able to show this love of neighbor only because first I must be able to accept my flawed and fragmented self enough to love myself; and I can love myself only when I can accept that God loves me, just as I am, without one plea.

One Lent, lost in the isolation of an attack of atheism, I wrote:

> *This is a strange place*
> *and I would be lost were it not for all the others*
> *who have been here before me.*
> *It is the alien space*
> *of your absence.*
> *It has been called, by some,*
> *the dark night of the soul.*
> *But it is absence of dark as well as light,*
> *an odd emptiness,*
> *the chill of any land without your presence.*
> *And yet, in this Lent of your absence,*
> *I am more certain of your love and comfort*
> *than when it is I who have withdrawn from you.*

I thank God for the characters who come to me in my stories, and who make me realize that the Institution is not the Church; the Church is all of us flawed and fallen people who make up the Body of Christ.

And so we are part of the Trinity, and that is an awesome thought, and the only thing to do is raise our voices and sing!

If I find the Holy Spirit the easiest person of the Trinity to understand, my faith in God the Father is also somewhat easier than my faith in God the Son; but it still involves the calm acceptance of mutually contradictory statements. He is infinite and wholly other and beyond mortal comprehension. And yet I reach out to hold his hand. I shelter under the shadow of his wings and know his nearness. No moral system, no personal rectitude, no code of ethics, is going to get me through this time we live in. I cannot do it alone, or even with the help of everybody around me, though it may be through their help that God is holding my hand.

It is always God the Son I find most difficult: the man Jesus of Nazareth, the dead Jew, is my stumbling block. It is easy to worship the Word who spoke the stars. But that Word made flesh?

There are books attempting to prove that he was an Essene

that he was married

that he was a homosexual

that he was a guerilla fighter, out to free Israel from Rome

that he was not dead when he was taken down from the cross (death by the slow strangulation of crucifixion usually took three days) but that his disciples hid him and produced him, in a horrible hoax, three days later

that he was a demiurge sent to clean up the mess God had made of the world

that he was only pretending to be human and didn't really share in human suffering

that he was a good rabbi with delusions of divinity

that it doesn't matter whether he was God or not

etcetera, ad infinitum, ad nauseam.

All these books mostly tell me what he is *not*. I can only guess at a few things which help show me what he is:

Jesus of Nazareth was a carpenter, which at that time meant that he was of the respectable middle class; he had a carpenter's strength; he had powerful lungs: he stood in a boat and spoke to thousands gathered on the shore (neither Ethel Merman nor Jesus Christ needed a throat mike), and the fact that he could cry out in a loud voice from the cross despite the strangling cords which compressed his rib cage is evidence of enormous physical power.

I don't know what he looked like, but he did *not* have blond curls and blue eyes. He was a Jew of Jews.

Since he did not fall for any of the temptations Satan offered him, he had no *hubris,* and so he is not a tragic hero. With the tragic hero there is always the question of what might have been, how the tragedy could have been averted. If Oedipus had not killed the old man at the crossroads; if Faust had not heeded the temptation of knowledge and youth; if Macbeth had not listened to the witches and lusted for the crown. . . .

With Jesus the might-have-been was answered when the Spirit led him into the desert to be tempted. There is an inevitability to his life, but it is not a tragic inevitability, because his will remained free.

He is hard for the consumer in the United States—or Soviet Russia —to understand, because he couldn't have cared less about the world's standards of success.

And this is the man who housed the second person of the Trinity.

But how? The impossibility bothered me, for a long time, and stopped bothering me only when I could rest with joy in 'the mystery of the word made flesh.'

There are analogies which help me to understand the first lines of John's Gospel. There are times when all of us willingly (and some-times unwillingly) limit ourselves for the sake of others. When my children were little I was hungry for adult conversation, for discussion of abstract ideas and concepts, but until they neared their teens our conversations had to be somewhat limited, even on our excursions up to nearby Mohawk Mountain to thrash out the problems of life and death. So I was only a part of my fuller self, but that part was still me; it was not something other than Madeleine, but it was not the whole Madeleine.

The week of Hugh's parents' golden wedding anniversary I was certainly a different, and perhaps better, Madeleine than the usual one, but the self I brought to Tulsa was still part of the whole me.

Analogies are never completely accurate. The willing limiting of the second person of the Trinity is far greater, and I struggled with it in writing, in Mary's voice, speaking these words from Ephesus when she was old and near time to die.

> *Now that I have spent these years in this strange place*
> *of luminous stone and golden light and dying gods,*
> *now that I have listened to the wild music*
> *of given-son, John, I begin to understand.*
>
> *In the beginning I was confused and dazzled,*
> *a plain girl, unused to talking with angels.*
> *Then there was the hard journey to Bethlehem,*

and the desperate search for a place to stay,
my distended belly ripe and ready for deliverance.
In the dark of the cave, night air sweet with the moist breath
of the domestic beasts, I laughed, despite my pains,
at their concern. Joseph feared that they would frighten me
with their anxious stampings and snortings,
but their fear was only for me, and not because of me.
One old cow, udders permanently drooping,
lowed so with my every contraction
that my own birthing cries could not be heard,
and so my baby came with pain and tears and much hilarity.

Afterwards, swaddled and clean, he was so small and tender
that I could not think beyond my present loving
to all this strange night pointed. The shepherds came,
clumsy and gruff, and knelt and bought their gifts,
and, later on, the Kings; and all I knew was marvel.
His childhood was sheer joy to me. He was merry and loving,
moved swiftly from laughters to long, unchildlike silences.
The years before his death were bitter to taste.
I did not understand, and sometimes thought that it was he
who had lost sight of the promise of his birth.

His death was horrible. But now I understand
that death was not his sacrifice, but birth.
It was not the cross which was his greatest gift;
it was his birth which must have been, for him,
most terrible of all. Think. If I were to be born,
out of compassion, as one of the small wood lice
in the doorsill of our house, limit myself to the comprehension
of those small dark creatures, unable to know sea or sun or song
or John's bright words; to live and die thus utterly restricted,
it would be as nothing, nothing to the radiant Word
coming to dwell, for man, in man's confined and cabined flesh.

This was the sacrifice, this the ultimate gift of love.
I thought once that I loved. My love was hundredfold less
than his, than is the love of the wood lice to mine,
and even here is mystery, for who dares limit love?
And has he not, or will he not, come to the wood lice
as he came to man? Does he not give his own self
to the grazing cattle, the ear of corn, the blazing sun,
the clarion moon, the drop of rain that falls into the sea?
His compassion is infinite, his sacrifice incomprehensible,
breaking through the darkness of our loving-lack.

Now I am old and sight and thought grow dim, limbs slow.
Oh, my son, who was and is and will be, my night draws close.
Come, true light which taketh away the sin of the world,
and bring me home. My hour is come. Amen.

I seek for God that he may find me because I have learned, empiri-
cally, that this is how it works. I seek: he finds. The continual seeking
is the expression of the hope for a creator great enough to care for
every particular atom and sub-atom of his creation, from the greatest
galaxy to the smallest farandolae. Because of my particular back-
ground I see the coming together of macrocosm and microcosm in the
Eucharist, and I call this Creator: God, Father; but no human being
has ever called him by his real name, which is great and terrible and
unknown, and not to be uttered by mortal man. If inadvertently my
lips framed the mighty syllables, entire galaxies might explode.

As I read the Old and New Testaments I am struck by the awareness therein of our lives being connected with cosmic powers, angels
and archangels, heavenly principalities and powers, and the groaning
of creation. It's too radical, too uncontrolled for many of us, so we
build churches which are the safest possible places in which to escape
God. We pin him down, far more painfully than he was nailed to the
cross, so that he is rational and comprehensible and like us, and even
more unreal.

And that won't do. That will not get me through death and danger
and pain, nor life and freedom and joy.

There is little evidence for faith in God in the world around me.
Centuries ago a man whose name is unknown to me cried out, "If God
were one whit less than he is, he dare not put us in a world that carries
so many arguments against him."

And, if I take the stories of the Bible seriously, when God's people
turn from him for too long, he withdraws. He has not answered my
knock for a long time, and this is beginning to make me angry. Why
isn't he there when I need him so desperately? So I write him another

LOVE LETTER

I hate you, God.
Love, Madeleine.

I write my message on water
and at bedtime I tiptoe upstairs
and let it flow under your door.

When I am angry with you
I know that you are there
even if you do not answer my knock
even when your butler opens the door an inch
and flaps his thousand wings in annoyance
at such untoward interruption
and says the master is not at home.

I love you, Madeleine,
Hate, God.

(This is how I treat my friends, he said to one great saint.
No wonder you have so few, Lord, she replied.)

I cannot turn the other cheek
it takes all the strength I have
to keep from hitting back

the soldiers bayonet the baby
the little boys trample the old woman
the gutters are filled with groans
while pleasure-seekers knock each other down
to get their tickets stamped first.

I'm turning in my ticket
and my letter of introduction
you're supposed to do the knocking.

How can I write to you
to tell you that I'm angry
when I've been given the wrong address
and I don't even know your right name?

I take hammer and nails
and tack my message on two crossed pieces of wood.

Dear God,
is it too much to ask you
to bother to be?
Just show your hindquarters
and let me hear you roar.

Love,
Madeleine.

I have often been told that when one first turns to God, one is greeted with brilliant Yes answers to prayers. For a long time, that was true for me. But then, when he has you hooked, he starts to say No. This has, indeed, been my experience. But it has been more than a No answer lately; after all, No is an answer. It is the silence, the withdrawal, which is so devastating. The world is difficult enough with God; without him it is a hideous joke.

The Trinity is unity in diversity; the Trinity is our model for Community.

What happened?

I turn again to that time when there was war in heaven, and Michael and his angels fought against the dragon. This is indeed a dark parable, this story of the breaking of the Original Community. Does it go as far back as the Big Bang? Or even further?

Once upon a time, back in *kairos,* so long ago that very likely it was before time, that strangeness where there wasn't even *once upon a time,* long before man was made and Adam was called to name the birds and the beasts, the most beautiful and bright of all the angels rebelled against the love of God, and his rebellion was put down by the Archangel Michael and his angels. But Michael's victory was only partial, at least for us human beings, because the bright angel walks our earth, lording it over us, bringing evil and distortion and hate in his wake, and even managing to make us believe that his power of non-ness doesn't exist.

It does. He does. If I can understand the truth of Love only through the Incarnation, so also I can understand destruction and annihilation only in particular. Satan is reasonable, tolerant, beautiful. If he were unreasonable, implausible, ugly, he would have no attraction for us; he would not be the Tempter, the one we pray that we will not be led to. He is immensely attractive and kind. He wants everybody to be happy, right here, right now. He can alleviate all poverty, cure all disease, and give us all the comforts of technocracy. As for free will, who needs that? Free will is a beastly burden a cruel creator has put on us, a creator whose ways are not our ways. If we have any sense at all we will follow the successful Prince of this Earth and reject the Lord of the Universe.

Free will is indeed a strange gift, fit only for the very mature. Why did he give it to us when we weren't ready for it?

When our three children were little, we had friends with one small boy, handsome, though tending to blubber because he ate nothing but ice cream. In the glow of their adoration for this creature of theirs, his parents gave him free will. He was allowed to decide what he should eat (ice cream), what he should wear, when he should go to bed. When there was a family decision to be made, they turned to this child, when he was three, four, five years old, to make it. As we watched this little boy turning into such a loathsome brat that our children groaned when they were forced to play with him, it seemed to us that his parents were not, in fact, giving him the free will they were talking about; they were making him God. They adored him as only God should be adored. They turned to him for decisions with the kind of expectation one should not have of any human being, and certainly not of a child.

So it became clear to us that this small boy was ending up with no free will at all. Somehow or other, the loving parents had swallowed one of the Tempter's hooks, and the child was given total self-indulgence, which is far from free will.

He still tempts. The ancient, primordial battle to destroy Community, to shatter Trinity, still continues. Creation still groans with the pain of it. Like it or not, we're caught in the middle.

Satan is the great confuser. I'm sure he whispered sweet reasonableness into the ears of the men who decided to build a city, and in the city put a tower that would reach heaven.

But the tower fell and they were divided and broken. Up until the time of the Tower of Babel, the children of Israel lived in close-knit communities. Each person, great or small, had an intrinsic share in the life of the community. When one suffered, everyone suffered. Oh, yes, there was sin and evil and too much wine and conniving and all the bad things which come from fallen man in a fallen world. But the paradoxes of human nature were still accepted. And wherever man went on the face of the known earth he spoke the same language; everybody could understand everybody else. It wasn't like that first Pentecost when everyone in that large group gathered together was suddenly able to understand each other's language as had not been possible since the days before the building of the Tower of Babel.

God broke his people at Babel and I doubt if I will ever understand this. But one of Satan's dirtiest devices is to promise infinite understanding to finite creatures. And so he has promised us success, and his success is delusion, and the breaking apart of community.

Those early communities of the Hebrew children were not successes. The people bickered. They turned away from God and worshipped a golden calf. They coveted each others' wives. But they knew that they could not get alone without each other. They accepted their interdependence. When they turned away from God and built their temples to Baal they knew how to repent and to say *I'm sorry.*

It is far more difficult for us to say *I'm sorry* today than it was for the Hebrew children, because to say *I'm sorry* implies admission of failure, and we live in a culture where failure is not tolerated. In school, for instance, a child is not allowed to repeat a grade more than a certain number of times; then he is automatically moved ahead, ready or not. A black student whose high-school education, to our shame, simply has not been adequate to prepare him for college must be admitted anyhow, and given a diploma, which thereby becomes a worthless piece of paper. Some of my college-age friends are discouraged from taking a course outside their field which nevertheless may fascinate them, because they may not get the high grade they need on their record if they're to go on to graduate school, and so they take the less challenging course in order to get the high grade which no longer has any real meaning.

When Hugh and the children and I were living in the country year round, I learned a lot about failure and about community, almost in the way that those old children of Israel learned about community.

I had already begun to understand failure as creative in terms of my marriage, and this understanding was tested with the coming of children. There's an odd law about families; they tend to grow; it may be dogs, or cats, or babies, or birds, or plants, but families need to blossom. Our family grew in all kinds of ways, for Hugh taught me early that a family with closed doors is not a family.

During our Crosswicks years, one of our baby sitters, aged thirteen, came for an evening and stayed two years. And because we lived outside the village, playmates for our children had to be fetched and carried, and we usually had at least three extra for the weekends.

Then there was the community of the church, the white-pillared, tall-spired church which stood directly across from our General Store in the center of the village. When we moved to Crosswicks, neither of us had been in church for a long time. For good reasons, of course. We found more real community in the theatre than we did in city churches. The church seemed to hold up to us a God who had nothing to do with the stars which crackled above us on cold nights, or with the frogs whose deep clunking announced that the iron earth would thaw and pussy willows come and the geese honk high and wild.

But our village church wasn't really like a city church. I'm not even sure that it was like what most of us think of as church. It was the center of the village geographically, and became so in our lives, though it had no relation to a social club, although it was the largest part of our social lives, too. In those days, before I'd ever heard of ecumenism, the Congregational Church in our village was truly ecumenical. The war was not long over; there was not one of us who had not in some way been touched by the war, participated in it, either abroad or at home, lost people we loved in it. Two of the women who were to become my good friends were English war brides. We all knew that mankind, left to its own devices, makes slums and battlefields and insane asylums, and many of us had settled in the little village looking for something else, something which bore little resemblance to the success-oriented cities and suburbs. Our doctor had deliberately chosen, when the war was over and he could leave the army, to be a village general practitioner instead of a big city specialist. Hugh and I, too, had rejected the values of the city, being too young and untutored to understand that city or country has little to do with the *symboles* by which we live.

We soon found ourselves swept into a tight-knit little band of struggling Christians. There were six or eight couples of us, all about the same age, all with small children, who threw our lives into the life of the church, guided by the young minister who, also, with his wife and baby, had left a big city church, and come to this small green and pleasant land. It was within the community of these people who sang in the choir, taught Sunday School, visited the sick, that I first experienced, without realizing it consciously, a truly Christian community. I doubt if I will ever experience it in the same way again, not only because I am now grandmother as well as mother, but because there are few villages in the Eastern United States as small as ours was then; it, too, has grown; we now have five hundred telephones and our phone number has had to be changed and I am finding it hard to remember the new one.

I understand the depth of our commitment better now than I did then. A community, to be truly community, must have a quality of unselfconsciousness about it. We knew that we were struggling to be Christian, and that we often failed, and we knew that we couldn't be community on our own, and so the grace of community was given to us.

Today I must seek community in a different way. Traveling along the fjords of Norway one autumn, Hugh and I passed many villages with no more than a dozen houses, and boathouses instead of garages; and I looked at these little clusters with longing, because such a village cannot exist without being a community. But in life as I must live it today, community must have a new form. I do not know what it will be, and I suspect that I won't know until memory tells me that I am having it right now without knowing it, just as we were unselfconscious about it when we lived year-round in Crosswicks.

I sympathize with experiments in communes, but any time we try to go back to the Garden it can mean being led by a Manson.

So I look back without too much nostalgia on those days when our children were young, but with gratitude for the experience, which helps me look to the future knowing in my blood and bones what Christian Community is about. We really did try to minister to each other, to pray together, moving through self-consciousness and embarrassment to freedom, and at first I was paralyzed with embarrassment. If one of us mothers was having a difficult pregnancy or had grippe, two or three of us would go and clean house (and I hated this job as much then as I do now and I was more often on the receiving than on the giving end, but I did try). We took turns taking the children, bringing in meals. Hugh rode the tractor in the summer to help a farmer friend with his haying and came home sunburned and streaked with honest sweat. In the autumn the women canned and froze vegetables together because we were going to need that food in the winter. We moved from house to house, working together, and surely my friends gave unstintingly in helping this city girl who had never before pulled a carrot from the ground, or plucked an apple from a tree. The land on which Crosswicks stands once gave all that was needed for life. Now we have only the orchard, the berries, and a mammoth vegetable garden. We do not render our own soap or dip our own candles. But the fertile land, the great beams of the house itself, cause me to remember—not just the community, which was essential for survival two hundred-odd years ago, but a glimpse of something unbroken, and of which we are still a part.

We were very loosely organized, our little group centered in the spired church, but we were organized by love.

Several years ago when all the rooms in the house had been wall-papered by us with paper we had carefully chosen, I announced that I was too old ever to hang wallpaper again, and if things got too shabby we'd have to bring in a professional. But a couple of years ago I started on the second round, and as I struggled with shears and wallpaper paste, I realized that I was still part of that community which physically was broken by time and distance long ago.

It is once again the joy of memory, for those days are real, and are mine to dip into. I do one of my rare cleaning out of closets and come across a baby's shoe; a little girl's sweater which I had washed in water too hot for it, so that it shrank so small that it was used for dolls; a small stuffed animal with one torn ear and one lost eye which I had once upon a time thought I was going to fix.

I cannot go to the bookshelves and pull out *The Secret Garden* without remembering a rainy weekend when it was our turn to have everybody at our house and I kept a charm of children quiet and happy by reading aloud until I was hoarse.

Our children all quickly grew used to being in half a dozen houses as freely as their own. When the father of one family was stricken with an acute form of cancer, his three little ones were already used to being in other houses, and during his last days they moved from house to house where they were already at home. Death was no less premature and shocking, but the children were not taken from familiar surroundings and sent to strangers, and I think the loving but calm concern given them did help; it helped us, too. I didn't know much about intercessory prayer then, but I do know that our prayers during that period brought healing for all of us, and it seems somehow appropriate that I was listening to Handel's lilting spring cuckoo concerto on the clear winter morning when the phone rang and someone told me that death had come at last.

There were joyful experiences as well as sad ones. On a night when I woke up early with labor pains, Hugh took our sleeping daughter, drove five miles to neighboring farmer friends, and put her in bed, still sleeping, beside her friend Chucky, and drove off without disturbing anybody, even the cows.

When Josephine woke up in the morning it would be in a familiar room, among people she knew and trusted. And everybody in the household would know that the new baby was on the way. Another friend among our community, who had left nursing not long before to stay home with her baby, simply announced that she was going to the hospital with me to be my special nurse—knowing that babies do not birth easily for me. Over this baby's birth she was on her feet for forty-eight hours straight, and that was as much a part of our church life as the Sunday services or the choir practices.

You can tell they are Christians by their love.

It wasn't until our full-time days at Crosswicks had been behind us for a number of years that as I looked back with the blessing of memory I saw that for nearly a decade I had experienced the kind of love described in the Acts of the Apostles, despite all our human flaws. The early Christians quarreled, and so did we. Once Hank got so mad at me during choir practice that he threw a hymnal at me. One wife came into the store one day at noon looking a bit dazed and said, "I just broke a plate over Stephen's head." But despite it all, we were there for each other.

There, in all our particularity. Just as my concern for the victims of starvation across the planet is awakened by my awareness of the hunger of my neighbor, who has a face and a name, so is my love for all humankind awakened by my love for any one part of it. My Christian God is not the exclusive God of the Christians. He is Lord of the Universe, and he notes the fall of the sparrow in every part of his creation, and he counts the hairs of every head, not just Christian or Jew. I learned something of this wider compassion when I lived with my friends in the country who were, except in our ministry to each other, often so different from me that we did not always understand each other. My rejection slips did not seem very cosmic to anybody but me, and I felt that most people thought that I was simply not quite good enough to be doing what I was doing. The things which were cosmic to them were alien to me.

That decade of community was important to me but it was not idyllic. It was for many reasons one of the most unhappy periods of my life. But I did experience Christian community, and it was this which kept much of what happened from being totally destructive.

There was nothing idyllic about the fact that four of our most intimate friends died within three years of each other, and that by the death of one couple we inherited a seven-year-old daughter, and on the same day that she came to us, we found a seventeen-year-old ex-baby sitter huddled in our garage, pregnant and unmarried and certain that we would not throw her out.

There was, for me, nothing idyllic about struggling to raise our children, trying to keep house in drafty old Crosswicks where the washing machine—once I had graduated from doing the laundry in the bathtub and had a washing machine—froze during the winter months at least twice a week, usually full of diapers; and we were never warm around the edges.

There was nothing idyllic in the violent conflict between Madeleine, wife and mother, and Madeleine, writer. I struggled to write under the worst possible conditions, after the children were in bed—that force field of concentration would have been a dangerous idea while they were awake and active. Like most young mothers I was constantly tired. Added to fatigue was struggling to cope with failure, which looked as though it would have no end. I was trying to develop as a writer, but I received from editors nothing but a long stream of rejection slips, mostly the impersonal printed ones, although I had already had several books published, and with moderate success. Theron, my agent, was worried that too much failure would kill my talent, and perhaps, in the end, it would have. I'm not sure how strong I am, and what would have happened if the chill rejections had never stopped.

The failure to sell my writing was coupled with failures within myself, as wife, mother, human being, faltering Christian. Failures must be accepted now, too, in the very different communities in which I find myself: in the Crosswicks summers, full of comings and goings and occasional days when I am completely alone with the animals and the garden; in our winter community in the city, the community formed by Hugh's work in the theatre and my community at St. John's Cathedral—it's a good combination, the theatre and the church, and an evening of friends from both communities works marvelously, and is full of stimulation and laughter.

The church in our village offered me community and so redeemed my failures as wife, mother, writer, and if our village church is different today, that does not change what it gave to me then, or say that the change is not as good as what was. It is simply normal change. And I, too, am different.

Our communities are joyful and creative for me only when I can accept my own imperfections, when I can rush out with my sins of omission and commission and hang them on the cross as I hang out the laundry.

If I could not hang my sins on the cross I might tend to withdraw, the responsibilities of community are so great. And far too often I have taken on myself a responsibility which is not really mine, because my faith is not strong enough, and I tumble, splat, into the do-it-yourself pit.

It is only when I am able to put the subtle whispers of the tempter behind me and accept failure that I am free to be part of a community, and part of that freedom is to accept that the community itself is going to fail—at the very least it is going to change, and it may die, and this, in worldly terms, in Satan's terms, is failure.

I think of my granddaughters learning to find it difficult to say, "I'm sorry," to accept having done something naughty, and I remember seeing the same thing in my own children, and I still struggle with the same error in myself. We are taught early, very early, to set up false expectations of ourselves, and when we fall away from the pearly-pink perfection we have supposed to be our 'real' self, and are faced with what is in fact our 'real' self, we alibi and rationalize and do everything we can to avoid seeing it. And far too often we succeed, and struggle unsuccessfully to live with a stranger who never was, and then we are like my psychiatrist friend's patients who are afraid to remember, because if their memories are true, then their present lives are false.

Charlotte, our younger granddaughter, used to withdraw completely into herself when she was scolded, even if it was just an "Oh, Charlotte!" as the milk was overturned for the fifth time, retreating as completely as though she had gone into another room. She stayed deep inside herself for however long she needed to accept, to herself, that she had been careless, that she was a child capable of overturning a mug; then, in one spontaneous burst, she returned to the community, flinging her arms around father, mother, grandparent, whoever was nearest, bursting with love.

On one of these occasions one of my children reminded me of something I had forgotten: there was a week when they were little when at least one glass of milk was spilled at every meal, and I finally got so irritated that I said, "Whoever spills the next glass of milk will leave the room." Shortly after which I reached for something and knocked over my glass. I left the room.

Our two little granddaughters have a sense of community which many adults have lost; people have developed less a sense of community than a loneliness which they attempt to assuage by being with other people constantly, and on a superficial level only. In both the literary and theatrical worlds Hugh and I are occasionally required to go to enormous cocktail parties, one of our most unfavorite activities (and I have now been introduced to the ecclesiastical sherry party). The cocktail party says something about affluent America, and reveals tellingly that affluence can blur the sense of joy in interdependence which is behind all true community. The loneliness, the namelessness of cocktail-party relationships surrounds us. We meet, but even when we kiss we do not touch. We avoid the responsibility of community.

But it is always a changing community.

The old four-generation Crosswicks community died with the death of my mother and the purchase of Jo's and Alan's house, aptly called Little Gidding. There is much going and coming between the two dwellings; the doors are open and the wind blows through and sometimes I am bold to think that it is the wind of the spirit. I sit lightly to denominations, but I am Anglican enough to think that our frequent house communions have done much to keep our communities living and loving.

There have been times, especially during the summer, when I have longed for solitude, and it took some hard lessons for me to learn that I needed to be what I had thought was selfish; that I needed to take time to myself to write, to go to the brook, to be. When I was able to accept the imperfect Madeleine who could not function without time to work, time to be alone, the summers became rich and Trinitarian for me.

After one of them I wrote

MRS. NOAH SPEAKING

I suppose under the circumstances
there's really no point in complaining
but really! Noah and I had just got accustomed
to living alone and having some peace and quiet
and fixing up the house the way we wanted it at last.
I brought up three boys, wiped their runny noses, changed their messy diapers,
*   washed, sewed, cooked, saw to it that they had the proper advantages,*
We got them safely married
*   (though if I didn't know it before I know it now:*
*   their wives leave a great deal to be desired).*
We liked having them come to visit us on the proper holidays,
*   bringing the babies, taking enough food home to feed them for a week,*
*   and Noah and I could go to bed in peace.*
And now look what has happened!

Sometimes I think it would have been simpler to have drowned
*   with everybody else—*
at least their troubles are over.
And here we are jammed in this Ark—
why didn't the Lord give Noah enough time to build a big enough ark
*   if he wanted him to build one at all?*
The animals take up almost all the room
and Noah and I are crowded together with Shem, Ham, and Japheth,
*   their slovenly wives and noisy children,*
and nowhere to go for a moment's peace.
Noah, of course, has hidden several elephant's skins of wine somewhere,
*   and when the rain and noise and confusion get too bad*
*   he goes down to the dirty hold with the beasts and gets drunk,*
*   sleeps it off on the dirty straw,*
*   and then comes up to bed smelling of armadillo dung and platypus piss.*

Not that I blame him.
It's my daughters-in-law who get me.
They insist on changing the beds every time I turn around.
They won't use a towel more than once, and they're always getting dressed up
*   and throwing their dirty linen at me to wash.*

The washing is easy enough—we've plenty of water—
But how do they expect me to get anything dry in all this rain?
I don't mind doing the cooking, but they're always coming out to the
*   kitchen to fix little snacks with the excuse that it will help me:*
*   "You're so good to us, Mother Noah, we'll just do this for you,"*
*   and they never put anything away where it belongs. They've lost*
*   one of my measuring cups and they never clean the stove and they've*
*   broken half of the best china that came down to us from Grandfather*
*   Seth.*
When the babies squall in the night, who gets up with them?
Not my daughters-in-law.
*   "Oh, Mother Noah'll do it. She loves the babies so."*
*   Ham's wife is always stirring up quarrels, playing people off against*
*   each other. Shem's wife, who never does anything for anybody, manages*
*   to make me feel lazy and mean if I ask her to dry one dish. Japheth's*
*   wife is eyeing Shem and Ham; she'll cause trouble; mark my words.*

Today that silly dove Noah is so fond of came back with an olive twig
*   on his beak. Maybe there's hope that we'll get out of this Ark*
*   after all.*

We've landed! At last! Now we can get back to normal and have some
*   peace and quiet and if I put something where it belongs it will stay there*
*   and I can clean up this mess and get some sleep at night and—*

Noah! Noah! I miss the children.

When I think of the phrase *The Coming of the Kingdom* it means
to me the restoration of community, the healing of brokenness which
will enable us to rejoice once more in being one—not a solitary,
isolated one, but whole, body, intellect, spirit at peace; mind, heart,
intuition in collaboration.

There are those who do not want this wholeness, who want to
continue the process of fragmentation, and this has to be fought, with
Michael and his angels by our side. If we care about wholeness, about
unity in diversity, we are in battle. But it isn't the same kind of warring
which confused our children when they were little: 'But I thought the
Germans were our enemy? Why are they our friends now?' 'But I
thought Russia was our ally? Why are we frightened of Russia now?'
It isn't like the kind of warring which polarized the country over
Vietnam. On the news not long ago I heard about firefighters who are
spending the Fourth of July weekend in continuing to fight a brush
fire in California which has already destroyed several homes and

threatens to destroy more. The fight against the Powers of Breaking has more in common with these firefighters than it does with battles over national boundaries. It is a hard fact that since Christendom wars have been far worse than they ever were before, but I don't think we can blame Christendom for the making of bombs and bayonets; it is the Destroyer who is at work here, and he has had to work all the harder since the coming of the second person of the Trinity to share in our lives.

Men and women are often happy and fulfilled when they are at war, when the community of warriors holds the life of each one in its care, but I'd guess that effectively stopping an out-of-control forest fire brings the same kind of community, and evokes as much bravery and far more satisfaction than wiping out a city.

I've always been ambivalent about the Fourth of July, that national holiday which falls early in what used to be the Trinity season. As an American, I need to take it seriously, because our forefathers did have a dream of community, of wholeness.

I miss the symbols of fireworks, and it would seem that the occasional injuries from carelessness with fireworks (not firecrackers and noisemakers, but the works of light and beauty) were minimal compared to the injury to personality caused by sitting in front of a television set, the Great Baby Sitter (yes, I used it too; in a world of the small family unit and no servants it is almost unavoidable), and learning passivity. When our children were little the Fourth of July meant a kind of fairy-land beauty, because even the little ones could hold a sparkler, and in the first dusk we would have a procession of a dozen or more children plus their respective parents, weaving through the apple orchard with the sparklers like a skyfall of stars.

At dinner, always a communal affair, one of the grownups would talk a little about the enormous privileges of freedom still open to Americans, and we would all hold hands to say grace, and we took seriously, in our small community, our American heritage.

But the world has changed. Sparklers are outlawed. We've had Vietnam and assassinations and Watergate. And apart from a Bicentennial year, we barely note the fourth. There is an ambiguity about the holiday which embarrasses us.

But it reminds me, with an unexpected jolt each year, that we are still at war, that creation still groans with the strain of it.

But the growing of the garden is on our side. The plashing of the brook is on our side. The green of grass and the brilliance of flowers and the song of the birds are on our side.

In *Dragons in the Waters* an old gentlewoman from South Carolina is rather unexpectedly in a Quiztano Indian village in Venezuela. In the morning before dawn she arises and walks across the greensward to the lake's edge:

Umar Xanai was there before her, alone, sitting in Charles's favorite position.

The old woman sat down silently, slightly to one side and behind him. Around her she could sense the sleeping village. Someone was moving on the porch of one of the Caring Places. Soon Dragonlake would be awake. All around her she heard bird song. A fish flashed out of the lake and disappeared beneath the dark waters. Above her the stars dimmed and the sky lightened.

When the sun sent its first rays above the mountain, Umar Xanai rose and stretched his arms upward. He began to chant. Miss Leonis could not understand the velvet Quiztano words, but it seemed to her that the old chieftan was encouraging the sun in its rising, urging it, enticing it, giving the sun every psychic aid in his power to lift itself up out of the darkness and into the light. When the great golden disc raised itself clear of the mountain the chanting became a triumphal, joyful song.

At the close of the paean of praise the old man turned to the old woman and bent down to greet her with the three formal kisses.

She asked, "You are here every morning?"

He nodded, smiling. "It is part of my duties as chief of the Quitzanos."

"To help the sun rise?"

"That is my work."

"It would not rise without you?"

"Oh, yes, it would rise. But as we are dependent on the sun for our crops, for our lives, it is our courtesy to give the sun all the help in our power—and our power is considerable."

"I do not doubt that."

"We believe," the old man said quietly, "that everything is dependent on everything else. The sun does not rise in the sky in loneliness; we are with him. The moon would be lost in isolation if we did not greet her with song. The stars dance together, and we dance with them."

Thou also shall light my candle, sings the psalmist. The Lord my God shall make my darkness to be light.

To sing this is already to choose sides.

To look for community instead of cocktail-party relationships is part of choosing sides in this vast, strange battle. To say, "I'm sorry"; to be silent; to say "I love you," "I care." It is these little things that are going to make the difference. For God chooses the foolish things of the world to confound the wise, the weak to overthrow the strong. Out of failure he brings triumph. Out of the grave he births life.

It is difficult for me not to make impossible demands on my communities as I sometimes make them on myself. It is difficult for me to accept that there is still war in heaven, and that I must join the battle lines on one side or the other, because the wars of the world's history have confused me about battle lines. It would be easy to fall into the Manichaean heresy, where good and evil were born simultaneously and have been battling since the beginning. But that takes away the Godness of God, and I can't live without God as one, God as all. There was war in heaven, part of God's creation turned against him, and like it or not, we are caught in it and we have to choose creation or destruction; and I might sometimes teeter on the edge of despair did there not shine for me that light in the darkness which the darkness cannot put out.

It is difficult to accept that all my beloved communities are going to die, and that even while they exist there are incredible spaces between human beings, even the closest. And, despite all my urgings toward community, I will always be, like Abraham, a wanderer, far from home. But the people who are most aware of their own impermanence are the most able to throw wide the doors of heart and hearth to the stranger, to hear his message, receive his blessing.

To make community misunderstood is a powerful weapon of the Destroyer—to promise permanence, to insist on perfection, to strangle freedom, so that instead of having community, we have a concentration camp.

Crosswicks may be noisy and on occasion extremely untidy, but it has never, thank God, remotely resembled a concentration camp. And it has taught me about Trinity, that *unity in diversity* which has been mouthed so often that it is now part of the jargon and has become as empty as *meaningful* and *relevant,* but it's still the kind of oneness I mean. The kind which comes when our wildly diverse family is gathered about the dinner table and Bion and Hugh differ noisily (within this unity) as to whether we'll eat entirely by candlelight or turn on one electric light bulb. The kind which I have known, and

Hugh still knows, in the theatre, where everybody is working together to bring a play to life. The kind I know when Alan and I play piano and violin, respectively and together, even the cacophony of our invented Bartók weaving its Trinitarian joy.

3 = 1.

1 is 3.

And this is good.

And this is God.

11... Setter and Swallow

THE EPIPHANY, the Transfiguration, Pentecost, all speak to me in the same luminous language. They are all lit with the same incredible gold light. And the story of Nathanael is also in a brilliant tongue, the language of the dark parable which cannot be comprehended by sunside alone, and I am not at all surprised that it is found in the first chapter of John's Gospel.

Once upon a time there was a man whose name was Nathanael. Jesus called Philip to follow him, and Philip went to Nathanael, and told him that he had found the one for whom they sought, Jesus of Nazareth. Rational Nathanael replied dubiously, "Can any good come out of Nazareth?" Philip replied, "Come and see!"

Jesus saw Nathanael coming to him and said, "Behold an Israelite indeed, in whom is no guile."

Nathanael said, "How did you know me?"

Jesus answered, "Before Philip called you, while you were sitting under the fig tree, I saw you."

Nathanael, his reason knocked out from under him, replied, "Rabbi, you are the Son of God."

One evening I was talking about this story to Hugh, and he said, "I don't understand it."

"What don't you understand?"

"What was so extraordinary about Jesus seeing Nathanael under the fig tree? Why would that make Nathanael say he was the Son of God?"

"Oh—" I said, and remembered and told Hugh about the fig tree in my grandmother's back yard in North Florida. When I was visiting her when I was a little girl and had had too much of the grownups and of the Florida heat, I would go out in the yard, smeared with lavender oil to keep the insects away, and lie in the cool shade under the fig tree and read until someone came out and called me in. Whoever it was had to call; I couldn't be seen in the deep shade of the fig leaves. "So it *was* extraordinary that Jesus saw Nathanael under the fig tree. He probably was sitting there just because it was private and he couldn't be seen."

"Well, maybe."

Nathanael, in any event, was astonished.

Jesus answered him, "Because I told you that I saw you under the fig tree you believe? You'll see greater things than this. I tell you in truth that you shall see Heaven open, and the angels of God ascending and descending upon the Son of man."

For Nathanael this was a moment of total reality, a moment when reasonable, chronological time was broken open, and he glimpsed real time, *kairos,* and was never the same again.

But that once upon a time two thousand years ago might equally well be today. I suspect that most of us are very like Nathanael, eminently reasonable people. Like Nathanael we see things the way they are—at least we think we do. And it's jolting to discover that our reasonable view of things just isn't the real view. When this happens to me, and it often does, I remember Nathanael, and try once again to be like him, not the reasonable Nathanael safe and hidden under the fig tree, but the astonished Nathanael who was told that he would see heaven open and the angels of God ascending and descending upon the Son of man.

He must have been frightened. How could he, how can any of us visualize angels of God ascending and descending upon the Son of man? When I try I get a mindscape, powerful though not very visual, of Jacob's ladder with the angels of God ascending and descending superimposed on Jacob himself wrestling throughout the night with the angel. And I get a vision of a special kind of brilliance, not golden, but like the light of the moon shining on diamond-coated branches and twigs after an ice storm. But that's not it. That's not even a glimpse of angels ascending and descending upon the Son of man.

And yet Jesus promised Nathanael that he was going to see them. And I ask myself exactly when was it that Nathanael actually came to see this promised vision? If I had to make a guess I'd say that it was probably on Good Friday when the sky darkened and the tree whose seed was buried with the first Adam held the second Adam. The old tradition that the cross on which Jesus was crucified stood on the same place, and grew from the very seed of the tree from which Adam and Eve ate the forbidden fruit, and that Adam's skull *(cal-varius)* is still there, under that tree, seems to fit in with the opening of Nathanael's eyes.

How can I see in the same way that Nathanael saw his extraordinary vision, a vision which had in it the promise of resurrection? It isn't easy to accept the fact that such a vision is more real, more true, than something within the realm of provable fact. But I'll never accept it if I stay safely hidden under my fig tree, and I want the courage to move out of the shadows so that I may have my own glimpses of transfiguration.

As always, they may be very small things, so tiny that it seems presumptuous to set them down beside something so grand as angels ascending and descending. But they are moments of revelation for me, when suddenly sunside and nightside know each other. This summer there has been the amazing friendship of Timothy, the red Irish setter, and his swallow.

Timothy was three and a half years old when he came to us, and for those first three and a half years he had been beaten. Dog and child abuse in whatever form are mysterious horrors to me. When we got Tim he was approximately twenty-seven in people years, and we were not at all sure we were going to be able to help this miserable, terrified creature who crawled abjectly on his belly. But within twenty-four hours he began to walk upright, and to come sit on the floor by me and hold up his paw to be held. It took him nearly two weeks to learn that it was safe to walk by Hugh to get to me, because whoever had beaten him was evidently a man, and he was still afraid of all men. There are times when Tim is in so paw-holding a mood that Hugh could wish he still inspired a little awe in the big red creature.

He came to us in the early autumn, and by Thanksgiving he had learned that he was allowed to come without a personal invitation into the kitchen with Hugh and me in the evening, while we had a drink and I cooked dinner. The kitchen is large for a city apartment, large enough for two comfortable, if shabby, chairs, and Timothy quickly took over the larger and shabbier—he gets away with things no other dog of ours has been allowed to do. Bion's first night home for the Thanksgiving holidays, he came out to the kitchen with us and sat comfortably in the old green chair. Tim poked his long red nose around the corner, ambled slowly across the kitchen, took a flying leap and landed, legs sprawling every which way, on Bion's lap. After all, Bion was in his chair.

So we knew that there was hope for him. We've had him nearly four years now and he's come a long way, but he's still a neurotic creature full of fears. Any man with stick or cane makes him cringe with terror. And it isn't a full year since he's come to trust the world enough to wag his tail, and only this summer that he's had the confidence to thump it on the floor.

For this summer Timothy has his swallow.

I think it was Bion who saw it first, but we've all seen it. Timothy will rush out to the big meadow, his once-timid tail waving ecstatically. He looks adoringly up at the sky, wagging, listening, and the swallow comes to him, flying very low, and then Tim will run along with the bird while it flies, back and forth, round and about, in great parabolas, all over the big meadow. Then the swallow will fly off and up, and Tim will stand looking upward, swishing his tail, and waiting for his friend to return.

It has been a great joy to us to watch this amazing friendship. Day after day they play together, and the game never palls. There is nothing of the stalker or hunter in Timothy's actions when he is with the swallow. Occasionally he will accidentally flush a pheasant, and then his tail goes straight out and still, and one forepaw curves up and he points. But with his swallow, his tail never stops waving. The two of them are lion and lamb together for me, a foretaste of Isaiah's vision. When I watch them playing together in the green and blue, it is a moment of transfiguration.

And it seems especially right that it should be shy, frightened, loving old Timothy rather than any of the other family dogs who are around Crosswicks during the summer. By and large they don't even seem aware of what is going on, and have shown only the mildest interest in Tim's atypical ecstatic behavior.

We often have friends visit us during the summer, and one weekend it was a family who live in our apartment building in the city. Their son was away at camp, but they came with their two little girls, the same ages as Léna and Charlotte, and their charming mop of a dog, Esau.

It was, despite showery weather, a lovely weekend. Between showers we went berrying, swimming in Dog Pond, walking down the lane. We ate and talked and were comfortable together. On Sunday afternoon when the sun came out we took the children and the dogs for a walk. It was much too wet to go through the high grasses and dripping bushes and brambles and trees to the brook, but we went down the lane and attacked some of the bittersweet which used to be a rare treasure, but which is now growing rampant and strangling the young trees. When we started back to the house we saw that Tim was already in the big meadow playing with his swallow friend. They were swooping about, Tim's nose heavenward, his tail wagging in a frenzy of joy.

Esau, the little mop, saw it too, and unlike the other dogs wanted in on the game. We human beings were so enchanted with Tim and the swallow that we paid no attention to Esau, until Tim saw him and very definitely did not want any interference in his private game.

We all began to run, but they were halfway across the meadow.

Timothy is a big dog and Esau is a small one. If Tim had wanted to, he could have broken Esau's neck with one shake.

The men with their longer legs reached the two dogs first. Bion, watching from the kitchen windows, said that it had looked to him as though Tim were simply standing over Esau, and evidently what he had been doing was simply keeping Esau away from his swallow. But he had drawn blood; there was a definite nick in Esau's neck.

It was not a tragedy. But suddenly we were in a fallen world again. It was no longer lion and lamb in peace and amity. It was the world of battlefields and slums and insane asylums.

What did I expect?

Until the eschaton our moments of transfiguration are essentially flashes of brief glory. To want Tim and his swallow to live in Eden is like Peter wanting to build tabernacles around Jesus and Abraham and Moses.

But while Peter was speaking, foolishly trying to trap glory in a man-made tabernacle, a bright cloud overshadowed them, and they were afraid, and a voice came out of the cloud saying, "This is my beloved son, in whom I am well pleased; hear ye him." And when they opened their eyes they saw Jesus as they were used to seeing him, Jesus of Nazareth, a man like themselves. And he told them not to tell anybody of the vision until the Son of man be risen from the dead.

> *Suddenly they saw him the way he was,*
> *the way he really was all the time,*
> *although they had never seen it before,*
> *the glory which blinds the everyday eye*
> *and so becomes invisible. This is how*
> *he was, radiant, brilliant, carrying joy*
> *like a flaming sun in his hands.*
> *This is the way he was—is—from the beginning,*
> *and we cannot bear it. So he manned himself,*
> *came manifest to us; and there on the mountain*
> *they saw him, really saw him, saw his light.*
> *We all know that if we really see him we die.*
> *But isn't that what is required of us?*
> *Then, perhaps, we will see each other, too.*

Too often we don't see each other. It takes something like Tim and the swallow, Tim and Esau, to open my eyes for a moment. When I watch Tim and his swallow now they are as beautiful as ever, and yet I watch them with a tinge of sorrow because we are still far from home.

When will we once again be one?

Not long after the episode of Tim and Esau, I was privileged to be given an experience of the kind of oneness seldom experienced. It was a spiritual oneness and helps me understand why the Song of Songs, that unabashedly physical love poem, is also the only language for spiritual love.

I have been blessed all the years of my life by the self-giving love of an English nanny known to us all as Mrs. O—for when I was a baby I could not say Mrs. O'Connell. Despite the name she acquired when she married a handsome Irishman, she never left anyone in doubt that her nationality was English. I was always comfortably certain that she loved me, but it was a typically Anglo-Saxon love which did not indulge in demonstrativeness. She did not, as I remember, kiss me at bedtime when I was a small child. One of our pleasant jokes, after my marriage, was Hugh's attempts to give her a kiss; despite much laughter, she managed to avoid the kisses. Nor was she ever a handholder.

Last spring she was ninety-five, and for the past several years has been in a home for elderly nuns, the Convent of Mary the Queen. Two of her three daughters are nuns, Sister Miriam Ambrose and Sister Anastasia Marie, and it was because of them that she was given her pleasant room and bath. During these years of her old age I have been called three times to her deathbed, and each time she has surprised doctors and nurses by recovering. It isn't that she is clinging to life, like a brown and brittle leaf clinging to the tree; she is very ready to go home. When she has been on the road to recovery she has each time remarked with good-humored resignation, "Well, God doesn't want me and the devil won't have me."

The Sisters call me regularly to report on her condition, and we all try to go see her as often as possible, and to bring the little girls for a state visit once a year. This spring she became very weak, and her mind began to wander, but the Sisters urged me not to come. "If there's a day when she's alert and will recognize you, we'll call."

In August I suddenly have a tremendous urge to go to her, and my friend Gillian says she'd love to take a day off from work and drive to the convent with me. So when Sister Ambrose calls to say that her mother seems a little stronger and might recognize me, we decide to go.

It is a brilliant summer day. There has been a lot of rain, so the leaves are a lush, rich green, not dry and dusty as they sometimes are in August. Gillian and I have shared much during the long years of our friendship, death and pain as well as birth and joy. There's nothing we can't talk about, and we've journeyed far together in our attempts to understand life and death and the increasing hope of a God of loving concern and faithful promise.

When we reach the convent I fall silent. A voice calls upstairs on a loudspeaker to announce our visit. We walk through a long room with two rows of rocking chairs where ancient Sisters sit to watch television. When Hugh comes to the convent with me it is an added glory for Mrs. O, for not only do the Sisters watch his show, but most of the nurses, and many of them come hurrying for autographs or simply to shake hands with 'Dr. Tyler.'

Gillian and I go up on the elevator to the fourth floor. Mrs. O's room is just around the corner where she has been able to watch all the comings and goings on the floor. It is hot in the summer, and we have wanted to give her an air-coonditioner, but she won't have one because she'd have to keep her door closed and thus be isolated from the life bustling around her.

Wherever she is, she has always brought with her the gift of laughter. The nurses on the night shift say, when they are tired or discouraged, "I think I'll go to Mrs. O'Connell's room. She's always good for a laugh." The orderlies and cleaning women love her; whenever there has been a crisis in her condition there have been tears, open and unashamed. Perhaps she is being kept here on earth for so long because her gift of laughter is desperately needed. Ill and difficult patients may well be treated with more tenderness because of Mrs. O.

Never very large, each year she has become smaller and smaller. But there is today a startling change since my last visit. She has eaten nothing solid for three months; a little tea, a little thin soup, the Holy Mysteries; on these she has been kept alive. But there is nothing now between skin and bones. The body on the hospital bed looks like pictures of victims of Belsen, Auschwitz, Ravensbrück.

When I first bend over her she does not know me. I wait while she makes the slow journey from the past to the present. I put my hand on hers and say, "It's Madeleine, Mrs. O. It's Madeleine." Suddenly she is fully with me, and she puts her arms around me as she would never have done in the old days, and says, "Oh, Madeleine, my Madeleine, oh, my Madeleine," and I no longer see the ancient wasted body. I have my arms about her so that I am holding her sitting up, with the fragile body leaning against me like a child's, and yet she is still holding me; we are both child, both mother.

She moves in and out of time. We talk in low voices and she asks me how the children are, does Bion still have his nice girlfriend? how are the little girls? She hasn't seen Gillian for at least fifteen years and yet she is completely aware of her presence and who she is, and asks about her family.

Once she gets lost in chronology and asks me, "Are you downstairs in your carriage?" But the next moment she is back in the present and says, "How's the boss?" (Her pet name for Hugh.) "How could I have forgotten to ask about the boss?"

I stay for an hour, much longer than I had expected, but we are in *kairos,* Mrs. O and I, in God's time, free, for the rest of the hour, from *chronos.* "And the extraordinary thing," I wrote in my journal, "was the electric current of love, powerful and beautiful, flowing back and forth between Mrs. O and me. Gillie had expected to step outside and write letters, but she too felt the lovely light of love which was uniting Mrs. O and me, so she stayed, remarking later what a privilege it had been for her to be present. I cannot set down in words the strength and joy of that river of love; it was something which can happen only in *kairos;* it was a time of Transfiguration—and in the octave of the Transfiguration, too—I just thought about that."

So we are given our glimpses of what it is really like, how things are really meant to be. There in that wasted body I saw at the same time the transfigured body, something visible to the spirit and not to the eyes.

These glimpses of reality are the foundation stones of faith.

12 ... The Day Is at Hand

THE MICHAELMAS DAISIES are purply blue in the fields; the goldenrod is tall. We come to Crosswicks only for weekends. The long weeks after Pentecost stretch out and it seems odd that schools and colleges have started, the house is emptying, and there are still six weeks till Advent.

Hugh and I are often alone on weekends, and we enjoy our companionable solitude. In the bedroom with the four-poster bed there are three rocking chairs, as well as the ancient chest across the foot of the bed, so that when the household gathers upstairs for a nightcap there will be plenty of places for everybody to sit. But now there are empty seats.

The big chest holds the sheets, the eiderdown for winter. It is often a receptacle for anything I feel like dumping down until I find time to put it away, and in the summer everything is casually swept to the floor if someone wants to sit there.

There was one spring when it was regularly an altar. A bad fall had me off my feet and in bed for six weeks. I was allowed to go, on crutches, to the bathroom, but otherwise I was not to get out of bed. Not easy for anyone as used to being as active as I am. It was late spring, and Alan and Josephine were free to be in the country, and Hugh's schedule was at that time fairly flexible, so that he could be more in Crosswicks than on West End Avenue, so I managed to talk the doctor into letting me be driven up.

The drive was typical. I sat in the back of the car with my leg on pillows and two dogs somehow or other stretched across me—one, a collie (Tim's predecessor); the other, half shepherd, half golden retriever (Jo's and Alan's first dog). They made a lapful. The cat perched on the ledge by the rear window. We stopped for something to eat, made the mistake of giving Thomas, the cat, some chicken, which he threw up, messily, before we'd gone another five miles. Much scrabbling for tissues and paper towels, with Josephine leaning over the seat and trying to help and Thomas crouching into his setting-hen position and feeling sorry for himself.

When we finally reached Crosswicks there was the problem of getting me upstairs. I had been warned that I must not touch my foot to the ground. Trying to go up the narrow front stairs of a New England farmhouse, facing forward, and on crutches, proved to be impossible for me, particularly because we were all laughing so hard at my efforts that it made me weaker than ever. I finally made everybody go away and leave me alone, sat down on the steps, facing downstairs, with my leg stretched out in front of me, and went up, step by step, on my bottom, and finally got into bed, no worse for wear.

Dinner was brought up to my room so that I would not have to eat alone, and at bedtime Alan looked at the top of the chest, which was fortunately clear of debris at that moment, and said thoughtfully, "I think I'll set up for Mass."

That became the pattern during those weeks when the house was frequently full of visitors. Anybody who was up in the early morning felt free to come in while Alan celebrated Communion; anyone who felt like sleeping in was free to sleep. And I was part of the Body, not isolated by being shuffled off in bed, but a full part of the community.

That belonging remains with me as I call the dogs and take my staff (a stripped young maple from a grove in need of thinning), and stride alone across the autumn fields.

Michaelmas. Summer is ending. We sniff the wind at night to see if the tomatoes and other tender plants in the garden need covering from early frost. The dragon which Michael fought brings frost with him, but it is not the natural frost for which the countryside is preparing and for which we sniff. The rich earth needs the long fallow months of winter, and the deep blankets of snow, known locally as poor man's fertilizer, to prepare for the full glory of spring.

A Deeper Cold once clutched this land. Even in the New World, where Crosswicks, nearly two hundred and a quarter years old, is young compared with the dwellings of the Old World, there are hints of a time beyond man's memory. The great glacial rocks I pass on the way to the brook are evidence that ice pushed across this land, inexorably grinding down palm trees and great ferns which stood as high as oaks; elephants fled before the coming of the ice, and other animals we glimpse only as rarities in zoos, or in the glossy pages of the *National Geographic.* Time is old, and our memory is lost down its winding labyrinths.

And so we tend to limit ourselves to the near past. We talk of Christianity as being not quite two thousand years old, and forget that the Second Person of the Trinity was, in his full glory, before time was made.

But we human creatures are in time, acted on by time, changed and dwindled and in our mortal aspect finished by it. The time that we 'tell' is as much an agreed-upon fiction as lower math; serviceable, but not very real.

The dwindling of our language reflects the assults of time. I am sorry that we no longer *tutoyer* in English; my little knowledge of French gives me glimpses of how this enriches relationships. When *you* becomes only *you,* we open the door to sexism; and we are taking *thee* and *thou* away even from our public worship. In some of the contemporary prayers I feel that we are speaking to God in much the same way that people used to call black servants 'Boy' and I don't like it any more with God than I do with his people.

In the beginning of Ibsen's play *Rosmersholm,* Rosmer and Rebecca West are on stage with a third person, and they use the formal *you.* When they are left alone on stage they switch immediately to *thee* and *thou,* and there is no question for the audience as to the depth of their relationship. There is no adequate way of getting this knowledge across in English. To have them call each other *dear* or *darling* does not do it; we are all deared and darlinged at the drop of a hat nowadays.

When we lose the ability to convey intimacy in speech, then it becomes easy for us to turn creatures into things; the English language knows things, unlike the Latin tongues, where there is nothing without gender. Maybe there are some who would prefer thingdom to gender, but I'm not one of them. And even the word *thing* has been changed and distorted, so that it no longer makes sense to speak of 'these Holy Things.' Or perhaps it makes the only and complete sense! (Remember the phrase "that holy thing which shall be born of thee" referred to Jesus.)

The Welsh say, "She is casting rain," rather than it is raining. In French, snow, too, is 'she.' And it has always amused me that in Spanish a woman's dress is masculine. But on the whole the male and femaleness of gender makes considerable sense in these so-called 'Romance' tongues. In the old days when one said "She is casting rain," one was referring to a goddess who had power over the clouds. And this is closer to the truth of love than our "It is raining," where *it* is simply part of a blind force over which we have no control. If we truly thought of the earth as Mother we could not do to her some of the things we have done. And if we think of everything in the created order as good, because God is Creator, then gender in rock and rose, tree and turnip, sea and seed, is a form of thanks and praise.

Alan told me that in Chinese folklore there is a mythical bird who is only half a bird: one eye, one wing, one leg. In order to fly, a left-hand bird must find a right-hand bird. Alone, they are earthbound, flopping clumsily about; together they can soar across the sky.

Interpret this Freudianly if you will, but that's only part of it—though it is a part. But it rejoices me to take it beyond that, into an understanding of a deeper wholeness. There are the two Chinese birds within each of us, seeking each other for completion.

How long ago was it that we were sundered from each other, and sundered from ourselves? so that dark, night, earth, mystery, intuition, all became feminine; and light (it's feminine in French!), day, sky, fact, intellect, became masculine? It's achingly sad for the male of the species that he has been taught to repress his intuitive side, his tears, his gentleness, his ability to grieve. When the ability to grieve is repressed, the ability to love is often repressed along with it—except in the roughest act of rutting which has little to do with love.

In interpreting myth and fairy tale, many psychologists see the mother of the hero as standing for the unconscious. The appropriate behavior for the hero is to outgrow this 'fairy tale' or unreal world, and move from the dark into the light. The longing for what the mother has to offer is a longing for the inertia and lack of consciousness of the fetus.

But this is a partial explanation at best. The unconscious aspect of the personality is anything but inert, and this is why it is so fearsome. The hero must fight tooth and claw for what the psychologists call his ego-consciousness, but this ego-consciousness is only a partial consciousness; full consciousness comes only when the ego can trust the subconscious enough to embrace it instead of doing battle; only when nightside and sunside are mediated instead of separated, and so become a whole.

When we limit ourselves to our ego-consciousness, then we close off that part of us which is capable of true prayer, poetry, painting, music. When we embrace the monster it may indeed devour us, and this is the genuine risk. It may also turn out to be the handsome prince or the beautiful princess for whom we have been waiting all these years.

It is only as we recognize and call by name all that we have relegated to the dark side of Mercury, to the deep black waters of the subconscious mind, that we have any hope of wholeness. All those moral virtues I was taught in my Anglican schools must be unlearned, because most of them were neither moral nor virtuous. And many of the things which I was taught to consider bad and nasty are bad and nasty only because we have made them so. For instance, a 'nice' woman, a 'lady,' was not supposed to enjoy sex; she was to do her duty to her husband, and bear children for him, but she was not supposed to enjoy it. The grandmother and great-aunt of a friend of my mother's were baptized Patience and Submit, which gives one a good idea of the frame of mind of their mother. Only the lower classes were supposed to enjoy the natural acts of love.

Even in this supposedly enlightened day and age, a young friend of mine, going to maternity classes when she was pregnant with her first baby, and planning to bear her little one with her husband beside her, and to nurse their child, reported with shock that more than half the young mothers in the class were not going to nurse their babies. One said, with considerable pride, "My husband is not going to have me going around with my boobs exposed." The language may be today, but the attitude, I had thought, was yesterday. But it isn't. Satan still manages to make us look upon that which is natural and beautiful and good, as perverse and ugly and nasty.

All that God created is good. It is only we who have taken this good, succumbing to the wiles of the Destroyer, and seen it as bad.

All the things which we have shoved down into the darkness of the subconscious were created to be good. The darkness itself is good, but we have distorted so many things within it that the Destroyer has taken it over and made it a power for evil, for the breaking and destruction of God's creatures.

I was mercifully spared some of the distortions I would otherwise have had to struggle to unlearn by the most negative aspects of my childhood. Because I was rejected by my peers, and had to accept to myself that I was unlike them, I found myself within, rather than without. Had I been happy and popular in school I would not have plunged deep into the archetypical world of fairy tale and myth, where the night is as important as the day, the dark as light, where there is acute awareness that male and female, when evil powers intrude, battle and struggle and try to possess, but that fulfillment is only in participation. I would not otherwise have devoured George Macdonald and so absorbed, without realizing it, some of his loving theology. One of my books, long lost, was stories from the Bible, and of these stories one of my favorites was Joseph with his coat of many colors—and his dreams; Joseph, the one the others didn't like, the one who understood the dark part of the personality. I would not otherwise have read the fantasies of E. Nesbit and the science fiction of H. G. Wells, so that the larger world of imagination and intuition was not closed off for me as it was for many of my contemporaries.

Had my teacher not ridiculed my homework I might have done my lessons instead of painting pictures, playing the piano, writing stories, and working out my real self, not in the outward self which was rejected by teacher and classmates, but in the interior self. Undoubtedly I neglected sunside for nightside, but that was taken care of when I was wrested out of the world of imagination and plunged into boarding school where I had to learn about the outer world in order to survive.

It was in boarding school that I learned to make my own solitude in the midst of the mob, to surround myself with a force field of concentration, in which I could dream and write stories and poems. The misery of a total lack of privacy during those years has been more than compensated for by the discipline of concentration I was forced to acquire. I wrote my first novel while I was on tour with a play, wrote in railway stations, in trains, in theatre dressing rooms which I shared, in hotel bedrooms which also I shared. I can write in any amount of sound and fury as long as I am not responsible for that sound and fury—as I discovered when I had children, and learned that I was not free to move into this kind of deep concentration until they were safely asleep in bed.

The difficulties of those early days have proven to be advantages which have helped me to be more integrated than I might have been otherwise.

And so, of course, does my profession, and my husband's. In acting and in writing, the artist has to struggle for wholeness, just as in painting, or making music, or sculpting, or making pottery, or weaving. Sunside and nightside, maleness and femaleness, must collaborate. A priest, too, had better be aware of both the masculine and the feminine qualities of the priesthood, the two working together, participating in one person to make the image of God.

The Reverend Alan W. Jones, in an article in *The Anglican Theological Review* (yes, it's the same Alan I've been talking about in these pages, but now I am quoting him and it is appropriate to be more formal), writes, "One of the ways I understand my priesthood is as a midwife—bringing Christ to birth in others. This is no way determines my specific sexual identity. It does, thank God, creatively affirm the feminine within me."

The image of God, feminine and masculine, is, as image, physical. Sarxy: of the flesh. And the sheer physicalness of the image has not been easy for me. I used to find it difficult to talk about the resurrection of the body because it was lots easier for me to think of the soul as being separate from the body, imprisoned by it, and released from it at death like a bright bird suddenly freed and flying from the bars of the cage.

But although Jesus was never recognized on sight after the Resurrection, he went to great pains to prove to his friends that he was indeed body. He ate fish—something not really possible for a disembodied spirit. He showed Thomas the marks of the nails in his hands, and of the spear in his side.

Perhaps he wasn't recognized on sight because we aren't used to seeing bodies as they ought to be, whole, undistorted, complete.

Complete does not mean finished. I cannot understand theologians who assert that when God created the universe it was not only whole and complete, it was finished. He'd done it, and that's that. No change allowed.

When I looked at and ran my hands over my newborn babies I checked to see that they were whole, complete, all ten fingers and toes, everything all there. And they were, praise God, magnificently complete and beautiful creatures. But not finished! Anything but finished! So why should we attempt to limit God to a finished creation? That assumption implies that God is even more limited than his creatures, whereas the God I reach out to has no limitations, and knows no dichotomy between light and dark.

As long as we are unwilling to admit great areas of ourselves into our lives, to conjoin sunside and nightside, it is difficult for us not to put our trust in that which will rust and decay, where thieves can break in and steal.

Is there anything in this life on which we can really and truly count? Certainly not our possessions. Nothing that money can buy. Not even human love. Even the most dependable is flawed and fallible. Participation is very good with Hugh and me right now, but I can't count on this continuing forever. Death, if nothing else, separates all lovers. It strikes a chill to my bones as I see marriages of thirty, thirty-five, even forty years, breaking up, long after the partners have survived the trauma of the fledgelings leaving the nest. We all betray each other. No human being is totally faithful. Of course God is, but I see God through his creatures. Perhaps I can sometimes see him more clearly on weekends when we come to Crosswicks and I go and sit on the big rock at the brook, because I can count on the rock being there; but even the rock could not keep the rifle from firing at the icon on the tree in front of it; even the rock could break apart if there was an earthquake.

So what can I put my trust in that I can really know, here and now? I used to think that when all else failed I would have my memories. Saint Exupéry said that in our old age we will sit under the sheltering branches of the tree of our memories. But I saw Grandfather's memory being taken away from him, and then Mother's, and that was the worst of all.

THE AIR BITES SHREWDLY

There is almost nothing a child cannot bear
As long as the image of its parent shines clear.
Age is acceptable, normal wear and tear,
But poison cannot fall into the ear.
The image distorts; safety is gone; is where?

Hamlet, after the death of his father,
Found, also, changes in his mother,
And it was this latter, rather,
It would seem to me, than the other
That caused the dark storm clouds to gather.

The person changed is blackly unacceptable
(Primeval fears of presence of a devil);
Soma, not psyche, may be corruptible.
How does the distorted one find grace in this black evil?
Help my mother to bear. God, make her able.

It was death, in the end, which enabled her.

The only thing we can count on completely is death. A friend of mine, a fine writer, said, "I am terrified of annihilation." A senior at Harvard wrote me, "What I am afraid of is not-being." I do not believe people who say they are not afraid of death. I do not believe people who say that they do not mind the thought of annihilation, that eternal nothingness sounds pleasant.

The Michaelmas daisies, the goldenrod, the turning leaves, tell me that this Christian year is drawing to a close, and the Christian is taught that death is *not* annihilation, that death leads us into fuller life, *not* non-being. But the promise remains too glorious, too infinite, for us finite, time-trapped creatures to comprehend.

The more I am enabled to give myself away, the more complete I become. When I can let go that part of me which struggles vainly to believe, then with my whole self I rejoice in knowing. The more I am enabled to abandon myself, the more full of life I am. So: death ought to be the ultimate act of self-abandonment in order that we may become wholly alive. To count on death as the only thing a human being can count on, is an affirmation of life.

I think I like this. But then I wonder: if death is the door to life, why not suicide? Is it that if we refuse what we are given in one life, we are not ready to accept another? The answer to 'why not suicide?'

lies, it has to lie, in the Incarnation, the fully lived life of Jesus of Nazareth as the essential prelude to his death and resurrection. He enjoyed life. Friends, food, drink. He took time to Be: when he was drained from all the demands his friends and neighbors made on him, he simply took off, abandoned them for as long as he needed to be alone with the Father and to be refilled—and often they did not like it. He did ask, in agony, to be spared the cross. But he accepted the No.

To abandon the right to put an end to our lives whenever and however we want to (pills and bullets are easier than cancer or the cross) is part of that self-abandonment which is necessary for full being.

I want to enter consciously into my own death. But hospitals and the 'advances' of medicine often deny this. Dearma and Grandfather in very different ways died in their sleep. Mother said that she would like to die as Grandfather did, just slip off quietly, unknowing, and in the end this prayer was granted her as she slipped out of life in Bion's arms.

I think that I would like to know.

But there are not many quiet and conscious deaths nowadays. Dearma, Grandfather, Mother, all died at home, and that is as it should be. Next best, Grandma Josephine, in the hospital, was allowed to die in a way no longer permissible; she said that the needles with the intravenous feedings bothered her; she asked Hugh and his sister Genevieve to have them taken out; and this was permitted; and she died knowing that she was going to meet her Lord Jesus. My mother-in-law's faith never faltered. She both believed and knew.

Euthanasia, I am convinced, is wrong. It becomes far too easy to get rid of the old or the unwanted; the needle is more painless and less expensive and more final than the Old People's Home. But what I call reverse euthanasia is equally wrong. Keeping a body alive which would under normal circumstances die is a kind of murder.

I did make the difficult decision not to force-feed Mother during her last weeks. When a body is no longer able to eat or, even worse, to breathe without machines, unless there is real hope of real cure, of return to full life, then that body should be allowed to die. Keeping permanent vegetables plugged into machines is, as far as I am concerned, sin. And this struggle to keep a mere lump of flesh 'alive' is a result of technology turned into technocracy. I am all for technology; I see because of technology. But technocracy is a symptom of a world where only man is God and death is the victor. Even during my worst periods of atheism I can't accept that.

Atheism is, for me, a virulent virus, put into the world by the Evil One for our destruction, and I come down with it as on occasion I have come down with flu. When the Michaelmas daisies and the goldenrod were gone this autumn, and the leaves stripped from the trees, I had a horrible attack. It was brought on by a long series of events.

Just before Thanksgiving and my birthday and the first Sunday of Advent, Mrs. O died. She had long been ready; we could only welcome her release into glory, and I am sure that there is more laughter in heaven now that she is there. But those of us who love her were very aware of how much we are going to miss her.

When one of the Sisters had called to tell me that her mother had died, I had thought to myself that if they asked me if there was anything of their mother's I would like to have as a keepsake, I would ask for her rosary; surely those glass beads, so prayed on with her fingers and heart, would contain something of her grace. But they were twined about the dead fingers in the coffin, so I said nothing.

At the last moment, just before the lid was shut down, Sister Anastasia went back to kneel before her mothers's body. When she came back she held out her hand, in which something was clasped. "Madeleine, would you like Mother's rosary?" And she dropped it into my palm. For this intuitive understanding, I will always be grateful.

We left the funeral parlor and went to the church. At first we did not realize why it was we could not go into the nave. Then we saw that another funeral was going on inside. When the mourners had filed out, we went in. Nothing can take away completely the beauty and comfort of the Requiem Mass, but it was given life only by the congregation of people who had loved the ninety-five-year old woman; the priest said words which had been repeated so often that they had become empty.

When I was a child I sometimes took a word or a phrase and said it over and over again until it had lost all meaning. The saying of the words of the Mass reminded me of this childish game. But that was my fault as much as the priest's, or even more. It wouldn't have bothered Mrs. O, because nothing could dim for her the reality of the glory.

When we left the church another hearse was rounding the corner for yet another funeral.

I went back to the Cathedral library and finished the work day, and then walked home with Timothy. There was quite a lot of mail and I sat down on the foot of the bed to read it. An extraordinary and unexpected blessing has been birthday cards and even presents from people who have read my books and become my friends, and I opened several of these, my heart melting within me with love and gratitude.

One card seemed to be full of what I took to be potpourri, a thoughtful gift. But then I noticed that it was a get-well card and not a birthday card, which struck me as strange since, thank God, I had not been ill. Then I sniffed the dried flowers and they had no scent. Then I looked closer.

I called Hugh, "Please come here." He got up from his chair and came at the tight urgency in my voice. "Are these cockroaches?"

They were. Someone had taken the trouble to collect about a cupful of cockroaches and put them in a get-well card, and send them to me. The timing couldn't have been more accurate, although I doubt if whoever it was knew that it was near my birthday, or the day of the funeral of the woman who had been a second mother to me.

For a moment I thought I was going to vomit, so physical was my reaction. Then I got the vacuum cleaner and vacuumed the bedspread, the rug, clean of all trace of the shiny brown deadness of the roaches. I said quite calmly to Hugh, "If life in an old building in New York were not a constant battle against cockroaches, this would be even more horrible."

It was horrible enough. It was a manifestation of a hate even more sick than the hate which had taken a rifle and shot through the icon at the brook. I do not know who it was, and I will probably never know, and this is just as well.

That night we had seats at the ballet, seats ordered months before. I took Mrs. O's rosary with me and held it in my hand all evening, tangibly holding off the powers of darkness. Because those small beads were icons of love, hate could not surround me entirely; the circle of love was stronger than the strangling bonds of hate.

But that day did nothing to help my attack of atheism.

Tallis was off to Australia to preach at the consecration of a mutual friend, otherwise I would have gone running to him. I did find myself telling a young friend, a religious staying briefly in New York en route to join her community, the Little Sisters of Jesus. She thought briefly, then said, "You are very much loved, and where there is great love there is also great hate," and her affirmation of the love made the hate less terrible.

And even in my atheism I could pray for this hate, this horrible sickness, could pray for its healing.

Another help came in a letter from France, from a friend who has often been in positions of authority and power, and who has received several anonymous poison-pen letters. "I was upset and hurt and shocked and angered by them, and I remember praying for the person who sent the ugly picture, for the men who drew it, printed it, and sold it. It doesn't worry me now, because it's all part of the dust anyone kicks up who sticks out his/her neck, takes a stand on anything significant, has any impact. If we had *more* impact, we'd probably be shot, like King and the Kennedys."

That lightened my perspective.

A few days later the phone on my desk in the Cathedral Library rang. Long Distance. The eighteen-year-old daughter of a friend of mine, in a small town in the Midwest, had been kidnapped as she went to her car with a bag of groceries, driven out of town, raped, and murdered. Not in New York. In a small town where everybody was known by name. A lovely child had her life taken away from her, brutally and slowly. And there was nothing I, at this distance, or indeed any of the friends at home, could do to help.

That afternoon a college-age friend of mine dropped in to see me as she usually does whenever she's in town. I was appalled at her appearance. Her skin was tinged with grey; there were deep circles under her eyes. She came to kiss me and she was trembling all over. I plugged the pot in for tea, and she told me that she had left the hospital the day before, after an abortion. There was no question of marriage; she had thought the boy loved her, but he didn't, and she did not want marriage under those conditions. But she did want the baby. Her parents, respectable, affluent, arranged the abortion, took her to the hospital with cold efficiency, and left her there for forty-eight hours. "And I knew, when I woke from the anaesthesia, that I had committed murder. I let them force me into it. I could have stopped them if I'd wanted to badly enough." Tears overflowed.

This was no time for reason. She flung herself into my arms like a small child and wept.

A few nights later the attack of atheism took hold. I could no longer fend it off.

I woke up in the night as I usually do with the words of the Jesus Prayer plashing up into my conscious mind like a little fountain, as they have been doing for years. And I thought bitterly, why on earth am I saying these meaningless and empty words? They mean nothing. Lord Jesus Christ is only an illusion. There is nothing. Nada. Nada. Nada.

I lay in cold isolation on my side of the bed, not even reaching out with hand or foot to touch the warm and sleeping flesh of my husband in my usual instinctive affirmation of incarnation.

Nothing. Nothing.

And then I flung myself onto the words of the prayer like a drowning person clutching at a rope thrown into the dark sea. I held onto it with all my strength and I was slowly pulled from the waters which had been sucking me under, pulled out of the dark and into the light and Lord Jesus Christ did indeed have mercy on me.

For a long time I was convalescent, recuperating slowly from the virulent attack, a little less feverish (as it were) each day. I was called to conduct a retreat and this was the best medicine I could have been given.

I know that I am not immune from further attacks. But I also know that the darkness cannot put out the light.

For an English friend I wrote, one winter when he was in New York and staying at the General Seminary:

> *Come, let us gather round the table.*
> *Light the candles. Steward, pour the wine.*
> *It's dark outside. The streets are noisy*
> *with the scurrying of rats, with shoddy*
> *tarts, shills, thugs, harsh shouting.*

And what comfort is cold within? We're able
to offer a slim repast. The taste of brine
warm from fresh tears, is in the glass. Choosy
guests will not come here. The bread is body
broken. The wine is dark with blood. I'm doubting

if half of those invited will turn up.
Most will prefer to choose a different table,
will go elsewhere with gentler foods to sup.
And yet this is indeed a wedding feast
and we rejoice to share the bitter cup,
the crumbs of bread. For O my Lord, not least
of all that makes us raise the glass, is that we toast
You, who assembled this uncomely group: our one mysterious host.

Bread. Wine. A dinner table. The firm clasp of hands as we say grace. The warm flame of candles. It is all an affirmation of incarnation, of being, versus non-being. Even the sender of those cockroaches was in a perverse and sick way affirming incarnation, while completely misunderstanding the act.

The Lord Jesus Christ whose very name has the power to pull me from the terror of non-ness came to earth in a vulgar affirmation that all creation is good; we can dirty it, turn it to evil, join the angel who fought against Michael, but creation itself, all matter, is good.

We are afraid of the physicalness of incarnation. Jesus of Nazareth was a total man, with every part and function of a man's body—even the parts which Paul described as "less honorable." The more shattering thing is that he was tempted in all ways, including temptations I've never known, some I've probably never even heard about. I worship a Christ who is fully God because he was incarnate more completely than anyone I have known.

This past week while we were in the city, Bobby came to the north field of Crosswicks and spread its browning clover and grasses with manure. During the weekend Hugh goes to the rotting mulch of the composte heap and spreads it over the garden before ploughing it in. And this is good.

Lift up your heads, O ye gates; and be ye lift up, ye everlasting doors; and the King of glory shall come in.

Who is this King of glory? It is the Lord strong and mighty, even the Lord mighty in battle.

Lift up your heads, O ye gates, and be ye lift up, ye everlasting doors, and the King of glory shall come in.

Who is this King of glory? Even the Lord of hosts, he is the King of glory.

Thus cries the psalmist. Thus I cry after him.

Who is this King of glory? A child born of a woman. A man betrayed by his friends as well as by his enemies. A failure who died ignominiously and who should by all logic have been immediately forgotten. A king of no glory on earth, a king who lost his battle with the Powers of this world, or so it would seem from the surface of the story. He performed a few miracles, but miracles were nothing new; others performed miracles. And he couldn't save himself at the end.

If I am to seek for answers to my questions, or even for the questions to ask in the first place, I must hold to this failure, but it isn't easy, so far have we strayed from the original vision. We don't understand the method in his madness. His coming to us as a human child, in total weakness, was the greatest act of warfare against the powers of hate and chaos that I know. And if I, too, am to fight in this battle, it is from his weakness that I must draw my strength.

The *symboles* by which I live are the answers to my questions, are themselves the questions, are the healers of our brokenness. When we deny our wholeness, when we repress part of ourselves, when we are afraid of our own darkness, then the dark turns against us, turns on us, becomes evil. Just as the intellect when it is not informed by the heart becomes vicious, so the intuition, the subconscious, when it is forcibly held below the surface, becomes wild, and until we look at it and call it by name, our own name, it can devour us.

Am I afraid to look down into the dark and acknowledge myself, and say: Madeleine! and know that this, too, is part of what I am meant to be? Yes, I am afraid sometimes, but I become less afraid as my trust in the pattern of the universe deepens. I, too, have my place, as do we all, with the greatest galaxies, the smallest particles. Perhaps it takes all of this, all of creation, to make the Body of Christ, and the bride.

The days are growing noticeably shorter; the nights are longer, deeper, colder. Today the sun did not rise as high in the sky as it did yesterday. Tomorrow it will be still lower. At the winter solstice the sun will go below the horizon, below the dark. The sun does die. And then, to our amazement, the Son will rise again.

> *Come, Lord Jesus, quickly come*
> *In your fearful innocence.*
> *We fumble in the far-spent night*
> *Far from lovers, friends, and home:*
> *Come in your naked, newborn might.*
> *Come, Lord Jesus, quickly come;*
> *My heart withers in your absence.*
>
> *Come, Lord Jesus, small, enfleshed*
> *Like any human, helpless child.*
> *Come once, come once again, come soon:*
> *The stars in heaven fall, unmeshed;*
> *The sun is dark, blood's on the moon.*
> *Come, word who came to us enfleshed,*
> *Come speak in joy untamed and wild.*
>
> *Come, thou wholly other, come,*
> *Spoken before words began,*
> *Come and judge your uttered world*
> *Where you made our flesh your home.*
> *Come, with bolts of lightning hurled,*
> *Come, thou wholly other, come,*
> *Who came to man by being man.*
>
> *Come, Lord Jesus, at the end,*
> *Time's end, my end, forever's start.*
> *Come in your flaming, burning power.*
> *Time, like the temple veil, now rend;*
> *Come, shatter every human hour.*
> *Come, Lord Jesus, at the end.*
> *Break, then mend the waiting heart.*

We have much to be judged on when he comes, slums and battlefields and insane asylums, but these are the symptoms of our illness, and the result of our failures in love. In the evening of life we shall be judged on love, and not one of us is going to come off very well, and were it not for my absolute faith in the loving forgiveness of my Lord I could not call on him to come.

But his love is greater than all our hate, and he will not rest until Judas has turned to him, until Satan has turned to him, until the dark has turned to him; until we can all, all of us without exception, freely return his look of love with love in our own eyes and hearts. And then, healed, whole, complete but not finished, we will know the joy of being co-creators with the one to whom we call.

Amen. Even so, come Lord Jesus.